William Henry Fitchett

Fights for the Flag

William Henry Fitchett

Fights for the Flag

ISBN/EAN: 9783337133405

Printed in Europe, USA, Canada, Australia, Japan

Cover: Foto ©ninafisch / pixelio.de

More available books at **www.hansebooks.com**

FIGHTS FOR THE FLAG

MARLBOROUGH

From a mezzotint by J. FABER, *after the portrait by* SIR GODFREY KNELLER

FIGHTS FOR THE FLAG

BY

W. H. FITCHETT
("VEDETTE")
AUTHOR OF "DEEDS THAT WON THE EMPIRE."

"*What is the flag of England? Winds of the world declare!*"
—KIPLING

WITH PORTRAITS AND PLANS

LONDON
SMITH, ELDER, & CO., 15 WATERLOO PLACE
1898
[*All rights reserved*]

Printed by BALLANTYNE, HANSON & CO.
At the Ballantyne Press

CONTENTS

	PAGE
BLAKE AND THE DUTCHMEN	1
MARLBOROUGH AT BLENHEIM	16
LORD ANSON AND THE "CENTURION"	33
GEORGE II. AT DETTINGEN	53
THE BATTLE OF MINDEN	71
RODNEY AND DE GRASSE AT THE BATTLE OF THE SAINTS	94
LORD HOWE AND THE FIRST OF JUNE	114
SIR JOHN MOORE AT CORUNNA	134
WELLINGTON AT SALAMANCA	158
THE SIEGE OF SAN SEBASTIAN	185
SIR EDWARD CODRINGTON AT NAVARINO	215
INKERMANN	233
FAMOUS CAVALRY CHARGES	268
THE MEN IN THE RANKS	294
"THE LADY WITH THE LAMP"	322

LIST OF PORTRAITS

DUKE OF MARLBOROUGH	*Frontispiece*
ADMIRAL BLAKE . . .	*To face page* 1
ADMIRAL VAN TROMP . .	,, 8
LORD ANSON	,, 33
GEORGE II.	,, 53
LORD STAIR	,, 71
PRINCE FERDINAND . . .	,, 73
LORD RODNEY	,, 94
LORD HOWE	,, 114
SIR JOHN MOORE	,, 134
DUKE OF WELLINGTON . .	,, 158
SIR AUGUSTUS FRAZER . .	,, 185
SIR GEORGE CATHCART . . .	,, 233
SIR JAMES YORKE SCARLETT . . .	,, 271
THE EARL OF CARDIGAN . . .	,, 284
MISS FLORENCE NIGHTINGALE	,, 322

LIST OF PLANS

	PAGE
THE BATTLE OF BLENHEIM	24
THE BATTLE OF DETTINGEN	55
THE BATTLE OF MINDEN	79
THE WESTERN ATLANTIC	99
RODNEY AND DE GRASSE, *April 12th*, 1782	102
THE BATTLE OF THE FIRST OF JUNE, 1794	120
THE SPANISH CAMPAIGN	138
THE BATTLE OF CORUNNA	151
THE BATTLE OF SALAMANCA	172
THE BATTLE OF SAN SEBASTIAN	189
THE BREACH AT SAN SEBASTIAN	207
THE BATTLE OF NAVARINO	226
THE BATTLEFIELD OF INKERMANN	237

FACSIMILE

LETTER OF MARLBOROUGH	*To face page* 17

ADMIRAL BLAKE

From a mezzotint by THOMAS PRESTON

BLAKE AND THE DUTCHMEN

FEBRUARY 1652-53

> "The spirit of your fathers
>   Shall start from every wave—
> For the deck it was their field of fame,
>   And Ocean was their grave:
> Where Blake and mighty Nelson fell
>   Your manly hearts shall glow,
> As you sweep through the deep,
>   While the stormy winds do blow;
> While the battle rages loud and long,
> And the stormy winds do blow."
>   —CAMPBELL.

A SPECTATOR standing on the wind-blown summit of Beachy Head on the afternoon of May 19, 1651-52, would have looked down on a great historic scene. In the famous strait beneath, some sixty great ships were engaged in the fiery wrestle of battle, and the sullen, deep-voiced roar of their guns rolled from the white English cliffs across the strait to the dunes of Calais, faintly visible through the grey haze. But the fleets engaged were in point of numbers strangely ill-matched. Running westward past the Downs before a fresh breeze came a great Dutch fleet of fifty ships under the flag of Van Tromp, the most famous of Dutch admirals. Beating up to eastward to meet them was an English fleet of fifteen ships under Blake, who was in no sense a seaman, but who comes next to Nelson himself in the greatness of his sea exploits. It is easy to picture the scene—the antique-looking ships, short-bodied, high-sterned, snub-nosed, the bowsprit thrust up at a sharp angle, and carrying a tiny mast with a square sail at its extremity. A modern seaman would gaze amazed at the spectacle of a seventeenth-century fleet, luffing clumsily into line, or trying to claw to windward.

And yet the fighting quality of these clumsy fleets was of a very high order. These Dutchmen, heavy-footed, solid, grim, were in the seventeenth century, to use the phrase of a French writer, "the Phœnicians of the modern world, the waggoners of all seas." They were the commercial heirs of Venice. The fire of their long struggle for freedom had given to the national character the edge and temper of steel. They had swept the Spanish flag from the seas. The carrying trade of the world was in their hands. They fished in all waters, traded in all ports, gathered the wealth of the world under all skies, and, as far as marine qualities were concerned, might almost have been web-footed. Holland to-day is a land without ambition, comfortable, fat, heavy-bottomed. In the middle of the seventeenth century Holland proudly claimed to be the greatest naval power in the world, and by daring seamanship, great fleets, famous admirals, and a world-encompassing trade, it went far to justify that boast.

Great Britain had just finished her civil war, and the imperial genius of Cromwell was beginning to make itself felt in foreign politics. The stern and disciplined valour of his Ironsides, that triumphed at Naseby and Worcester, was being translated into the terms of seamanship. The Commonwealth, served by Cromwell's sword, and Milton's pen, and Blake's seamanship, was not likely to fail in vigour by sea or land. But there is always a flavour of sea-salt in English blood, an instinctive claim to sea supremacy in the English imagination. England in 1652, released from civil strife, was feeling afresh that historic impulse, and was challenging the Dutch naval supremacy. The Commonwealth claimed to inherit that ancient patrimony of English kings—the sovereignty of the narrow seas, and the right in these waters to compel all foreign ships to strike the flag or lower the topsail in the presence of a British ship. Behind that question of sea etiquette lay the whole claim to naval supremacy and the trade of the world. That fight off Dungeness on that May afternoon nearly 250 years ago was really the beginning of the struggle betwixt the two maritime republics for the mistress-ship of the seas. To quote Hannay, "the greatest naval power of the day, and the greatest naval power of the future," were measuring their forces in the tossing lists of the narrow seas.

In this his first great naval fight Blake showed an individual daring like that of Collingwood when he bore down, far ahead of his column, on Villeneuve's far-stretching line at Trafalgar. In his ship—the *James*—that is, he outsailed his squadron, and met alone Van Tromp's compact line, with its swift-following jets of flame and blasts of thunder as each ship in turn bore up to rake the British admiral. But Nelson himself never showed swifter decision or cooler daring as a leader than did Blake when he unhesitatingly led his fifteen ships to meet Van Tromp's fifty. It is true that a British squadron of nine ships under Bourne, a gallant sailor, was lying in the Downs; and Blake, no doubt, calculated that the mere thunder of the engagement would quickly call up Bourne's ships to fall on Van Tromp's rear. This is exactly what happened; but this does not make any less splendid the courage with which Blake, with fifteen ships, faced the Dutch fleet of more than twice his own numbers, and led by an admiral of Van Tromp's fame and genius. For four hours the thunder of the battle rolled over the floor of the sea. Dutchman and Englishman fought and died with stubborn courage under the drifting smoke clouds; and the two fleets, a jungle of swaying masts and shot-torn sails, with all the tumult of their battle, drifted slowly westwards. Even in that early day, however, the British gunnery had those qualities of speed and fierceness which, somehow, seem to belong to it by right of nature; and, as night fell, the stubborn Dutch gave up their attempt to force the strait, and, leaving two of their ships as prizes, stood over to the Flemish coast; while the British, their flagship dismasted and with shot-battered sides, slowly bore up to Dover. It is characteristic, however, of the tireless and silent energy of Blake that, as war had now broken out, he instantly commenced to sweep Dutch traders off the seas. From every quarter of the compass Dutch ships, richly laden, were creeping homeward, unconscious that war had broken out; and Blake's frigates, instantly taking possession of all the trade routes, sent them as prizes up the Thames in scores. The British, in a word, showed themselves both nimbler-witted and nimbler-footed than the Dutch.

In his famous lyric Campbell links Blake with

"mighty Nelson"; and in point of fame and character Blake is not unworthy to stand beside him whom Tennyson calls—

"The greatest sailor since the world began."

And yet Blake was not, in any technical sense, a sailor. He was fifty years of age before he put foot on a man-of-war, and he stepped without an interval from being colonel of foot to being admiral of the fleet. Early in 1649 Parliament undertook to reorganise the fleet, and it issued a commission to three colonels—of whom Blake was one—to be "admirals and generals of the fleet now at sea." An admiral in topboots and spurs seems sufficiently absurd to the modern imagination; but in the sea tactics of the seventeenth century the men who fought the ship, and the men who sailed it, were totally distinct.

Of the sea-going qualities of the British sailors of that day there is no room to doubt. They were the descendants of Drake, of Frobisher, of Hawkins; as much at home on the sea as an aquatic bird; familiar with surf and storm; familiar, too, with perils of battle as with perils of tempest and rock. The British seaman of the seventeenth century mixed battle with trade. He fought with French privateers in the narrow seas, with Sallee rovers in the Strait of Gibraltar, with Algerine pirates all through the Mediterranean, with Dutchmen off the Spice Islands, Portuguese in the Eastern seas, and Spaniards everywhere. He was half bagman, half buccaneer, and, to quote Hannay, "carried a sample of woollen goods in one hand and a boarding-pike in the other." Macaulay says of the fleet of that period that "the gentlemen were not sailors, and the sailors were not gentlemen."

No doubt the British seaman of 1650 was a rough-looking figure, with tarry hands and weather-battered face. But he had a touch of the simplicity of a child behind his roughness; and in resource, in fortitude, and in practical seamanship he has never been surpassed. Now an infantry colonel, or a major of horse, suddenly, by a drop of official ink, transmuted into an admiral, he had, no doubt, some absurd limitations. He had to direct manœuvres of fleets when he scarcely knew "larboard" from "starboard." He did not know the very alphabet of sea dialect. It is said that Monck, who was another "admiral in spurs," in the middle of an action sent a shout of laughter round his own decks by giving the order, "Wheel to the left!"

But these Commonwealth veterans, suddenly sent afloat, were hardy, daring, and, in some cases, brilliant soldiers; and they soon learnt to manœuvre fleets as they used to deploy battalions. They brought indeed some useful soldierly traditions into marine use—order, discipline, close fighting, hard hitting. A French writer, less than twenty years afterwards, wrote, "Nothing equals the beautiful order of the English at sea. Never was a line drawn straighter than that formed by their ships; thus they bring all their fire to bear upon those who draw near them. They fight like a line of cavalry which is handled according to rule, whereas the Dutch advance like cavalry whose squadrons leave their ranks and come separately to the charge." It can hardly be doubted that Cromwell's soldier-admirals carried something of the steadiest discipline and terrible fighting power of the famous Ironsides into the naval tactics of their day.

Certainly Blake had all the moral and intellectual endowments of a great commander, either by sea or land. A little man, broad-faced, deep-eyed, chary of speech, melancholy of temper, he yielded no outward gleam of brilliance. Yet British history scarcely shows a nobler character. He was loyal, unselfish, humane. He possessed the indefinable art that makes the true leader—a spell that made his men trust him, believe he could never fail, and be willing to charge with him against any odds. He was a strange compound of the prudence which calculates all the odds, and the daring which scorns them. Courage in him spoke with gentle accents, and looked through quiet eyes; and yet it was as swift as Nelson's, as heroic as Ney's, as cool as Wellington's. And the keynote of Blake's character was that magnificent word DUTY, which Nelson spelt out with many-coloured flags to his fleet on the morning of Trafalgar, and which Henry Lawrence chose as his epitaph at Lucknow. The story of Blake's deeds is worth telling, if only for the sake of showing British youths from what a stock they are sprung, and what great traditions they inherit.

There is no time to tell of Blake's career as a soldier, though his defence of Taunton was perhaps the most brilliant single episode, on the Parliamentary side, in the great civil war. Of his sea exploits only the most picturesque and striking can be briefly sketched. He met Van Tromp again at desperate odds, with desperate courage and somewhat desperate fortune, off Dungeness, on November 29, 1652. The Dutchman had some eighty ships, Blake less than forty. Blake had discovered the secret which Nelson rediscovered afterwards, that the

British sailor fights to best advantage at close quarters. While the Dutch, like the French in the revolutionary war, fired at the masts of their enemy, Blake taught his men, as Hawke and Nelson taught theirs, to fire at the hull. In the wrestle off Dungeness, therefore, the Dutch suffered more damage than the British, but won the triumph that belongs to overwhelming numbers; and it was after this combat that, according to a popular but utterly unfounded tradition, Van Tromp sailed through the narrow seas with a broom at his masthead.

Blake and Van Tromp had their final trial of strength in the famous three days' battle off Portland in February 1653. Van Tromp, with a fleet of seventy-three men-of-war, was convoying some 200 merchant ships to Dutch ports. Blake, with about seventy men-of-war, sighted them coming up the Channel before a strong wind, a far-stretching continent of swaying masts and bellying sails. Blake, with the red squadron, lay directly in the enemy's path; Penn, with the blue squadron, was five miles to the south; Monck, with the white squadron, was nearly ten miles to leeward. Blake, however, with his twelve ships, bore steadily up to the attack; and round this tiny cluster of British ships Van Tromp's great vessels closed as a pack of wolves might gather round a handful of sheep. There was nothing sheeplike, however, in Blake's squadron. The roar of their guns rolled in one sullen sustained wave of sound over the sea; and, fast as the Dutchmen shot, still faster and more fiercely did Blake's men reply. Monck and Penn, who saw their commander-in-chief apparently swallowed up in the mass of hostile ships, beat furiously up to join

ADMIRAL VAN TROMP

From an engraving by J. HOUBRAKEN, *after the portrait by* LIEVENS

in the fight. The close and desperate fighting told sorely on both sides; 100 men were killed or wounded on the British admiral's flagship, its masts were gone, its hull little more than a wreck, and other ships of his squadron were in little better condition. But of the Dutch ships one was burnt, one blown up, and seven taken or sunk.

Night by this time had fallen. Van Tromp swept past the British line, and, a fine tactician, threw his own fleet into a half-moon formation, with the huge convoy held in its embrace, and steadily drifted, a great island of canvas, along the French coast. But at daybreak the English, bringing the wind with them, were thundering on the Dutch rear, and striving fiercely to pierce their line. All day long the fleet ran, with the tumult and roar of battle, eastwards. The advantage was slightly with the British, and the Dutch rear-admiral's ship was captured. A Dutchman, however, according to Penn, is never so dangerous as when he is desperate, and never was sterner fighting than on that historic Saturday. When the next day dawned, Tromp, still holding his steadfast half-moon formation, was bearing up for the shallows off Calais, the inexorable Blake, with loud-bellowing guns, thundering on his rear. One Dutch captain, grappled on each side by an English ship, set fire to his own vessel that the three might sink together. The British, however, drew off, and left the Dutchman to blow up in solitude. At last Penn, with a cluster of his faster ships, broke through the stubborn line of the Dutchmen, and when Sunday night fell, the British frigates were ravaging like wolves amongst the helpless merchantmen. During the night Van Tromp gave his captains orders to scatter, and when day broke again the Dutch ships had disappeared, or were discoverable only as tips of vanishing sails on the sea rim. That great three days' fight off Portland—a "stupendous action," as Clarendon calls it—was the turning-point in the long duel for the sovereignty of the seas betwixt Great Britain and Holland.

In 1654–55 Blake sailed with a powerful fleet for the Mediterranean. Cromwell had demanded from Spain the right of trade with America, and the exemption of Englishmen from the jurisdiction of the Inquisition. "My master," said the Spanish ambassador in reply, "has but two eyes, and you ask him for both!" Drake, some eighty years before, had "singed the King of Spain's beard," and Blake was now despatched to put out one or both of the King of Spain's eyes! For Cromwell's foreign politics were of a daring temper. "I will make the name of Englishman," he said, "to be as much dreaded as ever was the name of *civis Romanus*." Blake's commission was, in general terms, "to see that the foreigners do not fool us." Blake extracted from the Duke of Tuscany, and even from his Holiness the Pope, solid sums in compensation for wrongs done to British commerce. He visited Tunis, then, as in Lord Exmouth's time, the torment and scandal of the civilised world, and his performance anticipates and outshines even Exmouth's great deed at Algiers a hundred and fifty years later.

Finding negotiation useless, Blake, on April 4, led in his ships, anchored within half musket-shot of the Dey's batteries, and opened a terrific fire on them. Nine great ships of war lay within the harbour. When the cannonade was at its height Blake lowered his boats, manned each with a picked crew, and sent them in to fire the Dey's ships. The British boats rowed coolly, but at speed, through the eddying smoke, fell upon the enemy's ships, and fired them. The flames leaped up the masts, and spread from ship to ship, and when night fell the skies above Tunis shone, as bright almost as at noonday, with the flames of the burning ships and batteries. Taking warning by the fate of Tunis, Algiers hastened to surrender its Christian captives. Blake's cruise in the Mediterranean was epoch-making.

Clarendon, speaking of the fight at Tunis, says that Blake "first taught British sailors to despise castles on shore"; and that is true. But Blake first carried the British flag, as a symbol of terror and power, round the Mediterranean ports, and established in the great midland sea a supremacy which has never been lost since. His cruise, indeed, marks that assumption of what may be called the police of the seas which Great Britain has ever since maintained.

Blake's object, next, was to strike at the Spanish plate-ships. The great galleons creeping eastward to Spain, with their freight of sugar and dye-wood, of quicksilver and precious stones, of gold and silver and pearls, fed the financial strength of Spain. To cut them off was to snap all the sinews of its strength at a stroke. Blake, through most of 1655-56, was blockading Cadiz, and watching for the plate-ships to heave in sight from Santa Cruz. For a great fleet to keep the sea through the winter was, at that period, a thing undreamed of. Yet, practically for twenty-seven months, in spite of scurvy and tempest, Blake maintained his iron blockade of Cadiz.

Every few days a storm would blow his ships across the foam-edged horizon; but when the storm had blown itself out the British topsails surely hove in sight again. The ships' hulls grew thick with barnacles and sea grass, their rigging rotted, their supplies were exhausted, and scurvy raged through the crews. The men, for two months, ate their vegetables boiled in sea water. "Our ships," wrote Blake, "are extremely foul, our stores failing, our men fallen sick through badness of drink. Our only comfort is that we have a God to lean upon, although we walk in darkness and see no light." And yet Blake's iron will kept the ships for nearly two years on their watch outside Cadiz. Nelson's long watch off Toulon, or Collingwood's off Cadiz in the year previous to Trafalgar, is not so wonderful as Blake's blockade in the seventeenth century.

Then came that amazing dash at Santa Cruz, which formed the last and greatest of Blake's exploits. Stayner had intercepted one squadron of treasure-ships immediately off Cadiz. With three ships he had attacked six, sunk some, and captured the rest. They were a magnificent prize, no less than £600,000 being found in one ship alone. But the largest squadron of plate-ships lay at Santa Cruz, under the great peak of Teneriffe, kept by the terror of Blake's name from attempting to reach the Spanish coast, and upon these Blake made his famous dash.

Santa Cruz is a deep and narrow bay, guarded by heavy batteries, with a difficult approach. Owing to the high land a fleet might easily be becalmed under the heavy guns of the batteries and so be destroyed; or if the wind carried the ships into the bay, while it prevailed there was no chance of escaping out of it. It was at Santa Cruz that Nelson suffered his one defeat and lost his arm. It is not the least of Blake's titles to fame that he succeeded where Nelson failed.

On the morning of April 20, Blake, with his squadron, appeared off the bay. A fleet of sixteen great galleons was drawn across the bottom of the bay, and Blake's swift soldierly glance told him in a moment that these ships would act as a screen betwixt his own squadron and the great Spanish batteries on the shore. Blake led into the attack with the same lightning-like decision Nelson showed at the Nile. The British fleet ran, with all sail spread, but in grim silence, past the batteries at the entrance to the bay. The fire was loud and fierce, but the Spanish markmanship bad. His leading ships, under his favourite officer, Stayner, Blake launched at the galleons, but with the remainder of the squadron Blake himself rounded on the flank of the batteries, covering Stayner from their fire. For four hours the 700 guns of ships and batteries sent their tremendous waves of sound up the slopes of Teneriffe. The Spaniards fought with great courage, but Blake's fire, by its speed and deadliness, was overwhelming. At two o'clock the fleet of galleons was in flames; by three o'clock nothing was left of them but half-a-dozen drifting blackened wrecks. Then came a sudden change of wind, and Blake's ships ran safely past the forts again to the open sea. They had done their work. They had not merely "singed the King of Spain's beard"; they had emptied his pockets and broken his strength. "The whole action," says Clarendon, "was so miraculous that all men who knew the place concluded that no sober man, with what courage soever endued, would ever undertake it." Yet Blake did this "miraculous" thing, and the daring that inspired the exploit is not so wonderful as the genius which kept this scurvy-wasted, barnacle-covered fleet in the heroic temper which made it eager to accomplish whatever Blake planned.

Nothing is more pathetic than the story of Blake's home-coming. On an August afternoon in 1657 the fleet—the battered flagship, the *George*, leading—was in sight of Plymouth. The green hills of Devonshire, the spires and roofs of the smoky city, the masts of the ships were in full view. The piers and shores were crowded with thousands waiting to welcome the greatest sailor of his generation back to England. All the church bells in Plymouth were ringing. But at that moment Blake lay dying in his cabin. His captains, with those rare and reluctant tears that brave men weep running down their weather-beaten faces, were standing round his bed bidding farewell to their great chief. Just as the slow-moving *George* dropped her anchor Blake breathed his last. Never has England had a braver, a less selfish, a more simply and nobly loyal servant. His corpse was rowed by his sailors up the Thames, carried in state to Westminster Abbey, and laid in Henry VII.'s chapel—the noblest bit of human dust in even that mausoleum of kings. It is one of the things to be remembered against Charles II. that, after the Restoration, he had Blake's bones dragged from their resting-place and cast into some nameless grave. The English monarch, however, who sold Dunkirk and filled his pockets with French gold could hardly be expected to respect, or even to understand, Blake's fame. Perhaps, indeed, the fame of the noblest and bravest of English sailors was a secret sting to the conscience of the worst of English kings.

MARLBOROUGH AT BLENHEIM

August 13, 1704

> " 'It was the English,' Kaspar cried,
>   'Who put the French to rout ;
> But what they fought each other for,
>   I could not well make out.
> But everybody said,' quoth he,
>   'That 'twas a famous victory.' "
>   —Southey.

AMONG the historical treasures of Blenheim House is a slip of paper on which are scribbled a dozen lines in pencil. Those lines were written by the Duke of Marlborough at the close of the fierce death-wrestle at Blenheim. The tumult of battle was rolling westward, where French and Bavarians were in disordered retreat, with Marlborough's cavalry riding fiercely on their rear. The smoke of the great fight yet hung black in the heavens. The slopes of the hills to the right, where Prince Eugene had four times over made his fiery onset, and the marshy plain in the centre where Marlborough himself, by a cavalry charge worthy of Murat—8000 cavalry joined in one furious onset of galloping hoofs—had broken through the French centre, were strewn with nearly 30,000 killed and wounded. But Marlborough, with the rapture of the great fight still dancing in his blood, pulled up his horse on one of the little rustic bridges across the Schwanbuch, and

August 13, 1904

I R

I have not time to
say more, but beg
You will give my Duty
to the Queen, and let
her know Her Army
has had a Glorious
Victory. Mons*r* Tallard
and two other Generals
are in my Coach and
I am following the rest
the bearer my Aid de Camp
Collo Parkes will give her
and account of what
has pas[se]d. I shall goe
it in a day or two by
an other more att
large

Marlborough

Reduced facsimile of the Note written in pencil by the Duke of Marlborough to the Duchess, on the field of battle at Blenheim.

scribbled these dozen lines to his imperious and bitter-tempered wife in London, to tell her of the great event.

Marlborough, apparently, borrowed the scrap of paper from some member of his staff, for on the back of it are the faded items of a tavern bill. He used the parapet of the bridge for a writing-desk; he had been seventeen hours in the saddle, most of that time riding in the very heart of one of the greatest battles in all history; yet the firm shape of the letters is a curious testimony to that serenely unshakable temperament which was Marlborough's most striking characteristic. This scrap of paper, tavern bill on one side, martial despatch on the other, with its few lines scribbled on the parapet of a German bridge, is the record of one of the greatest victories in British history —a victory which has profoundly affected the development of the British Empire. Southey, it is true, affects to doubt whether Blenheim has any genuine historical value:—

> "'With fire and sword, the country round
>   Was wasted far and wide;
> And many a childing mother then,
>   And new-born baby died;
> But things like that, you know, must be
>   At every famous victory.
>   .   .   .   .
> 'And everybody praised the duke,
>   Who this great fight did win.'
> 'But what good came of it at last?'
>   Quoth little Peterkin.
> 'Why, that I cannot tell,' said he,
>   But 'twas a famous victory.'"

But then Southey's politics coloured his poetry. Creasy,

with justice, places Blenheim amongst the fifteen decisive battles of the world. It was a battle in the seventeenth century, which, for a time at least, destroyed the military fame and power of France almost as completely as Sedan did in the nineteenth century. "A hundred victories since Rocroi," says Green the historian, "had taught the world to regard the French army as invincible, when Blenheim, and the surrender of the flower of the French soldiery, broke the spell." But this was the least result of Blenheim. Its great merit is that it shattered absolutely and finally the attempt of Louis XIV. to establish a sort of universal empire. Louis XIV. is looked at to-day through the lens of his defeated and inglorious old age, and the true scale of his intellect, and of his ambition, is not realised. But in the qualities of an imperious will, a masterful intellect, and an ambition which vexed the peace and threatened the freedom of the world, Louis XIV. comes nearer Napoleon than not merely any other character in French history, but any other character in modern European history. "To concentrate Europe in France, France in Paris, and Paris in himself," was the ideal of Louis XIV., exactly as it was of Napoleon. The two best-remembered epigrams of Louis—"L'état, c'est moi," and "There are no longer any Pyrenees"—perfectly express the temper of his intellect and the daring of his schemes. And he came almost as near achieving success as Napoleon did. The great Bourbon had forty years of nearly unbroken triumph. He had at least one faculty of genius, that of choosing fit instruments. Louvois organised his finances, Vauban built his fortifications, Turenne and Villars and Berwick led his armies.

Louis' ambition was not less perilous to the world, because through it ran a leaven of religious intolerance. His revocation of the Edict of Nantes drove 400,000 of the best citizens of France into exile, while another 100,000 perished of hardship, or of imprisonment, or on the scaffold. When his grandson ascended the throne of Spain and the Indies, it seemed as if the French King's dream of a world monarchy was about to be realised. The "Spain" of that date, it must be remembered, included the Netherlands, Sicily, Naples, Milan, half Italy, in a word, and more than half America. Here, then, was the menace of an empire which in scale exceeded that of Cæsar, and in temper was inspired by the policy which drove the Huguenots into exile, and would have kept the Stuarts, as French pensioners, on the throne of England. As Alison puts it, "Spain had threatened the liberties of Europe at the end of the sixteenth century; France had all but overthrown them in the close of the seventeenth." What hope was there for the world if the Spain that launched the Armada against England, and the France which drove the Huguenots into exile, were united under a monarch like Louis XIV., with his motto, "L'état, c'est moi"?

Our own William III. headed, with much ill fortune, but with quenchless courage, the confederacy of England, Holland, Austria, and the other independent powers against the ambition of Louis XIV. When he died, Marlborough brought to the same great task a happier fortune, and yet more splendid abilities; and Blenheim is the victory which changed the face of history, turned to thinnest air the ambitious dreams of Louis XIV., saved Protestantism throughout Europe, and secured for the English-speaking race that freedom of development it could never have found under a Stuart dynasty, and which has made possible the British Empire of to-day.

In 1703 Bavaria joined France as an ally, and opened the door for the French generals into the very heart of Germany. At the beginning of 1704 Louis had no less than eight separate armies on foot, and his field of war stretched from Portugal to Italy. But Louis himself shaped the lines of a campaign which, in boldness of conception, is worthy to stand beside almost any of Napoleon's. One French army was already wintering in Bavaria in combination with the army of the Elector there. Louis' plan was to wage a purely defensive war at all other points; a second French army, under Marshal Tallard, on the Upper Rhine, was to march through the Black Forest into Bavaria; Villeroy, with forty battalions and thirty-nine squadrons, was to move from Flanders on the Moselle, and thence to the Danube; Vendôme, with the army of Italy, was to penetrate through the Tyrol to Salzburg. Thus four great armies were to converge to a given point in the valley of the Danube, and march upon Vienna, and there finally overthrow the Confederacy.

Marlborough penetrated this design. To be waging a few more or less inglorious sieges in Flanders, while the French generals were marching on Vienna, was, he clearly saw, to suffer hopeless and final defeat. He met Louis' strategy by a great counter-stroke: a march from Flanders through the rough country of the Upper Rhine to the Danube, gathering as he went reinforcements from every side. But the British general had to win a victory in half-a-dozen Cabinets before he could put a single soldier on the march. He had to persuade Dutch deputies, English ministers, and Imperial statesmen to consent to his strategy, and he obtained that consent by concealing its real scale from them almost as completely as he did from Louis XIV. himself. Only, perhaps, to Prince Eugene, a soldier of like spirit to himself, now in command of the Austrian armies, to Heinsius, his faithful ally in Holland, and to Godolphin, his brother-in-law at the English Treasury, did Marlborough unfold his complete design. The Dutch would never have consented to fight the French on the remote Danube; but they were lured into the scheme of a march to Coblentz, for the purpose of a campaign on the Moselle.

Marlborough's movements curiously puzzled the French generals. When he reached Coblentz, everybody believed he was going to fight on the Moselle. When he reached Mayence it was guessed that he was about to attack Alsace. But when he crossed the Neckar, and kept on his steadfast march through Würtemberg, his plan stood disclosed. There was wrath in Holland, alarm in Paris, and much agitated riding to and fro betwixt the head-quarters of the various French armies; but it was too late for the Dutch to object, and also too late for the French generals to intercept his movement, and it was clear that the combination of three French armies under Tallard, Marsin, and the Bavarian Elector, Max Emanuel, on the Danube, would be met by a counter concentration of three armies under Marlborough, Prince Eugene, and the Margrave Louis.

Marlborough's march to the Danube was a grand scheme grandly executed. Part of the route crossed the great chain of rugged hills in Würtemberg known by the name of the Rauhe Alp—the rugged Alps—but through wild passes, across swift rivers, and, in spite of tempestuous weather, the steadfast Englishman pressed on. The strength of Marlborough's force consisted of 16,000 British, sturdy infantry, equal in endurance and warlike temper to Wellington's Light Division in the Peninsula, or to the foot guards who held the Sandbag battery at Inkermann. Amongst the British cavalry was a regiment of Scots Greys and another of Royal Dragoons, equal in valour to those who, more than a century afterwards, charged across the sunken road upon the French cuirassiers at Waterloo. Their officers were men like Cutts and Rowe and Kane and Ingoldsby, not, perhaps, great generals, but soldiers who, in fighting quality, in the stubborn bulldog pluck that never recognises defeat, were equal to the Pictons, and Craufurds, and Colin Campbells of a later date.

Marlborough crossed the Rhine on May 26; on June 10, at Mondelsheim, he met Prince Eugene, and began one of the most loyal and memorable friendships in military history. Three days later the junction with Margrave Louis was effected at Grossheppach.

The tree still stands under which, nearly two hundred years ago, the three commanders sat and planned the campaign which ended at Blenheim. Of that historic three the Englishman was, no doubt, intellectually the greatest, and certainly stands highest in fame. He was fifty-four years of age; he had won no first-class battle yet, but during the next seven years he was to win a series of the greatest victories in British history. He lacked, perhaps, Wellington's fighting impulse. Marlborough, during ten campaigns, fought only ten pitched battles; Wellington, in seven, fought fifteen. But Marlborough never fought a battle he did not win, nor besieged a fortress he did not take, and in many respects he is the greatest military genius the British race has produced.

The Margrave Louis of Baden owed his place in the group under the historic tree at Grossheppach rather to his rank than to his military skill; but Prince Eugene of Savoy was in every respect a great soldier. As Stanhope puts it, he was an Italian by descent, a Frenchman by training, and a German by adoption; and in his signature, "Eugenio von Savoye," he used to combine the three languages. A little man, black-haired, black-complexioned, with lips curiously pendulous, and mouth semi-open; but with eyes through which looked a great and daring spirit. Eugene was a soldier as daring as Ney or Murat, and with their delight in the rapture of the onfall, the thunder of galloping hoofs, and the loud challenge of the cannon. But he was also one of the most loyal and generous of men, and if Marlborough was the brain of the great campaign just beginning, Eugene was its sword.

There is no space to dwell on the intermediate movements, nor even on the desperate fight round the Schellenberg, and the stern courage with which the British at last carried it, but carried it at a loss of nearly one-third their number. On August 11, 1704, the two great armies confronted each other at Blenheim.

Blenheim is a little village on the bank of the Danube; a stream called the Nebel, gathering its sources from the roots of the wooded hills to the west, runs in its front, and, curving round, so that its course is almost from north to south, falls into the Danube. From Lutzingen, on the lower slope of the hills, to

Blenheim on the Danube is a distance of four and a half miles. Blenheim formed the right wing of the French, and in it Tallard had packed nearly 16,000 infantry, the flower of his troops, fortifying the village with strong palisades. Lutzingen, on the extreme left, was held by Marsin and the Bavarian Elector, and, from the nature of the ground, was almost impregnable.

Betwixt these two positions was a marshy plain through which the Nebel flowed; in the middle of it stood a village called Oberglauh, held by fourteen battalions, amongst which were three Irish regiments destined to play a great part in the fight. Tallard covered his centre by a long screen of cavalry, strengthened by two brigades of infantry. His position thus was of great strength at either extremity, but his centre, though covered by the Nebel, and strengthened by the village of Oberglauh, was of fatal weakness, and through it Marlborough burst late in the fight, winning his great victory by a stupendous cavalry charge. It is curious, however, that Marlborough, though he had a military glance of singular keenness, did not discover the flaw in his opponent's line till the battle had been raging some hours.

Eugene, with 18,000 men, was to attack Tallard's left; Marlborough himself, with his best troops, nearly 30,000 strong—9000 of them being British—was to attack Blenheim and try and turn the French right. His cavalry was to menace the centre. Tallard had under his command 60,000 men, with ninety guns; Marlborough had 56,000 men and sixty-six guns. Marlborough's weakness lay in the strangely composite character of his forces. The battle, in this respect, has scarcely any parallel in history. To quote the historian Green, "The whole of the Teutonic race was represented in the strange medley of Englishmen, Dutchmen, Hanoverians, Danes, Würtembergers, and Austrians who followed Marlborough and Eugene." Nothing less than the warlike genius and masterful will of Marlborough could have wielded into effectiveness an army made up of such diverse elements.

Day broke on August 13 heavy with mist; and under its cover the allied forces moved forward to the attack. Tallard was quite unprepared for an engagement, when the fog, lifting for a moment, showed the whole landscape before him peopled with moving battalions and fretted with the gleam of steel. Marlborough waited till Eugene could launch his assault on the left wing of the French, and so difficult was the ground that not till nearly twelve o'clock did an aide-de-camp, galloping at speed, announce that the Prince was ready to engage. The fighting on the wooded ridges round Lutzingen was of the fiercest. Four times Eugene launched his troops in furious onset on the enemy, but such was the strength of the position held by the French and Bavarians, and with such steady valour did they fight, that Eugene's assaults were all repulsed, and he himself was only saved from disaster by the iron steadfastness of the Prussian infantry, on whose disciplined ranks the Bavarian cavalry flung themselves in vain.

The chief interest of the fight belongs to the left wing and centre, where Marlborough commanded in person. He first attempted to turn Tallard's right by assailing Blenheim. He launched against it a great infantry attack, consisting of five British battalions, with one Hessian battalion, under Rowe, supported by eleven battalions and fifteen squadrons under Cutts.

Nothing could be finer than the onfall of the British. They carried with a single rush some mills, which acted as a sort of outpost to Blenheim; then, dressing their ranks afresh, they moved coolly forward to attack the broad front of palisades which covered Blenheim. The village was crowded with 16,000 of Tallard's best troops, behind the palisades knelt long lines of infantry, while a second line standing erect fired over the heads of their kneeling comrades.

The broad red column, its general, Rowe, leading, came on with iron steadiness, the tramp of the disciplined battalions every moment sounded nearer and more menacing. When the British were within thirty yards the French fired. The long front of palisades sparkled with flame, a furious whirlwind of white smoke covered the whole front, and this was pierced again, and yet again, by the darting flames of new volleys. The British front seemed to crumble under that tempest of shot; yet it never swerved or faltered. On through smoke and flame it came. Rowe led it, moving straight forward, till he struck the palisades with his sword, and bade his men fire. The whole British front broke at the word into flame. Then the men, their officers leading, tried to carry the palisades with the bayonet. The great breach at Badajos did not witness a more fiery valour; but Blenheim was held by a force double in strength to that attacking it, with every advantage of position, and a front of fire more than double that of the British, and the attempt was hopeless from the outset. Rowe fell badly wounded; the two officers in succession who took command after he fell were slain. The men, under the whirling smoke, and scorched with the flames of incessant volleys, were trying to tear up the palisades with their hands, or clamber over them by mounting on each other's shoulders.

Suddenly through the smoke on their left came the thunder of galloping hoofs, and with a long-sustained crash twenty squadrons of French horse broke in on the British flank. The men fought in broken clusters and with desperate courage, but Rowe's regiment was almost destroyed, and its colours fell into the enemy's hands. Cutts, however—nicknamed by his men "the Salamander," from his lust of fighting, and habit of always being found where the fire was hottest—had brought up the second line, and the French cavalry recoiled before the stern valour with which the infantry fought. As they recoiled, some squadrons under Lumley came upon them in a gallop, recaptured the colours of Rowe's regiment, and drove the Frenchmen in disorder back to their lines.

Marlborough watched the furious strife around Blenheim with steady eye, and was satisfied that in Blenheim itself Tallard was impregnable. He withdrew his troops from the attack, the men falling sullenly back, full of unsatisfied eagerness for a new assault; but Marlborough had discovered the flaw in Tallard's centre. He kept up the feint of an attack on Blenheim, but commenced to push his cavalry and some battalions of infantry through the marshy ground and across the Nebel which covered Tallard's centre.

It was a difficult feat. Tracks through the marshy bottom had to be made with fascines and planks, and along these the mud-splashed cavalry crept, in single file, and floundered through the Nebel, or crossed by temporary bridges. Tallard committed the fatal mistake of not charging them till they had crossed in great numbers; then, while they were busy re-forming, he flung his squadrons upon them. But Marlborough had stiffened his cavalry with some battalions of infantry, and while the French and Bavarian cavalry broke in furious waves of assault upon them, these stood, like steadfast islets ringed with steel and fire, with exactly the same immovable valour the British squares showed at Waterloo more than a century afterwards. Tallard's horse recoiled, Marlborough's squadrons re-formed, and the moment for the great cavalry assault, which was to break the French centre and win Blenheim, came.

First, however, the village of Oberglauh, which stood as a sort of rocky barrier in the line of the coming charge, and was strongly held by an infantry force, had to be carried. Marlborough launched the Prince of Holstein-Beck, with eleven battalions of Hanoverians, against the village; but part of the force which held the village consisted of the celebrated Irish Brigade, the last survivors of the gallant and ill-fated battalions who followed Sarsfield into France. Their departure was long remembered in Ireland itself as "the flight of the wild geese," but the Irish regiments played a brilliant part in continental battles. After Fontenoy, where the Irish regiments alone proved equal to the task of arresting the terrible British column, George II. is reported to have said, "Cursed be the laws which deprive me of such subjects." And at Blenheim the Irish regiments seemed likely, at one moment, to play a part as great as at Fontenoy. They broke from Oberglauh upon the Prince of Holstein's column, tumbled it into ruin, took the Prince himself a prisoner, and hurled his men a mere wreck down the slope. For the moment Marlborough's centre was broken by that wild charge.

The Irish, with characteristic recklessness, were pursuing the routed Hanoverians, when Marlborough broke upon their flank with some squadrons of British cavalry.

The Hanoverians themselves, a mere tumult of flying men, swept round the flank of a line of steady British foot, drawn across the line of their retreat, and this, too, opened a close and deadly fire on the Irish brigade as, breathless and disordered, it came down the slope. With horsemen on its flank, and unbroken infantry scourging it with fire in front, the Irish brigade was flung back in defeat to Oberglauh. Then came the great cavalry charge which decided the fight.

Marlborough resembled Hannibal in his use of cavalry for the deciding stroke in a great battle, and he had now no less than 8000 horse, a long line of nodding plumes and gleaming swords, ready to launch on Tallard's centre. Behind were steady battalions of infantry, under the cover of whose fire the horsemen might re-form if the attack failed. In front was the long slope, soft with grass and elastic to the stroke of the galloping hoofs, an ideal field for a great cavalry charge. Tallard had drawn up his cavalry in two lines and had interlaced them with batteries of artillery and squares of infantry. These were drawn up slightly below the crest of the ridge, so as to exactly cover the summit with their fire.

At five o'clock Marlborough launched the great attack. Slowly at first, but gathering momentum as they advanced, the long lines of horsemen came on. The air was full of the clangour of scabbard on stirrup, the squadrons were just stretching themselves out into a gallop, as they reached the summit of the ridge, when they were smitten by the fire of the French infantry and artillery. So deadly and close was the volley that the leading squadrons went down before it, and for a few wild minutes, under the canopy of whirling smoke, Marlborough's horsemen were in fierce confusion. That was the moment for a counter-stroke! Tallard saw it, and gave the word to his cavalry to charge. They were more numerous than the British, yet they faltered. "I saw an instant," wrote the unfortunate Tallard afterwards, "in which the battle was gained if——" his cavalry, in brief, had charged! But it failed to charge. The moment of possible victory vanished, and over the crest, with bent heads and wind-blown crests, the gleam of a thousand swords and the thunder of innumerable galloping hoofs, came the British cavalry.

Tallard's centre was broken as with the stroke of a thunderbolt! His infantry was swept into ruin, his cavalry hurled into disordered flight, and his army fairly cut in twain. His left wing fell back, fighting desperately; but his right, the *élite* of his army, was hopelessly shut up in Blenheim itself. As night fell Marlborough drew his lines closely round the village. Webb, with the Queen's regiment, blocked one avenue of escape, a cavalry force—one regiment of which consisted of Scots Greys—guarded the other. The French general in command of Blenheim, believing the situation to be desperate, ignobly abandoned his men and tried to swim his horse across the Danube, and was very properly drowned in the attempt. For a time the fight round Blenheim was furious. Part of the village took fire, and in the light of the red flames Frenchmen and Englishmen fought hand to hand with fiery valour. But with the centre destroyed, and the left wing in full retreat, the condition of Tallard's right, shut up in Blenheim, was hopeless, and 11,000 French infantry laid down their arms as prisoners of war. The great French army, 60,000 strong, composed in the main of veterans and familiar with victory, practically ceased to exist.

That battle changed the course of history. It destroyed the dream of a universal empire which Louis XIV. had cherished so long; it secured for the Anglo-Saxon race that opportunity of free development which has made the Empire of to-day possible.

LORD ANSON

From a mezzotint by J. M'Ardell, *after the portrait by* Sir Joshua Reynolds, P.R.A.

LORD ANSON AND THE "CENTURION"

1740-44

> "Anson could not himself settle the Spanish war; but he did, on his own score, a series of things, ending in beautiful finish of the Acapulco ship, which were of considerable detriment, and of highly considerable disgrace, to Spain; and were, and are long likely to be, memorable among the sea-heroisms of the world. Giving proof that real captains, taciturn sons of Anak, are still born in England; and sea-kings, equal to any that were. . . . That memorable Voyage of his is a real poem in its kind, or romance all fact; one of the pleasantest little books in the world's library at this date. Anson sheds some tincture of heroic beauty over that otherwise altogether hideous puddle of mismanagement, platitude, and disaster; and vindicates, in a pathetically potential way, the honour of this poor nation a little."—CARLYLE.

IN one of the wards of Greenwich Hospital there stood until the year 1870 a huge lion rampant, carved in wood, at least sixteen feet high. It was, from the artist's point of view, a very bold and spirited figure; but the contours were blurred, the finer lines of the 'graver's chisel were almost obliterated by the sea-winds of many years. It was the figure-head of the *Centurion*, a ship scarcely inferior in fame to Drake's *Golden Hind*, in which Anson, one of the great sailors of our race, made his immortal voyage round the world in 1740-44. In 1870 it was transferred to the playground of the hospital school, and fell to pieces from decay in 1873. That fierce, bold lion's head, that for four stormy years groped its way round the globe—before it the waste seas of the

New World, behind it such a freight at once of perishing lives and of heroic hearts as before or since, perhaps, the sea-winds never blew upon—might well have been preserved. It was one of the most honourable relics of British history. On no other bit of carved wood had fiercer tempest blown, or a wilder smoke of battle eddied. The one surviving fragment of Drake's *Royal Hind*, it will be remembered, is in the shape of a chair in Oxford University, and to it Cowley addressed the fine and oft-quoted lines:—

> "To this great ship, which round the world has run,
> And matched in race the chariot of the sun,
> This Pythagorean ship (for it may claim,
> Without presumption, so deserved a name,
> By knowledge once, and transformation now),
> In her new shape, this sacred port allow.
> Drake and his ship could not have wished from Fate
> A more blest station, or more blest estate,
> For, lo! a seat of endless rest is given
> To her in Oxford, to him in heaven."

The figure-head of the *Centurion* was threatened for a while with a more ignoble fate. When the famous ship, after a cruising and fighting career of thirty years, was broken up, the figure-head was sent to George III. His prosaic German brain discovered no charm in a relic so wooden and so big, and he passed it on to the Duke of Richmond, then Master-General of the Ordnance, who allowed it to be turned into the sign of a public-house on his estate. William IV. was sailor enough to value this memorial of one of the most famous ships that ever flew the British flag; he begged the figure-head from the duke, and placed it at the head of the grand staircase in Windsor Castle. And for years, beneath the grim lion's head that had looked out so long on tempest and battle, flowed the dainty and idle figures that people a court. Presently the superfine taste of some gentleman-in-waiting quarrelled with this storm-beaten relic, and it was conveyed, like other sea-battered hulks, to Greenwich Hospital. It stood for many years in what is called the Anson Ward, lifting its warlike head high above the beds tenanted by many an old salt. On its pedestal were inscribed some lines plainly suggested by Cowley's:—

> "Stay, traveller, awhile, and view
> One who has travell'd more than you:
> Quite round the globe, through each degree,
> Anson and I have plough'd the sea;
> Torrid and frigid zones have past,
> And—safe ashore arrived at last—
> In ease with dignity appear,
> He in the House of Lords, I here."

Whoever desires to read a story which illustrates all the finest qualities of the English sailor—his cool fortitude, his bulldog tenacity of purpose, his magnificent fighting energy—which have made the British flag the supreme symbol of power in every sea, cannot do better than listen while, in the briefest fashion, the story of Anson's immortal voyage and his capture of the great Mexican galleon is told afresh.

Anson, born in 1697, was a lawyer by descent, but a sailor by some imperative necessity in his very blood. He was a sailor, however, not in the least of Nelson's or of Dundonald's type—dazzling, brilliant, with a gleam of genius running through his imagination like a thread of gold through rough canvas. He was a sailor of the school of Howe and of Collingwood; plain, sagacious, homely, dogged: to whom seamanship was a sort of seabird's instinct, and downright hard-fighting courage as natural as breathing—the stuff out of which the finest sailors and the most terrible fighters in history are made. Anson was an almost absolutely inarticulate man. Scarcely a letter is in existence written by his hand. He sat for years in the House of Lords, yet never made a speech. A familiar epigram says of him that he went round the world, but was never in it. Although he filled one of the greatest posts in the State —he was Vice-Admiral of Great Britain, and First Lord of the Admiralty during the Seven Years' War—he had none of the arts of the courtier, and no touch of the politician's adroit pliability. He was as much out of place in the gaieties of society as a seagull would have been in a cage of canaries.

But he was a great administrator as well as a great sailor. He stamped the impress of his practical seamanship on the navy of Great Britain. He formed, without the least intending it, a distinct school of British sailors; and the men he trained—Howe, Saunders, Byron, Hyde, Parker, Keppel, &c.—won many glories for the British flag. "The lieutenants and midshipmen of his ship and squadron," says Barrow, "were the admirals of the Seven Years' and the American Wars." Anson, too, was modest, humane, simple-minded, with an heroic standard of duty. His life is rich in the record of stirring deeds, but no chapter is more dramatic and stirring, or more characteristic of the qualities which have built up the British Empire, than that which tells the story of his famous voyage round the world and his capture of the great galleon.

Anson, though parted by two centuries from Drake, is, in reality, Drake's lineal successor, and the *Centurion* was the second British ship that circumnavigated the world. Anson, too, curiously repeated Drake's fortunes. Drake sailed from Plymouth at the end of 1577 with five ships, the largest of 100 tons, the smallest of 15 tons burden. He returned in a little less than three years, rich in treasure, but with only a single ship, and two men out of every three who sailed with him had perished. Anson sailed from Spithead, September 18, 1740, with six vessels, the *Centurion*, of sixty guns, being his flagship; his voyage lasted nearly four years; he came back, like Drake, rich in treasure won from the great foe of the British flag of that day—the Spaniard; but, like Drake, he brought back only one ship of his squadron and the losses amongst his crews were even more tragical than in the expedition of Drake.

The despatch of Anson's squadron was one of the direct results of the storm of passion awakened in England by the familiar story of "Jenkins's ear." The expedition was designed to round the Horn, carry battle and reprisal along the Spanish coasts in the South Sea, ravage, for example, the coast of Peru, make a dash at Callao, capture the great Acapulco galleon conveying the annual tribute of gold from Mexico to Spain, and return to England by the way of China. The squadron was to be strengthened by Bland's regiment of foot, and three independent companies of infantry, each 100 strong. From the outset, however, the same almost incredible stupidity of administration which afterwards destroyed the Walcheren expedition and produced the tragedy of the Crimea, did its evil best to wreck Anson's squadron. It was delayed until winter had made the passage round the Horn perilous. The news of the expedition was allowed to filter through to Spain, and a strong squadron under Admiral Pizarro was despatched to lie in wait for the British ships. Anson could not get seamen for his crews; and, instead of Bland's regiment and the independent companies of foot, 500 invalids, out-pensioners of Chelsea Hospital, were detailed for the squadron. Anson's remonstrances were vain. Only 259 of these unfortunate invalids, it is true, were actually got on board, for "all those who had limbs, and strength to walk out of Portsmouth, deserted"; and never was seen such a collection of cripples as that which the astonished crews of Anson's squadron saw emptied upon them. Many of them were over seventy years of age; many were blind; nearly all were bent with sickness, twisted with rheumatism, &c.

The ships, in brief, intended for a long and desperate expedition, were, by way of preliminary, turned into floating infirmaries! Not one of these unfortunate invalids, it may be added, lived to return to England! To supply the place of the 240 more vigorous invalids who had hobbled off in alarm, an equal number of newly recruited marines—most of them boys who had never fired a shot or worn a uniform—were drafted on board. Thus laden with sickness and infirmity at the very outset, Anson's squadron set out on its ill-fated yet splendid voyage.

Anson's squadron consisted of the *Centurion*, of 60 guns, the *Gloucester* and the *Severn*, of 50 guns each, the *Wager*, of 28 guns, and the *Tryal*, a sloop of 8 guns, with a couple of victuallers—ships intended to follow the squadron with supplies during the early stages of the voyage. The *Wager* is the ship whose wreck constitutes one of the best-remembered tragedies of the British navy. The squadron took forty days to reach Madeira, and sailed thence, on November 3, for St. Jago, one of the Cape Verde islands being appointed as a rendezvous. The weather continued fine, but already scurvy had broken out in the squadron, and Anson commenced to cut air-scuttles in all the ships to sweeten, if possible, the gloomy, unlit, evil-smelling decks where his unfortunate invalids were already beginning to die like sheep in pestilence. Anson's ships, it must be remembered, were of the old type—short-bodied, high-sterned, with bluff bows and low deck, and square yards on their jib-booms—ships almost as unsinkable as a bottle, but about as weatherly and as well-ventilated as so many corked bottles.

One piece of good fortune at this early stage of the voyage befell Anson. The Spanish squadron under Pizarro, despatched to intercept Anson's ships, had cruised for some days off Madeira; then, being seized with a sudden spasm of prudence, had sailed for Cape Horn, Pizarro having resolved to wait for Anson in the South Seas—if he ever reached those waters. Anson would, no doubt, have fallen with bulldog courage on Pizarro if the squadrons had met off Madeira, and, though the Spanish ships were more heavily armed and strongly manned than his own, would have sunk or captured them. But the mere business of clearing for action would have required Anson to jettison half the provisions with which his ships were packed, and his voyage must have been sacrificed—a disaster for which victory would have been a poor compensation. The Spanish ships, however, had effaced themselves, and unmerciful disaster followed them so fast and so furiously that the story of Pizarro's squadron is more tragical than even that of Anson's. One Spanish ship foundered at sea, a second was wrecked on the coast of Brazil. Famine stalked, gaunt and hungry, betwixt the decks of the Spanish ships, and mutiny followed hard on the heels of famine. A tiny cluster of Indians, eleven in all, being cruelly treated on board the Spanish flagship, the *Asia*, suddenly seized that ship one night off Buenos Ayres, slew many of the crew and officers, and there was witnessed the amazing spectacle of a ship carrying 66 guns and 500 men being held by eleven Indians. The Spanish admiral barricaded himself in his cabin for safety, part of the crew in wild terror escaped into the tops, and the rest were battened down between decks. For two hours the Indians held possession of the ship, but, their chief being shot, the rest jumped overboard. Pizarro, with this single surviving ship, reached Spain early in 1746, having spent nearly five years in distracted and tragical wanderings, and bringing back a single ship out of a squadron, and less than 100 survivors out of crews which originally numbered over 3000!

Anson's ships, meanwhile, with scurvy fermenting in the blood of every second man in the crews, were running down the Strait of Le Maire. Scarcely had they cleared the Strait, when the wildest weather of which the gloomy latitudes of Cape Horn are capable broke upon the unfortunate squadron. Never were fiercer seas or blacker skies, or gales more cruelly edged with sleet and ice. The very sails were frozen. The rigging was turned into mere ladders of ice. The decks were slippery as glass, and the great seas dashed incessantly over them. The groaning and overstrained ships let in water in every seam, and for over fifty days each furious gale was followed by one yet more furious. The *Centurion's* courses were actually kept reefed for fifty-eight days! The squadron was scattered, the *Severn* and *Pearl* never rejoining. On May 8, Anson himself was off the island of Socorro, and for a fortnight he hung there in the hope that some other ship of the squadron would make its appearance.

It was the wildest of scenes. Fierce westerly gales raged. The coast, a line of jagged precipices, was one mad tumult of foam. When the low, black skies were for a moment rent asunder, they only revealed the Cordilleras of the Andes, gaunt peaks white with snow, and torn with scuffling winds. All this time, too, Anson's crew was perishing fast with scurvy of the most malignant type. The body of a poor scurvy-smitten wretch was mottled with black spots. Limbs and gums were swollen to an enormous size, and broke into putrid eruptions. Old wounds broke out afresh. Bones that had been fractured, and had set firmly again for years, parted, the new bone dissolving into mere fluid. On the body of one veteran, who had been wounded fifty years before at the battle of the Boyne, the wounds gaped bloody-red, as though just inflicted. The men died so fast, or sickened so hopelessly, that by the middle of June from the *Centurion* alone more than 200 corpses had been thrown overboard, and, to quote the chaplain's record, " we could not at last muster more than six foremast men in a watch capable of duty." On

May 22, a new gale broke on the sorely buffeted *Centurion*, in which the fury of all the tempests that ever blew seemed to be concentrated. The *Centurion* survived, and, a lonely, half-wrecked ship, full of sick and dying men, bore up for Juan Fernandez.

In practical seamanship Anson and his officers were unsurpassed among the sailors of all ages and of all seas; but the appliances of navigation in 1740 were rude, and the science of it imperfectly understood. Anson intended "to hit the island on a meridian," and, believing himself to be on the required parallel, on May 28 he ran it down, until, at the exact moment, when they expected to see Juan Fernandez, there broke upon his look-outs the vision of the snow-clad summits of the Cordilleras of Chili! Anson, in a word, had missed the island, and it took him nine days to claw back to the westward and come in sight of Juan Fernandez. And during those nine days his men died so fast that "out of two hundred and odd men which remained alive we could not, taking all our watches together, muster hands enough to work the ship on an emergency, though we included the officers, their servants, and their boys." The next day the *Tryal* made its appearance; out of her crew of 100 men, 34 had died. Only the captain, lieutenant, and three men were able to stand by the sails. On June 21 the *Gloucester* hove in sight of the rendezvous. On that unhappy ship two-thirds of the crew had already perished; only the officers and their servants were capable of duty. Anson sent off provisions and men to her; but the wind was unfavourable, the *Gloucester* little better than a wreck, and she actually hung in sight of Juan Fernandez for a month without being able to make the anchorage, alternately flitting ghost-like beyond the sea-rim, and then reappearing! It seemed likely, indeed, that she would be left at last to drift a mere ship of the dead on the sea. When at last the sorely tried ship dropped its anchor, out of its original crew of 300 men only 80 remained alive.

Anson's squadron was now reduced to a couple of shattered, half-manned cruisers and a sloop, and Anson devoted himself to refitting his ships, and restoring the health of his men. The *Pearl* and the *Severn* had been driven back to the coast of Brazil, and had given up the expedition. The *Wager* had been wrecked; and the story of the tragedy, with its mingled heroism and horror, is told in the familiar narrative by one of its two midshipmen, afterwards Admiral Byron, and the grandfather of Lord Byron, the poet.

Anson remained for over a hundred days at Juan Fernandez. The three ships with him had crews amounting to 961 men when they sailed from England, and of these already 626 were dead. There remained of his squadron only three shattered vessels, with 335 men and boys divided betwixt them. How could he hope with these to face Pizarro's squadron, to attack any of the Spanish possessions, or to capture the great Acapulco galleon? Anson, however, was of that stubborn and resolute courage which only hardens under the impact of disaster. He despatched the *Tryal* to cruise off Valparaiso, and the *Gloucester* off Paita, while the *Centurion* cruised betwixt the two points. Some valuable prizes were captured, and then Anson with his three ships made a dash at Paita itself, a gallant feat worthy of Drake or of Hawkins.

Paita was respectably fortified, and held by a considerable garrison. Anson despatched three boats and fifty-eight men, under Lieutenant Brett, against the town, keeping his ships out of sight of land. Brett pulled with cool daring through the dark night, and almost reached the fort before the alarm was given. Then lights flashed through the awakening town, the church bells rang, the garrison ran to arms, the guns of the fort flashed redly through the darkness over the boats. But Brett, pulling with silent speed across the bay, leaped ashore, carried the fort with a rush, the governor and the garrison fleeing; and sixty British sailors remained in undisputed possession of the town, only one man of the attacking party being killed and two wounded! Anson's ships by daybreak were off the town, and more than £30,000 in coined silver was carried on board from the public treasury, and the whole town was burnt, though no injury was offered to the inhabitants.

Anson next proceeded to lay a trap for the Acapulco ship, scattering his tiny squadron in a semicircle—but out of sight of land—off Acapulco. The Spaniards, however, somehow caught a gleam of the white topsails of one of his ships over the edge of the horizon, and at that signal of terror the sailing of the galleon was postponed for a year! Anson, discovering this, turned the stems of his vessels to the wide and lonely Pacific. He would cruise off the coast of California, and intercept the Manilla galleon, on its voyage to Acapulco. He destroyed all his prizes, and began his voyage with two ships, the *Centurion* and the *Gloucester*. Scurvy broke out afresh. A furious gale smote the two English ships. On July 26, the captain of the *Gloucester* hailed the *Centurion*, and reported that his mainmast was sprung, and discovered to be completely rotten; he had seven feet of water in the hold; only ninety-seven of the crew, including officers and boys, remained, and out of this whole number only sixteen men and eleven boys were capable of keeping the deck.

Anson's dogged purpose never swerved. He transshipped to the *Centurion* the *Gloucester's* crew and part of her stores, and then set fire to her. Anson's squadron of five ships was thus reduced to a single vessel, a floating speck on the tossing floor of the wide and empty Pacific. The men, too, were dying at the rate of ten or twelve a day. The ship was leaky. Provisions were bad, and the supply of water almost exhausted. Still Anson kept steadfastly on his course, and on August 28 sighted Tinian, one of the Ladrone islands. Twenty-one of the crew died after the island came in sight, and before the sick could be landed; but the pure water and fresh fruits of Tinian arrested the raging scurvy as if by magic. Anson himself was down with scurvy amongst the sick on the island, when, on September 23, a furious tempest tore the *Centurion* from her anchorage, and she vanished over the horizon, amidst raging seas and driving rain. Anson seemed to be abandoned utterly, without resources or help. His steadfast courage, however remained unshaken. He crept from his tent with the poison of scurvy still in his blood, and set the men to work to lengthen a tiny twelve-foot boat they had. He would sail in it across the 600 leagues of trackless sea, without compass or chart, to Macao! On October 11, however, the storm-rent canvas of the *Centurion* was visible once more over the sky-line, and she crept back slowly to her anchorage.

Anson refitted his ship, sailed from Tinian on October 21, and reached Macao on November 12. It was two years since he left Spithead—two years into which had been packed as much of suffering and hardship, of tempest, and plague, and death, and of the heroism, which not tempest, nor plague, nor death itself could shake, as can be found, perhaps, in any other sea story extant.

Anson remained at Macao till April 19, 1743; then, with ship refitted, though not remanned, and stores renewed, he set sail ostensibly for Batavia, and thence to England. But when out of sight of land he called his men aft, told them there must be two galleons sailing from Acapulco this year, and he intended to capture them both! Each galleon, it might be added was double in weight of artillery and fighting force to the *Centurion*; but that circumstance Anson regarded as an irrelevant detail, to be dismissed without further consideration! Anson's men, hardened by suffering, and careless of peril, and full of confidence in their silent, much-enduring captain, welcomed the announcement with a shout, and the stem of the *Centurion* was turned towards the Philippine Islands, one of the way-marks in the course of the gold-ships of Spain. Anson's crew, at that moment, consisted of 201 hands, including officers, idlers, and boys; he had only forty-five able seamen. Each galleon, on the other hand, carried a crew of about 600 men. Anson warned his crew that the galleons were "stout ships and fully manned"; but Jack Tar's arithmetic, when applied to the business of reckoning up an enemy's force, is of curious quality; and Anson's men felt as cheerfully confident of capturing the wealth of the Spanish treasure-ships as though the yellow gold were already in their breeches' pockets! Anson's chaplain, indeed, tells an amusing story in proof of this. A few Chinese sheep were on board, intended for the officers' table, but for some days no mutton made its appearance there. The ship's butcher, on being interrogated, explained that only two sheep were left, and he was reserving those for the entertainment of "the generals of the galleons" after they were captured!

On May 30, the *Centurion* reached the desired cruising ground off Cape Espiritu Santo, and day by day, during all the month of June, the sky-line was searched by keen look-outs from the mastheads of the *Centurion*. The days went tamely by, and offered only the same spectacle of azure sea and azure sky, and a horizon broken by no gleam of white sail. On June 20, however, a quick-eyed middy, at the main topmast of the *Centurion*, caught a point of gleaming silver on the sky-line too steady for a seagull's wing. The news ran through the ship. It was early dawn, and soon in the glittering sunlight—a little south of where the day was breaking—the long-looked-for sail was visible. Only one ship, however, was in sight. Where was its consort? At half-past seven the galleon fired a gun, and took in her topgallant sails; this surely was a signal to her consort, still out of sight! And it shows the amazing audacity of Anson that he bore steadily down to attack two ships, each of which was double his own in strength. As a matter of fact, however, there was only a solitary galleon before him—a great ship with heavy guns, huge quarter-deck galleries, and a crew of over six hundred men. Its captain, a gallant Spaniard, bore steadily down, the standard of Spain flying at the masthead, and at noon, being about a league distant from the *Centurion*, brought to under topsails, and waited resolutely for the *Centurion* to begin the fight.

Anson stood on in perfect fighting rig. He had placed thirty of his best marksmen in his tops, and expected with them to scourge the Spaniard's decks with fire and drive the men from their guns. He had not one-fourth the number of hands necessary to work his broadside, and he detailed two men to each gun, whose sole business it was to load it; the rest he divided into gangs of ten, whose business it was to pass from gun to gun as it was loaded, run it out, aim, and discharge it. He thus kept up a constant fire of single guns, instead of firing whole broadsides; and his method had an unsuspected advantage. "It is common with the Spaniards," writes his chaplain, "to fall down upon the decks when they see a broadside preparing, and to continue in that posture until it is given; after which they rise again, and, presuming the danger to be for some time over, work their guns, and fire with great briskness, till another broadside is ready." Anson's plan of a continuous fire of single well-aimed guns, however, quite spoiled these Spanish tactics and abated their "briskness."

A squall of wind and rain broke over the two ships as they neared each other, and Anson could see through the driving rain that his antagonist was caught unprepared. The Spaniards were still busy throwing overboard cattle and lumber to clear their decks for the fight. Anson's original plan was to engage at pistol-shot distance, but he at once opened fire, in order to increase the confusion of his enemy. Steadily the *Centurion* came on, till, through the smoke, its lion's head could be seen gliding menacingly past the Spaniard's broadside. Then, having overreached the galleon, Anson swung into the wind, across his enemy's bows, and raked the Spaniard with a deadly fire. The galleon had not only hoisted her boarding netting, to prevent the English boarding, but, in addition, had stuffed the netting with mats, as a protection against musketry. But Anson was engaging so closely that the flame of his guns—or their burning wads—set fire to the mats, and these broke into a fire which blazed up half as high as the mizzen-top, and Anson slackened the fury of his guns, lest his prize should be destroyed. The Spaniards then cut their netting adrift, and the whole flaming mass fell into the sea.

Anson's marksmen in the *Centurion's* tops had, meanwhile, shot down their immediate antagonists in the tops of the galleon, and were, by this time, pouring a deadly fire on the galleon's upper deck. Only one Spanish officer, in fact, remained unhurt on the galleon's quarter-deck. The *Centurion*, however, had lost her advantage of position on the galleon's bows, and the two ships, lying broadside to broadside, at half pistol-shot distance, pelted each other with heavy shot for a full hour. But the trained skill and obstinate courage of the English proved irresistible. The ships had drifted so near that the Spanish officers could be seen running about with brandished swords trying to keep their men from deserting their guns. At last the great yellow flag of Spain fluttered sullenly down, through the smoke, from the masthead of the galleon, and Anson stepped on to the blood-stained deck of his prize.

Just at that moment one of the *Centurion's* lieutenants whispered in his ear that the *Centurion* was dangerously on fire near the powder-room. At the same moment, too, the galleon, with no steersman at its wheel, rolled heavily on the starboard quarter of the *Centurion*, and the crash shook both the ships from stem to stern. It was a crisis to shake the nerves of the bravest men, but Anson's coolness was above proof. The galleon was quickly got under control; a few quick, calm orders mastered the fire, and Anson's victory was secure. His prize had lost nearly a hundred and fifty men, killed and wounded. Her masts were splintered stumps; one hundred and fifty shot had passed through her hull—a sufficient testimony to the deadly quality of the British fire. Only fifteen shot, on the other hand, had pierced the hull of the *Centurion*, and its killed and wounded numbered only thirty-one. Anson's difficulties, in a sense, were increased by his very success. He had, with his handful of men, to navigate two large ships through dangerous and unknown seas, and to keep guard over four hundred and ninety-two prisoners. His prisoners, too, were restive, when they saw how slender was the crew of the *Centurion*, and how many of them were mere striplings. They became furious with shame at having been beaten, as they said, by "a handful of boys"! At any moment, too, for aught Anson knew, the sister galleon might heave in sight.

Anson, however, took his measures coolly. He put his lieutenant, Saumarez, in charge of the prize, transferred the bulk of the prisoners to the *Centurion*, and bore up for Canton, guarding his hatchways with swivel-guns loaded with musket bullets, a sentry with a lighted match standing day and night beside each gun. Every English officer, meanwhile, remained on constant guard, lying down, when his turn came, for a brief sleep, dressed, and with a weapon by his side. Thus guarding his prize, Anson reached Canton on June 30. There he liberated his prisoners, and started on his voyage home by the Cape of Good Hope, casting anchor at Spithead on June 15, 1744.

The last incident of the voyage was perhaps as dramatic as any during its whole course. War had been declared betwixt France and England, and a French fleet was cruising in the chops of the Channel. When the much-buffeted *Centurion*, however, crossed their cruising-ground, a thick grey fog lay on the Channel; and, all unconscious of his peril, and catching from time to time the faint muffled sound of bells from unseen ships, Anson moved on his course and reached Spithead in safety, thus completing a voyage more amazing in its incidents than that of Drake two centuries before.

The galleon, of course, was a very rich prize. In its strong-room were 1,313,843 pieces of eight, and more than 35,000 ounces of silver plate, or of virgin silver. Drake's expedition had its profitable commercial side. The British sailor of that period was, in fact, an odd compound of bagman and of buccaneer: and the *Golden Hind* expedition paid a dividend of £47 for every £1 invested in it. There are some very golden patches of prize-money in British naval history. In 1799, for example, the *Ethalion* captured the *Thetis*, with 1,400,000 dollars on board. The *Naiad* and *Triton* captured the *Santa Brigida*, with an equal amount of treasure. Each captain received as his share of the prize-money £40,731, 18s., each lieutenant £5091, 7s. 3d., and each seaman £182, 4s. 9d.! Yet earlier, in 1762, the treasure-ship *Hermione* was captured off Cadiz by the *Actæon*, of 28 guns, and the *Favourite*, of 18 guns. Each captain, in this case, received £65,000 as prize-money, each lieutenant £13,000, each petty officer £2000, and each seaman £500! Anson's galleon, however, shines resplendent in even such golden records as these. Yet the gold won by the *Centurion* was its least precious gain. The voyage of the great ship added enduring fame to the British flag, and its record remains as a shining example of the fortitude and the valour which have built up the British Empire.

GEORGE II.

From an engraving by J. C. ARMYTAGE

GEORGE II. AT DETTINGEN

June 27, 1743

TOWARDS the close of the month of June 1743, a great army of 40,000 gallant men, under a British general, Lord Stair, lay bewildered and helpless in the narrow valley, some eight miles long, betwixt Dettingen and Aschaffenburg. It seemed a doomed army. In the judgment of their exultant enemies, at least, the shadow of swift-coming surrender and captivity lay upon it. In that German valley, the tragedy of the Caudine Forks, they thought, was to be translated into modern terms at British cost! An English king, too, the last crowned British monarch who commanded an army in actual battle, was in that imperilled host. And to the light-tripping French imagination there had already arisen the golden vision of a captive English king, with his subjugated troops, being led in triumph through the streets of Paris; thus compensating distressed French pride for the disasters of Crécy and of Poitiers, and the promenade of John I. as a captive through London!

France, it is to be noted, has enjoyed few "consolations" of this character. Great Britain is not generally looked upon as a "military" nation; her true field is the sea. Yet, to quote Alison:—

"She has inflicted far greater *land* disasters on her

redoubtable neighbour, France, than all the military monarchies of Europe put together. English armies, for one hundred and twenty years, ravaged France, while England has not seen the fires of a French camp since the battle of Hastings. English troops have twice taken the French capital; an English king was crowned at Paris; a French king rode captive through London; a French emperor died in English captivity, and his remains were surrendered by English generosity. Twice the English horse marched from Calais to the Pyrenees; once from the Pyrenees to Calais; the monuments of Napoleon in the French capital at this moment owe their preservation from German revenge to an English general. All the great disasters and days of mourning for France since the battle of Hastings—Tenchebray, Crécy, Poitiers, Azincour, Verneuil, Crevant, Blenheim, Oudenarde, Ramillies, Malplaquet, Minden, Dettingen, Quebec, Egypt, Talavera, Salamanca, Vittoria, the Pyrenees, Orthes, Waterloo—were gained by English generals, and won, for the most part, by English soldiers. Even at Fontenoy, the greatest victory of which France can boast since Hastings, every regiment in the French army was, on their own admission, routed by the terrible English column, and victory was snatched from its grasp solely from want of support on the part of the Dutch and Austrians. No coalition against France has ever been successful in which England did not take a prominent part; none in the end has failed of gaining its objects, in which she stood foremost in the fight."—Alison's "Life of Marlborough," ii. 432.

By all the known and ordinary rules of war, the

position of the allied army at Dettingen was hopeless. To the north rose, steep and trackless, and black with pines, the Spessart hills. To the south—its banks here and there liquefying into a sour morass—flowed the river Maine. The strip of valley betwixt river and hills averaged not more than half a mile in width; and

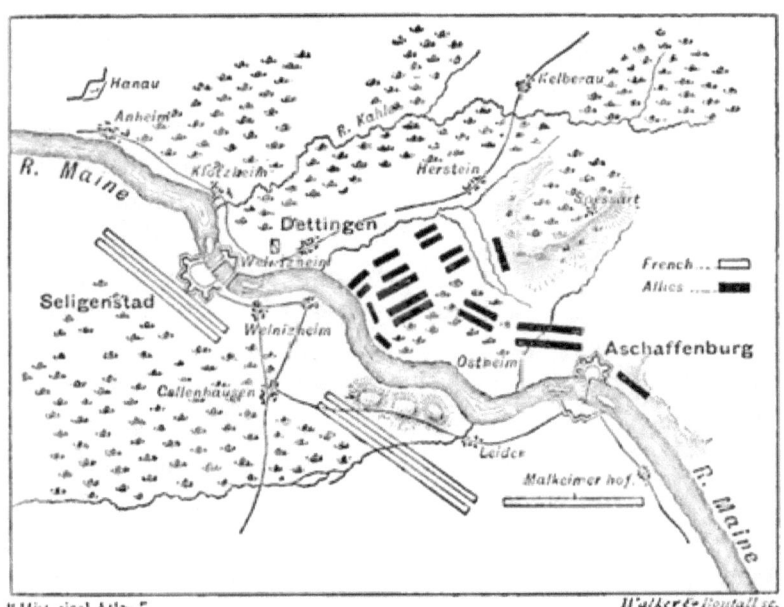

PLAN OF DETTINGEN.

on the high southern bank of the Maine, which commanded, as the broadside of a frigate might command a yacht, the low and narrow valley, wet and treacherous with bogs, where the British were stranded, was a great French army, 70,000 strong, under the most famous of living French generals, the Marshal de Noailles. A master of the art of war, De Noailles had thrust a strong force over the bridges at Aschaffenburg across the van of the allied army, barring its march. He had drawn 23,000 men across the Maine at Dettingen, cutting Lord Stair from his base at Hanau. And from Dettingen to Aschaffenburg French batteries, perched on the high southern bank of the Maine, stood ready to scourge with fire the narrow valley opposite, crowded with a stranded and starving army.

The most serious feature in the position of the allied army was the fact that its communications were cut, and its supplies exhausted. An army, according to Frederick the Great, "moves on its stomach," and the British stomach, in that strait little valley north of the Maine, had got past the marching stage. There was a scanty supply of unripe rye for the horses, and a yet scantier supply of unnutritious ammunition bread for the men; but the interval betwixt that host of 40,000 hungry soldiers and mere famine was measurable by hours. De Noailles, in a word, was applying, in 1743, to the British army he had caught in so pretty a trap, the very treatment which Bismarck applied to Paris in 1870. He was allowing it to "stew in its own juice," and was superintending the process with a dainty ingenuity which, from the abstract military point of view, was altogether admirable.

Of that imperilled 40,000 only 16,000 were pure British; the rest were Hanoverians, Hessians, &c., hired and nourished by British gold. But the experiment of trying to starve into tame surrender 40,000 soldiers of British or German stock, with muskets in their hands, is a somewhat perilous business for even the most adroit of military artists. Soldiers of British or kindred blood, their native courage edged and made dour by hunger, are very apt, in such straits, to turn on their tormentors, and, in violation of all the rules of war, tumble them into ruin. As Carlyle puts it, "40,000 enraged people of English and other Platt-Teutsch type would have been very difficult to pin up into captivity or death, instead of breakfast. . . . The hungry Baresarks, their blood fairly up, would find or make a way through somehow." And the story of the battle of Dettingen is the tale of how those 16,000 hungry and angry British soldiers—for they did most of the fighting—with all generalship and all the advantages of ground against them, by sheer, dogged, unscientific, and what their enemies complained was mere "stupid" fighting—the fighting of the rank and file, the actual push of reddened bayonets, and the blast of volleys delivered so close that they seemed to scorch the very flesh of their enemies—burst through De Noailles' toils, tumbled that ingenious general in mere ruin across the Maine, and turned starvation into victory.

The unhistorical reader may wonder how it came to pass that in 1743 a British army, with a British monarch at its head, was running the risk of capture in Central Germany, and under the shadow of the Bavarian hills. Carlyle somewhat unkindly pictures the typical modern Englishman demanding of the universe in mere amazement, "Battle of Dettingen, Battle of Fontenoy—what in the devil's name were we doing there?" He adds that the only answer is, "Fit of insanity, delirium tremens, perhaps furens.

Don't think of it!" An educated man is expected to know " who commanded at Aigos-Potamoi, and wrecked the Peloponnesian War. But of Dettingen and Fontenoy, where is the living Englishman that has the least notion, or seeks for any?" With one consent we have tumbled the Austrian succession war into the dustbin, and are cheerfully content that it should lie there. It belongs to those wars which may be described as "mere futile transitory dust whirlwinds, stilled in blood;" spasms of pure distracted lunacy on a national scale. "The poor human memory," Carlyle adds, "has an alchemy against such horrors. It forgets them!"

But this is only an example of Carlyle's too energetic rhetoric, and his own more sober judgment may be quoted against his swift and sword-edged epithets. In the war with Spain, picturesquely labelled from "Jenkins's ear," the statesmanship of England was on one side; the dim, inarticulate instinct of its common people was on the other. And the people were wiser than the statesmen! Walpole was forced into war against his will; and, as he listened to the bells of St. Paul's ringing in exultation when war broke out, he said, bitterly, "They may ring their bells now; before long they will be wringing their hands!" Yet, if ever war was justifiable, that against Spain in 1739 was.

Spain claimed to be mistress, by decree of the Pope, of all the seas and continents covered by the vague title of "the Spanish main"; and so for two centuries, whatever was the case in Europe, perpetual war raged in the Tropics. South of the line the British trader was driven by stress of necessity to become a buccaneer, and from the days of Drake the unfortunate Pope's decree had been slashed with cutlasses and rent with sea-cannon till it became a thing of rags. The claim of Spain to keep half the world locked up, from the common life of the race, under an ecclesiastical seal, was a menace to civilisation. "To lie like a dog in the manger over South America," reflects Carlyle, and say, snarling, 'None of you shall trade here, though I cannot,' what Pope, or body of Popes, can sanction such a procedure? . . . Dogs have doors for their hutches, but to pretend barring the Tropic of Cancer—that is too big a door for any dog!"

By the Assiento treaty the British were allowed to despatch one ship, not exceeding 600 tons, to the Spanish main each year; but what parchment skin of treaties could keep the volume of the world's trade flowing through such a petty squirt! Illegal traders in the Spanish main abounded, and Spanish guarda costas were not gentle in their method of suppressing them. Captain Jenkins, with his vessel the *Rebecca*, sailing from Jamaica to London, was stopped and searched off the coast of Havanna, by a Spanish revenue cutter. Jenkins was slashed over the head with a cutlass, and his left ear half chopped off. A Spanish officer then tore off the bleeding ear, flung it in its owner's face, and bade him "carry it home to his king, and tell him what had been done." The story of how that little morsel of brown, withered human flesh turned out a spark which kindled the inarticulate slow-burning wrath of the English nation into a flame, and swept England itself into war, is told in the following chapter. Carlyle himself says:—

"The 'Jenkins's ear' question, which once looked so

mad, was sane enough, and covered tremendous issues. Half the world lay hidden in embryo under it. 'Colonial Empire'—whose is it to be? Shall half the world be England's for industrial purposes, which is innocent, laudable, conformable to the multiplication table, at least, and other plain laws? Or shall it be Spain's, for arrogant, torpid, sham-devotional purposes, contradictory to every law? The incalculable 'Yankee nation' itself, biggest phenomenon (once thought beautifullest) of these ages,—this, too, little as careless readers on either side of the sea now know it, lay involved. Shall there be a Yankee nation, shall there not be? Shall the new world be of Spanish type, shall it be of English? Issues which we may call immense! Among the then extant sons of Adam, where was he who could in the faintest degree surmise what issues lay in the Jenkins's ear question? And it is curious to consider now, with what fierce, deep-breathed doggedness, the poor English nation, drawn by their instincts, held fast upon it, and would take no denial, as if they had surmised and seen. For the instincts of simple, guileless persons (liable to be counted stupid by the unwary) are sometimes of prophetic nature, and spring from the deep places of this universe."

But to the "Jenkins's ear" question was added yet another, of scale almost as huge. In 1733 the Bourbon houses of Paris and Madrid framed betwixt themselves the famous "Family Compact," one of a series of such compacts which Burke has described as "the most odious and formidable of all conspiracies against the liberties of Europe that have ever been framed." By this "Compact" the foreign policy of two great nations, it was agreed, should be "guided exclusively by the interests of the House." France was to aid Spain with all her forces by land and sea, whenever Spain chose to warn England absolutely off the Spanish main. The two branches of the Bourbons, in a word, were secretly pledged as allies in a policy which threatened the freedom of Europe in general; and England, as the chief Protestant and freedom-loving Power, was specially menaced. Its maritime supremacy was to be ruined. The attack on the Austrian succession was but an attempt to carry out the hateful principles of the "Family Compact." Frederick of Prussia, bribed by the hope of Silesia, had joined France and Spain. France claimed the Netherlands, Spain half Italy, and Gibraltar was to be wrested from Great Britain. In wise self-defence England was aiding with purse and musket the gallant fight Maria Theresa was making for the patrimony of her child. Yet nominally there was no war betwixt England and France when the battle of Dettingen was fought; and this explains Horace Walpole's famous epigram, "We had the name of war with Spain without the thing, and war with France without the name."

On June 19, 1743, George II., with his son the Duke of Cumberland, who won an evil fame afterwards as "the butcher of Culloden," rode into Lord Stair's camp at Aschaffenburg. Royal father and son, betwixt them, had not military intelligence enough to make up a twentieth-rate general; but both had an abundant stock of that primary element in a soldier, mere fighting courage. George II. Carlyle describes grimly enough as "a mere courageous Wooden Pole with cocked hat on top"; while of his son, the Duke of Cumberland, he declares that he "knew little more of war than did the White Horse of Hanover." But the quality of bulldog courage has been the attribute of the Welf race since the days of Henry the Lion, and both father and son possessed this in a shining degree. The second George, it is true, had not many other titles to human respect. Thackeray describes him as "a dull little man of low tastes." He had neither dignity, learning, morals, nor wit. He was "a little red-faced, staring kinglet"; there was no external signature of royalty upon him. Bielfeld, quoted by Carlyle, has drawn a curious little pen picture of this second of the Georges: a little man, of violent red complexion, with eyebrows ashy-blonde, and parboiled blue eyes, flush with his face, nay, even standing in relief from it, "after the manner of a fish"! George had the manners of a clown, and the morals of a "welcher." Every one remembers how, when his dying wife bade him marry again, this remarkable monarch replied, through his sobs, "No, no! I will have mistresses"! The Duke of Cumberland, morally, was, no doubt, an improvement on his father. At least, he had that rudimentary sense of honour which teaches a man to scorn a lie. But he was "of dim, poor head," and had not the faintest vestige of military skill. But he was "as brave as a Welf lion." Both father and son, indeed, would have shone as hard-swearing, hard-fighting, red-faced privates.

And yet it may be doubted whether father and son were not, on the whole, exactly the leaders which the desperate task before the allied army needed. Neither had military science enough to know how desperate the situation was. A better general might have tried manœuvres, and De Noailles, with all his advantages of numbers and position, would have beaten him hopelessly. The case was one which needed not so much brains as hard-pushing bayonets. "In Teuton populations," says Carlyle, "on that side of the Channel, or on this, there is generally to be found, when you apply for it, an unconscious substratum of taciturn inexpugnability, with depths of potential rage almost unquenchable. Which quality is, perhaps, strengthened by their 'stupidity' itself—what neighbours call their 'stupidity'—want of idle imagining, idle flurrying; nay, want even of knowing." For mere fierce, dogged, hard-thrusting, close-pressing combat—the business in which lay the one hope of the allied army—George II. and his 'martial Fat Boy,' the Duke of Cumberland, were not unfit leaders."

For the rest, the British troops at Dettingen were of fine fighting quality. The mere names of the regiments stir one like the rolling cadences of a passage from Homer: "Ligionier's Horse," "Onslow's Foot," "Cope's Dragoons," "the Horse Guards Blue," "the Scots Greys," "the Grenadier Guards," "the King's Regiment," "the Scotch Fusiliers," "the Welsh Fusiliers," &c. The Earl of Stair himself was a Scottish veteran, familiar with battles, though not a "lucky" soldier. Perhaps the finest soldier amongst the British was Ligonier, who had played a gallant part in Marlborough's campaigns. In the battle of Malplaquet, he had twenty-three bullets through his clothes, and was unhurt! But Ligonier had a genius for discipline, and he did for what is now the 7th (Princess Royal's) Dragoon Guards, what Sir John Moore did for the Light Division—he made it a fighting instrument of singular power. He became its colonel when it was on the Irish establishment and was known as the 8th, or "Black Horse"; afterwards it was called Ligonier's Horse, then the 4th Irish Horse, and now the 7th Dragoon Guards. Under Ligonier it was composed almost exclusively of Irishmen, and he so tempered and shaped it by discipline that it became, perhaps, the finest single regiment of horse in Europe.

Carlyle says, somewhat unkindly, that at Dettingen the English officers "behaved in the usual way, without knowledge of war, and without fear of death; cheering their men, and keeping them steady upon the throats of the French." But that may be fairly described as the whole duty of a British officer in such a fight as that of Minden!

The logic of hunger compelled the British leaders to come to prompt and resolute decision. Hanau was their base of supplies, and they determined to fall back upon it through Dettingen. George believed that when this movement was detected, De Noailles would fall with his utmost force upon his rear, so he kept his British regiments as a rearguard, and took command of them himself. On June 27, the allied forces began a slow and sullen retreat. But De Noailles had thrust his nephew, the Duc de Grammont, with 23,000 men, across the bridges at Seligenstadt, and seized Dettingen, thus barring George's retreat.

It would be difficult to imagine a stronger position than that held by De Grammont. The village of Dettingen stands in a defile; it is crossed in front by a stream, with treacherous and marshy banks; this, in turn, is covered by a morass. De Grammont had under him the *élite* of De Noailles' army, with strict orders not to move from his position, but to hold it to the death. The British must straggle through the morass, and flounder across the brook to reach the hollow way barred by the village, and held by 23,000 of the choicest troops of France, with a cross-fire of artillery covering their front. The valley, in a word, was a bottle, of which Dettingen was the cork!

As soon as George II. discovered that, to save his army, way must be won with steel and bullet through Dettingen, he changed the formation of his forces, and brought the British and Hanoverians to the front. The process took four hours, or from eight o'clock to twelve o'clock, to accomplish, and for the whole of that period the moving troops were scourged with fire from the French guns on the high southern bank of the Maine, a fire against which the British cavalry, drawn out in a long and slender line, formed a human screen of very penetrable quality. "Our regiment," wrote an officer in Bland's Dragoons, "was cannonaded for nearly three hours by batteries in front, flank, and rear; and then," he adds, "our three broken squadrons had to charge nine or eleven squadrons of the French Household Guards." The relief of charging anybody, however, after standing so long to be helplessly shot at, was so great to Bland's Dragoons, that they dashed through the splendid French Guards, as through a brush fence, "though," adds the officer we have quoted, "it is a miracle one of us escaped!"

By noon George had got his front in fighting shape. He had religiously put on the coat and hat he had worn at Oudenarde, thirty-five years before, when he had personally led a brilliant cavalry charge; and the solemn encasing of his stumpy little body in that old-fashioned, powder-stained uniform, with its faded tints, was a touch of sentiment quite unusual in George's prosaic and sulky nature. Just at this moment came the one French blunder which gave to the British a magnificent opportunity. De Grammont was little better than a rash and gallant youth, and there rode beside him French nobles as daring and as reckless as himself. French genius, as a thousand battles prove, lies rather in attacking than in waiting to be attacked. De Grammont had watched for four intolerable hours the allied forces slowly forming before him, till he could watch the business no longer. He sallied out from his stronghold, crossed the stream, picked his uncertain way through the morass, and came charging down to sweep the British off the face of the earth! Had he moved earlier while George II. was laboriously changing his formation, the stroke might have succeeded. But the British were now ranked in order of battle. They formed the spearhead of the long column of 40,000 men, straggling over six miles, of which the other troops were but the wooden staff.

They were, too, in grim fighting mood, hungry and wrathful. The French batteries had opened fiercely on the British lines, the balls falling thick round the post where George stood, and he was entreated to "go out of danger." "Don't tell me of danger," he said, "I'll be even with them!" His horse, alarmed by the tumult and the crash of shot, bolted. George succeeded in stopping it, and then dismounted; he would fight on foot, "he could trust his legs," he said, "not to run away with him!"

The Duke of Cumberland, with General Clayton and General Sommerfeldt, led the first line; the second was led by the Earl of Dunmore and the Earl of Rothes; Ligonier and Honeywood commanded the first line of horse, Cope and Hawley led the second.

The French line came on swiftly and with confused tumult. The British moved forward with dogged slowness, but with the air of men who did not propose to go back. When within some sixty yards of the enemy they halted for a moment, that the lines might be dressed, and then there broke from the steady ranks that sudden shout, deep-throated and challenging—what Napier describes as the most menacing sound ever heard in war—the hurrah of the British soldier as he meets his foes in battle—"a thunder-growl edged with melodious ire in alt," as Carlyle put it! From the French lines there came a tumult of shrill sounds; but after the fight was over, prisoners declared that the volume, the angry, challenging menace of that deep shout from the steadily moving British, shook the French lines as no blast of musketry could have shaken them!

The leading squadrons of cavalry on both sides dashed through the intervals of infantry; and, with one long, sustained, and crackling sound of crashing blades under which rolled like some deep bass the shouts of the contending horsemen, the squadrons met in full charge betwixt the moving lines of infantry. At first the French horse prevailed by mere dint of numbers and the speed of their charge, and the broken English squadrons were driven back on the infantry.

These wheeled quickly to let the broken horse through, and formed up again.

On came the steady infantry line, the tramp of disciplined feet sounding louder and yet louder. The French opened fire first, and from a distance; but the British strode doggedly forward, not firing a shot. An officer in the Welsh Fusiliers says, "Our people, marching in close order, as firm as a wall, did not fire till we came within sixty paces, and still kept advancing." The men, as a matter of fact, never halted, or broke step while they reloaded, but marched and fired with such resolute swiftness on their foes, that, as the officer we quoted wrote, "When the smoke blew off a little, instead of being among their living, we found the dead in heaps by us." "It was the regiment of Navarre that we met, one of their prime regiments; but our second fire turned them to the right about, and upon a long trot. We engaged two other regiments afterwards, one after the other, who stood but one fire each, and their blue French footguards gave way without firing a shot." This officer notes that other British regiments who opened fire at a greater distance, sustained more loss than did the Fusiliers; "for," he adds, "the French will stand fire at a distance, though it is plain they cannot look an enemy in the face. What preserved us was keeping close order, and advancing near the enemy ere we fired."

It was the dogged oncoming of the British infantry, without pause or falter, resistless as fate, with one far-running ceaseless spray of flame, and the roll of unceasing musketry—before which the first French line was simply shattered to atoms. And still on, ever on, came that astonishing infantry. Through the eddying white smoke the French caught glimpses of a moving human wall, that never wavered or halted, but, with perpetual roll of musketry, moved steadily and grimly forward.

Upon that wide front of footmen, De Grammont, as his only hope, launched his whole force of cavalry in one furious charge. And more gallant cavalry never, perhaps, joined in the shock of battle than those squadrons which, through the white smoke, broke on the long front of British infantry. The Black Musketeers were there, the Gendarmes, with breastplates and backpieces of steel, and long, cutting swords; the Maison du Roi, &c. With gleaming helmets, and thunder of galloping hoofs, and long line of tossing horse-heads and wind-blown manes, the French cavalry burst through the white smoke on the British footmen, and, by the mere impact, the slender red line was instantly broken. But every human atom of it thrust and shot as doggedly as ever, as the fierce horseman rode past him or over him! On to the second line, but with diminished impact, the French cavalry rode. But it was like riding into the flames of a furnace. The ceaseless musketry scorched them on every side. The English lines might be broken, but they fought as fiercely in fragments as they did in battalions. The second and third British lines, in fact, in the very climax of the tumult and thunder of the struggle, fell swiftly into a formation which speaks volumes for their resource, and discipline, and coolness, and which proved fatal to the rushing squadrons of French horse. They fell into "lanes," down which—merely because they offered an opening—the galloping squadrons of the French cavalry swept as with the fury of a sea-tide.

But each side of the "lane" was a front of perfectly steady and swiftly firing infantry; and on that comb-like formation, steady and of unshaken valour to its least unit, the French cavalry charge exhausted itself. Back, out of smoke and tumult, and the thunder of unceasing volleys, the French cavalry came—riderless horses, solitary flying horsemen, or broken, desperately-fighting, clusters, still striking, perhaps, with their long swords across the muskets at the British infantry, but falling as they struck.

De Noailles had watched with astonished wrath his nephew abandon the impregnable post he was ordered to hold, and sally out to meet the British in the open. "Grammont," he exclaimed, "has ruined all my plans;" and he hurried to the scene of action to remedy the blunder. But it was too late! Before the advance of the British lines, with their ceaseless blast of flame-edged musketry, De Grammont's force was simply wrecked. The stately, resonant sentences, indeed, in which Napier, more than seventy years afterwards, described the charge of the Fusiliers at Albuera, might be applied, without varying the tint of an adjective, to the men who fought at Dettingen: "Nothing could stop that astonishing infantry. . . . . Their flashing eyes were bent on the dark columns in front; their measured tread shook the ground; their dreadful volleys swept away the head of every formation; their deafening shouts drowned the dissonant cries that broke from all parts of the tumultuous crowd."

The fight lasted four hours, and then the French

regiments broke into mere flying, disordered panic. De Grammont tried to make a flank attack on the British with the Gardes Françaises, but even that *élite* corps threw away their arms, and, preferring water to fire, plunged into the river, drowning by whole companies. French barrack-room wit named them afterwards, "canards du Mein"—"ducks of the Maine!" De Noailles tried to withdraw his forces with some degree of order across the two bridges to the southern bank; but an army mad with panic, and with discipline temporarily dissolved, cannot be manœuvred, and, as British mess-room wit afterwards put it, the French that sad June evening "had, in reality, three bridges, one of them not wooden, and carpeted with blue cloth!" Even a French account describes the regiment of Guards as "running with great precipitation into the Maine, when nearly as many were drowned as were killed in the fighting." The French left 6000 dead and wounded on the field, and many standards and prisoners were taken by the British, whose loss did not exceed 3000.

Their victory left the British exhausted. They hurled themselves, indeed, on the French with such overmastering fierceness, chiefly because these stood betwixt the 16,000 hungry Englishmen, Scotchmen, and Irishmen and their dinner! But they could not pursue the broken French; and, camping all night on the field of battle, they marched slowly and sullenly, when the next day broke, to Hanau and their supplies. Stair, who was eager to pursue De Noailles, summed up the battle to a French officer with bitter wit. "You advanced when you ought to have stood, and we stood when we ought to have advanced." But "small as was the victory," says Green in his "Short History of the English People," "it produced amazing results." It drove the French out of Germany. It shattered into mere dust the "Family Compact" betwixt the two branches of the Bourbons. And the fight is memorable as showing, once more, how the dogged, all-enduring courage of the British rank and file will, in the last resort, almost compensate for the lack of brains in British generals. "If I blundered," said Wellington, long afterwards, "I could always rely on my soldiers to pull me through." That is an ancient and undying characteristic of the British soldier!

PRINCE FERDINAND

From a mezzotint by R. HOUSTON

THE BATTLE OF MINDEN

August 1, 1759

THE battle of Minden might almost be described as having been won by a blunder, and a blunder about so insignificant a thing as a mere preposition! Prince Ferdinand, who commanded the allied army, had placed the six regiments of British infantry, who formed the flower of his force, in his centre, and had given orders that they were to move forward in attack "on sound of drum." The British read the order, "with sound of drum." The seventy-five splendid squadrons of horse who formed the French centre were in their immediate front. The British saw their foes before them, line on line of tossing horse-heads and gleaming helmets, of scarlet and steel, and wind-blown crests. What other "signal of battle" was needed? Obeying the warlike impulse in their blood, they at once moved forward "with sound of drum"— every drummer-boy in the regiments, in fact, plying his drum-sticks with furious energy, and those waves of warlike sound stirred the dogged valour of the British to a yet fiercer daring! Prince Ferdinand never contemplated such a movement; it violated all the rules of war. What sane general would have launched 6000 infantry in line to attack 10,000 of the finest cavalry in Europe in ranked squadrons? It is on record that the Hanoverian troops placed in support of the British regiments watched with dumb and amazed alarm the "stupid" British moving serenely forward to a contest so lunatic. But to the confusion of all critics, and to the mingled wrath and shame of the French generals, these astonishing British regiments tumbled Contades' splendid cavalry into mere distracted ruin, and left his wings disconnected military fragments, and won, in the most irregular manner, the great battle of Minden!

Minden is, for Englishmen, not the least glorious fight in that long procession of battles we call the Seven Years' War—a war which, from the English standpoint, has much better moral justification than most people suppose. The Seven Years' War itself was but a sort of bloody postscript to the war of the Austrian Succession; this, in turn, was merely the second act in the great struggle labelled picturesquely from "Jenkins's ear." This, again, was but the final syllable in that long dispute, argued with the iron lips of guns and the glittering edges of swords, which runs back to the days of Drake and of Hawkins, and of "the singeing of the King of Spain's beard." Spain claimed, as the gift of the Pope, the exclusive lordship of the New World. One-half the planet, in brief, was shut, with a bit of ecclesiastical sealing-wax, against everybody but Spaniards! A British ship found trading in the Spanish Main was treated as a smuggler or a pirate, or as a combination of both. So it came to pass there was "no peace south of the Line."

But the situation at last grew intolerable. Captain Jenkins, of the good ship *Rebecca*, sailing innocently, as he declared, from Jamaica to London, was boarded by a *guarda costa* off Havanna; his ear was slashed or torn off, and thrown in his face, and he was bidden "carry it home to his king and tell him how British traders in Spanish waters were treated." Jenkins did so, quite literally; and that little bit of amputated sea-going flesh turned out to be the picturesque and concrete symbol about which the slow-beating British imagination kindled to a white fire of wrath. The statesmen of England were against war; the people were for war; and no one doubts to-day that the people were wiser than the statesmen. The inarticulate common-sense of the masses divined more truly the real questions at stake than did the wit of politicians. The commercial supremacy of England, its colonial empire, the question whether America was to be developed on the British or on the Spanish type, were amongst the issues involved. There might, indeed, have been no United States but for that slash at Captain Jenkins's ear! The northern half of the great American continent to-day might have been, like the southern half, a cluster of shrewishly wrangling, half Indian, half Latin republics.

But another dispute poured its gall into the quarrel. The two branches of the Bourbon House in Paris and Madrid were linked together by the secret and infamous Family Compact, a compact described by Burke as "the most odious and formidable conspiracy against the liberties of Europe" which history records. It was practically a secret alliance for the partition of Europe in the interests of the Bourbons, and it was certainly fraught with deadly peril to England, whose commercial freedom—whose very right to exist—it menaced. The Family Compact brought France into the war, first as a tributary, then as a principal: the war of "Jenkins's ear" expanded into the war of the Austrian Succession; and England, fighting on the Main or the Weser, was really fighting for her colonies, her trade, her very existence. She was contending, indeed, for the whole future of civilisation, though probably her statesmen very imperfectly understood the real scale of the great drama in which they were taking part. George II. certainly saw Hanover rather than America. The Treasury benches bounded the intellectual horizon of such politicians as Newcastle or Pulteney. Only Pitt, with his kingly brain and piercing vision for the remoter causes and ultimate issues of events, understood the real scale of the great contest in which England was engaged.

On the French side the contest was planned on great lines, and fought over a very wide area. Belleisle was the French minister of war, and his strategy was almost as spacious and magnificent as that of Napoleon himself. He fed the war in India and America; he menaced England herself with invasion by the mighty armament he assembled at Brest; and with 50,000 choice French troops on the Weser, under Contades and Broglie, he threatened to overrun Hanover. Clive in India, Wolfe at Quebec, Hawke off Quiberon, shattered the armies and fleets and hopes of France. On the Continent, however, England had brave troops, but no general. Pitt, who had a great statesman's gift for choosing fit instruments, determined to borrow a commander for the allied forces. He found his man in Prince Ferdinand—a fine soldier, trained in the school of Frederick the Great. Ferdinand had something of Marlborough's miraculous tact in dealing with men, and much, too, of

Prince Eugene's gallant fighting quality. A tough, swift-visioned, cool, and high-minded soldier, of unconquerable patience and exhaustless resource, and with a true genius for war. Wellington said a general's business consisted chiefly in guessing " what was happening on the other side of the hill "; and few soldiers have ever surpassed Ferdinand in the faculty for reading the thoughts and plans of the generals with whom he was contending. How serene and invincible must have been the quality of Ferdinand's patience may be judged by the fact that he achieved the feat of successfully commanding a miscellaneous host of Austrians, Prussians, Hanoverians, and British. And if the British soldier of 1759 had all the fighting qualities of his breed—the headlong daring of the men who swept up the great breach at Badajos, the iron valour of the unconquerable infantry who held the squares at Waterloo—yet he had, in addition, a good many of the troublesome qualities of his race. The British soldier is not very docile to a commander who has the bad taste not to be an Englishman himself, and who delivers his orders with a foreign accent.

Carlyle quotes a description, given by Mauvillon, of the British soldier of the last century, as seen through the spectacles of German officers, which shows how enduring are the characteristics of the type. " Braver troops when on the field of battle, and under arms against the enemy," wrote Mauvillon, " you will nowhere find in the world—that is the truth; and with that the sum of their military merits ends.' The British infantryman, Mauvillon says, in effect, is sulky and stubborn; the cavalry private has " such a foolish love for his horse" as makes him "astonishingly plunderous of forage." The British officer was totally unequipped with either knowledge of war or fear of death. "They have," says Mauvillon, "a quiet, natural arrogance which tempts them to despise the enemy as well as the danger; and as they very seldom think of making any surprisal themselves, they generally take it for granted that the enemy will as little." "It is well known," adds Mauvillon, "how much these people despise all foreigners"—especially, it may be added, when they are Hanoverians! Yet Ferdinand managed his British exquisitely. He asked of them only what they could give him, and what a good general most values, magnificent fighting service. Ferdinand subtly flattered them, indeed, by always thrusting them into the place where hard knocks were most abundant. In Contades and Broglie—the "war-god Broglie" of Carlyle, who, thirty years afterwards, flitted briefly and tragically across the smoky sky of the French Revolution—he had opponents of very high quality; yet Ferdinand out-generalled them as completely in the strife of wits before Minden as his gallant British regiments overthrew them by actual push of pike and bayonet in the battle itself.

Contades and Broglie, whose united forces were a little short of 70,000 men, were threatening Hanover; Ferdinand, with some 54,000 men, had the task of defending it. Contades had taken up a position of great strength in front of Minden. His right wing was on the Weser, his left was covered by a morass, impassible to either cavalry or artillery; the Bastau, a black, slow-creeping stream with treacherous banks, served as a sort of natural wet ditch to his front; and here, with 30,000 men and a powerful artillery, Contades sat unassailable, while Broglie, with a force of almost

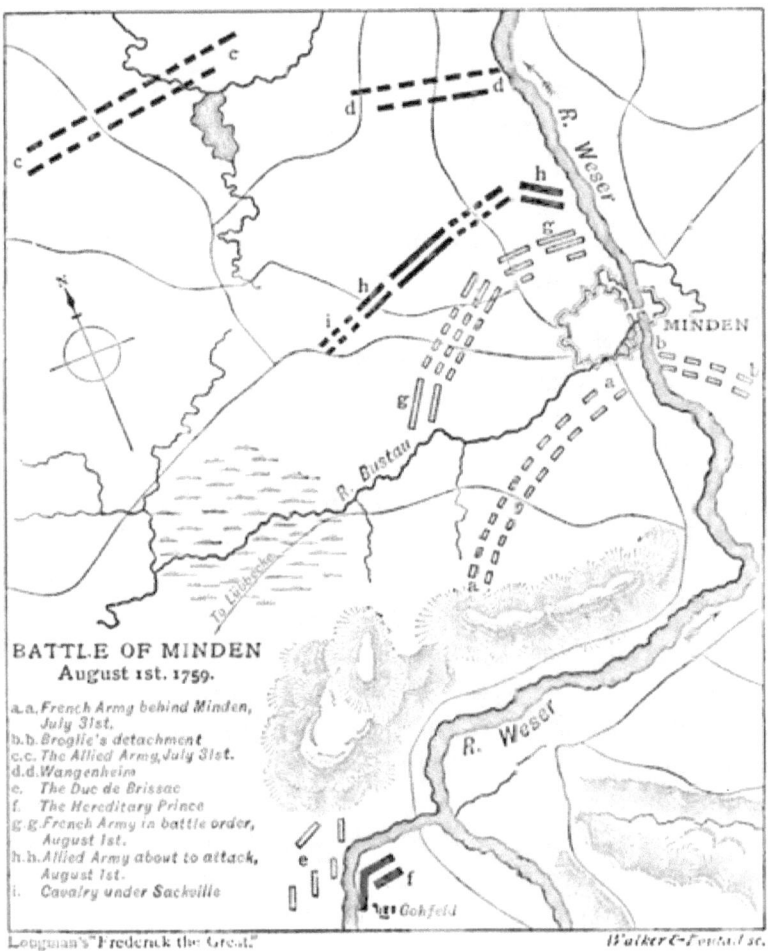

BATTLE OF MINDEN
August 1st. 1759.

a.a. *French Army behind Minden, July 31st.*
b.b. *Broglie's detachment*
c.c. *The Allied Army, July 31st.*
d.d. *Wangenheim*
e. *The Duc de Brissac*
f. *The Hereditary Prince*
g.g. *French Army in battle order, August 1st.*
h.h. *Allied Army about to attack, August 1st.*
i. *Cavalry under Sackville*

equal strength, was in touch on the farther bank of the Weser. Ferdinand could not attack the position held by the French in front of Minden; he dared not expose his own flank to the counter-stroke of Contades, while he marched off to prevent Broglie overrunning Hanover; it only remained to tempt Contades out of his ring of sheltering morasses. And the story of the cool daring and light-handed skill with which this was done makes a very pretty study in tactics.

In brief, Ferdinand detached 10,000 men under his nephew, the hereditary Prince of Brunswick, a gallant, hard-hitting soldier, to make a snatch at Gohfeld, ten miles to the rear of Contades, and so cut off his meal waggons, lumbering slowly down from Cassel. Next he thrust out his left wing, under Wangenheim, leaving an apparently careless and fatal gap of three miles betwixt wing and centre. Ferdinand, that is, committed—or seemed to commit, and with ostentation—under the very eyes of the eagerly watching French generals, two unpardonable military blunders. He divided his force in the presence of the enemy by despatching 10,000 to attack Gohfeld; he permitted his left wing to lie within actual stroke of the foe, and left it without support. Contades resembled, in a word, a wary and much experienced trout at the bottom of a deep pool, and Ferdinand's left wing was the fly with which the trout was being daintily tempted to make a dash out. The 10,000 men marching on Gohfeld, of course, gave the impression that the allied army was divided, as well as ill-placed. On the evening of July 31, 1759, Contades held a council of war, and it was determined to attack, suddenly—before dawn—and with the whole strength of the French army. The sound of the tattoo that night was to be the signal for movement. Contades' army was to cross the Bastau by nineteen bridges, already constructed, form into eight columns, and push, like the thrust of a spear, through the apparent gap betwixt Ferdinand's left wing and his centre. Wangenheim would thus be caught betwixt the main body of the French and the Weser; and Broglie, marching along the banks of the Weser, was to crush that truncated left wing into powder, and then join Contades in a victorious assault on Ferdinand's main body. But Ferdinand divined the plans of the French council of war as accurately as though he had assisted to make them. He guessed, indeed, the very hour and method of the attack. At one o'clock that same night his cavalry was saddled; and while the stars yet shone in the misty heavens, and while the French, with much confusion and tumult, were pouring across their nineteen bridges, Ferdinand's troops, in perfect silence and order, marching on converging lines, had filled up the apparent gap, and stood in order of battle ready for the fight.

Day broke, grey and uncertain, with fog, and the French moved stumblingly, and with many halts, across the heath, rough with undergrowth, in front of Minden. Broglie, with the bank of the Weser to guide him, reached Wangenheim's front just as the eastern sky began to whiten with the dawn, but he would not attack until he had seen Contades' columns marching past Wangenheim's flank. About eight o'clock Contades, riding in front of his slowly advancing battalions, mounted the low empty ridge which marked the apparent gap in Ferdinand's position, and from which he expected to see Wangenheim's undefended flank, lying open to his stroke. The grey mist, slowly lifting and

F

blown into eddies by a faint wind, still stretched over the plain, but through it there broke on Contades' astonished vision the outlines of a great army in steadfast battle array—far-stretching lines of solid infantry, punctuated with batteries, and edged with ordered squadrons of horse. The "gap" had vanished. Ferdinand's apparently abandoned left wing on the Weser was knitted by a chain of marshalled battalions to his centre. This was formed of three far-extended lines of British infantry, a long ribbon of steel and scarlet; while yet farther to the right, ranked in menacing squadrons, was the British and Hanoverian cavalry. With a stroke Prince Ferdinand had cancelled all the advantage of position on the part of the French, and drawn them out to meet him in the open.

Contades could not retreat; to cross those nineteen bridges with Ferdinand thundering on his rear would have been ruinous. He had, after all, great superiority in numbers, and, as quickly as might be, he made his disposition for battle. Contades adopted a very ominous precedent—the formation of Tallard at Blenheim. He placed his cavalry—a magnificent force of 10,000 horsemen—in his centre, covered their front by the fire of his powerful artillery, and formed his infantry on either wing. A small wood screened the British and Hanoverian cavalry on Ferdinand's right; some rough ground served to protect the Hanoverian and Prussian battalions that formed his left. But the centre was clear. Across a narrow interval of heath the crowding squadrons of French horsemen and the steadfast lines of British infantry gazed at each other. Nothing separated them but a few hundred yards of dry heathy soil, across which, with thunder of galloping hoofs, and the glitter of 10,000 brandished swords, the French cavalry might ride in one mad, breathless, overwhelming charge, which would break through those triple lines of exposed infantry as through a screen of bulrushes. In the opportunity for a sublime and apparently resistless cavalry charge, indeed, Minden anticipated Waterloo, and exceeded it; with this further advantage that the French horsemen had to hurl themselves, not against stubborn and moveless squares, with their double lines of steadfast bayonets, and flame of musketry fire from four faces. They had before them a long slowly-moving front of infantry in line. For now came the amazing "blunder" which makes the wonder the glory of Minden. This astonishing infantry was advancing, with flags uncased, and loud roll of drums, and steady tread of disciplined feet to attack the cavalry!

The six Minden regiments are the 12th (or East Suffolk), the 23rd (or Royal Welsh Fusiliers), the 37th, the 20th (or East Devonshire), the 25th, and the 51st. Of these, the three first named, under Colonel Pole, formed the first line; the last three, under Generals Kingsley and Waldegrave, formed the second line; they were supported by a Hanoverian brigade of three battalions. According to the "Historical Records of the 12th Foot," at a later stage in the fight the second line of British foot was formed on the right of the first line, and the Hanoverian brigade on its left, thus making one far-stretching and slender infantry line. But this movement is not reported in other accounts of the fight, and must be considered very doubtful. It is always difficult to translate into literary terms the tumult and confusion, the charges and retreats of a great fight; but a hundred years ago the art of accurately reporting the movements of a great battle had certainly not been invented, and what took place under the roof of battle-smoke can, as far as details are concerned, be only guessed. On the whole, it must be accepted that Ferdinand's centre, where the decisive struggle took place, consisted of three lines of infantry, of which the first and second were British, and the third Hanoverian.

Soon after eight o'clock on the morning of August 1, a not too vigorous attack on Hahlen, a hamlet on the extreme left of Contades' position, was made by some Hessian regiments, and while this splutter of fight was still in progress, the British regiments, who formed the centre of the Allied forces, put themselves in movement, and, with all their drums beating loudly, and flags uncased, moved forward to attack the 10,000 gallant cavalry opposed to them. Contades had covered his centre by the cross-fire of some sixty-six guns, and these at once smote the steady British lines with a sleet of iron hail; the British artillery, moving quickly to the front, opened, with fierce energy, on the French batteries in reply, and for nearly half-an-hour the great artillery duel raged, deep calling unto deep from either line. Presently the English line, steady as if on parade, was visible through the artillery smoke. A gust of wind swept the landscape for a moment clear, and the French cavalry saw before them a stretch of turf, over which a long slender line of infantry was moving coolly forward to attack them. The French cavalry was under the command of Prince Xavier of Saxony, and in its crowded squadrons were some of the finest regiments in the service of France—the Carbineers, the Black and Grey and Red Mousquetaires, the Gendarmes—armed like the French Life Guards at Waterloo with steel breastplates and back-pieces. The leading division of French cavalry consisted of the Carbineers and the Black and Grey Mousquetaires; and, with tossing manes and wind-blown plumes, with the ring of scabbard on stirrup, and the thunder of innumerable hoofs, the Carbineers leading, they swept down on the British line.

That line halted for a moment, dressed its front daintily, and then, from end to end, ran a darting line of flame. It was covered, as by some stroke of magic, with a foam of grey smoke, rent by quick-following blasts of sound, and shining with glancing points of flame. But from that smoky screen broke a flying spray of lead, through which no cavalry, however daring, could force a way. So deadly was the British fire, that the leading French squadrons went down, man and horse, before it, and what a moment before was a disciplined front of charging cavalry, became one wild mass of fallen horses and slain riders. The squadrons thundering on their rear had to break their order, and swing to right or left to escape the struggling mass in their path. The impact of the charge was thus broken, and the new squadrons, coming fiercely up, but wheeling as they rode to clear their fallen comrades, were, in turn, smitten with a cruel flank fire, and fell by scores. No cavalry could break through that front of fire and steel, and the French cavalry fell back shattered and half destroyed. Then the British line coolly resumed its movement and once more moved on. But ere many minutes had passed, through the smoke came a long line of tossing horse-heads and bent helmets and flashing sword-blades—it was the French cavalry in the unchecked fury of another charge! Once more the British along their whole front, broke into the flame of musketry volley, so close and deadly that it broke the line of galloping horsemen as though a procession of aerolites had swept through it. Then again the British line resumed its steady, inexorable advance. Some of the veterans of Fontenoy were in the Minden regiments, and the "terrible column" of Fontenoy, which with its "slow inflexibility" broke Saxe's army in two in that great fight, did not surpass in its fierce valour, or its torrent of deadly and continuous fire, the marvellous line of infantry that was now pushing into ruin the gallant French cavalry that formed the centre of Contades' line.

The French horse certainly did not fail in courage. They rallied again and again; six times they hurled themselves in wrathful charge on that steadily moving British front. One gallant regiment, the Mestre-de-Camp, gallantly led, did, according to one version, break through the British line, and through the gap a torrent of galloping horses and exultant men stormed. But the broken line, swinging slightly back, tore the flanks of the galloping squadrons with one deadly volley after another, while the second line coolly, as though on parade, scorched its head with the flame of its musketry, and the Mestre-de-Camp, smitten with fire on flank and front, simply shrivelled into ruin. The French infantry opened fire on either extremity of the British line, and men fell fast. But this did not arrest the steady flow of the British battalions, and the blasts of rolling musketry with which they smote into ruin everything in their path. Contades' seventy-five squadrons of cavalry, in brief, were pushed back, or blown back, in one mad tumult of broken, struggling, swearing horsemen. Contades himself describes the scene in an oft-quoted sentence, which compresses into its wrathful syllables the whole story of Minden. "I have seen," he wrote, "what I never thought to be possible—a single line of infantry break through three lines of cavalry ranked in order of battle, and tumble them into ruin!"

Still moving onward, the British line found itself met by a column of Swiss infantry, hastily brought up to arrest the terrible British advance. The Swiss are gallant soldiers, and their leading files moved steadily up to within forty paces of the British line, and then deployed. But the British fire caught them deploying, and though the steady Swiss, with obstinate courage, maintained the fight for a few minutes—until, indeed, the hostile lines were almost touching—yet the fire from the long British front proved resistless, and the two Swiss brigades in turn were driven into broken and disordered retreat.

At this moment Ferdinand despatched an aide-de-camp at full gallop to order the cavalry that formed his right wing to charge the broken French centre. Lord George Sackville commanded the cavalry, with the Marquis of Granby as second in command. He had under him a splendid body of British and Hanoverian horse, and an opportunity lay before him such as few battles have ever offered. Contades' whole army, indeed, lay at his mercy. But Sackville was in no mood for charging. He cavilled at his orders; he affected to misunderstand them. Was he to attack with the "whole cavalry," or with the "British cavalry"? He discovered offence in the eagerness which marked the bearing of the second aide-de-camp, Colonel Fitzroy, who came up with the urgently repeated order to charge. Fitzroy replied that "galloping had put him out of breath," and added that "it was a glorious opportunity for the British cavalry to distinguish themselves." Thrice an aide-de-camp rode up to Lord Sackville with the order to charge, without inducing him to move. Finally he announced that he would himself ride to Prince Ferdinand and ascertain his wishes. He accordingly rode up to the Prince and asked "how he was to come on," and it is a proof of the exhaustless patience of Prince Ferdinand that he calmly replied, "The opportunity is now past, my lord." Sackville, who never lacked audacity, presented himself with unabashed front that night at the Prince's headquarters and talked as loudly of the battle as any one; but in his general order on the day following the battle Prince Ferdinand distilled two sentences that had the corrosive power of gall on Lord George Sackville's head. "If," he said, "he had had the good fortune to have had Lieutenant-General the Marquis of Granby at the head of the cavalry of the right wing, his presence would have greatly contributed to make the success of the battle more complete and brilliant." "His serene highness," the general order further ran, "desires and orders the generals of the army that upon all occasions when orders are brought to them by his aides-de-camp, they be obeyed punctually and without delay."

Lord George Sackville resigned his command and

returned to London, where he was received with almost as furious and deadly an outburst of popular rage as that which met Byng when he returned after the loss of Minorca. British public opinion can forgive a general many faults, but the sin which in its eyes hath never forgiveness is the fault of being slack to charge when a charge is ordered. If the British infantry had covered themselves with glory at Minden, the British cavalry had made themselves the jest of half Europe, and Sackville alone was responsible for an incident which, by its shame, scorched as with fire the national self-respect. Lord George Sackville bore himself fiercely, and in stentorian tones challenged a full investigation. He was dismissed from all his posts as a preliminary, and in February 1760 was tried by court-martial. The six months' delay had, of course, told in his favour, and he bore himself not merely with courage, but with haughty arrogance, as though not he, but his judges, were the true criminals. Sackville's defence was that Prince Ferdinand's orders lacked clearness, and that, as a matter of fact, he used all reasonable diligence in executing those orders. Three aides-de-camp—two of them British, Captain Ligonier and Colonel Fitzroy, and one a German officer—brought the order to charge to Lord George, and their evidence was definite and fatal. The commander of one of the British cavalry regiments, Colonel Sloper, gave evidence that he noticed Lord George's reluctance to carry out his orders at the time, and said to Ligonier, "For God's sake repeat your orders to that man, that he may not pretend not to understand them. It is near half an hour since he received orders to advance, yet we are still here. But you see the condition that he is in." The court-martial, which consisted of eleven lieutenant-generals and four major-generals, found that Lord George had disobeyed his orders, and was unfit to serve his Majesty in any military capacity whatever. George II. struck the culprit's name, with his own hand, from the list of privy councillors, and directed that the sentence of the court-martial should be "published in the public orders of every regiment, not only in Britain, but in America and every quarter of the globe where British troops happen to be, that officers being convinced that neither high birth nor great employments can shelter offence of such nature, and that, seeing they are subject to censures worse than death to a man who has any sense of honour, they may avoid the fatal consequences arising from disobedience of orders."

This sentence might have seemed sufficient to ruin any one; but Horace Walpole, the very day the sentence on Lord George was published, wrote to Sir Horace Mann, with characteristic shrewdness, "This is not the last we shall hear of him. Whatever were his deficiencies on the day of battle, he has at least shown no want of spirit either in pushing on his trial or during it. I think without much heroism I could sooner have led up the cavalry to the charge than have gone to Whitehall to be worried as he was; nay, I should have thought with less danger of my life." Grey, in a letter about the same date, notes that when Lord George Sackville heard his sentence read, "his unembarrassed countenance, the looks of revenge, contempt, and of superiority that he bestowed on his accusers, were the admiration of all." As a matter of fact, it is nothing less than absurd to accuse Lord George Sackville of not possessing the soldier's rudimentary virtue of courage. He led his regiment gallantly into the tempest of fire at Fontenoy, and fell wounded in the breast among the tents of the French camp. He fought more than one desperate duel. He was a man of great and varied abilities, but cursed with a jealous and overbearing temper. He had a distinct genius for quarrelling with everybody. Mr George Coventry wrote an elaborate volume to prove that Lord George was the real author of "The Letters of Junius." Nobody entertains that theory now; but in the quality of suspicious and malignant temper, in the faculty for secreting gall, and then sprinkling it on everybody about him, Lord George Sackville might well have vied with "Junius." He had the gall of that bitter satirist, if not his pen. It is probable that on the morning of Minden, Lord George Sackville was in a ferment of sulky British jealousy at being under the command of "a d—— foreigner" like Prince Ferdinand; and he allowed the gall in his blood to so disorder his reason, that he forgot both his duty as a soldier and his honour as a gentleman.

What increased the unpopularity of Lord George Sackville, with his arrogant temper and sword-edged speech, was the contrast betwixt him and his second in command, the Marquis of Granby. Granby was everything which a British crowd expects an officer—and especially a cavalry officer—to be. Not too clever, perhaps, but handsome, gallant, generous; open-handed to his friends, adored by his soldiers, dreaded by his enemies. The portrait of Granby by Reynolds represents him bareheaded and conspicuously bald; and, as Carlyle reminds us, there is a bit of history behind that patch of bald

scalp shown in Reynolds' picture. In the fight at
Warburg in 1760 Ferdinand's advance was faring very
badly. Granby, at the head of the Blues, his own
regiment, rode at a sharp trot for five miles to join the
fight, broke into a gallop when the scene of action was
reached, and dashed at speed into the *mêlée*. Granby's
hat had blown off, and bareheaded, like Clarke leading
the heavy brigade into the fight at Balaclava, Granby
rode with his bald head among the helmets and sabres
of Warburg. Walpole scarcely burlesques the popular
craze when, on the news of Minden reaching London,
he wrote: "Lord Granby has entirely defeated the
French. The foreign gazettes, I suppose, will give this
victory to Prince Ferdinand; but the mob of London,
whom I have this moment left, and who must know
best, assure me that it is all their own Marquis's doing."
No wonder that the British mob, who were willing to
send Lord George Sackville's head to the block, painted
the Marquis of Granby's head on innumerable public-
house signs. The "Markis o' Granby," the haunt of Mr.
Weller senior, owed its title to the hard-riding, hard-
fighting cavalry leader who fretted and swore at Minden
when his leader delayed to charge.

But Lord George Sackville survived the court-
martial. As Lord George Germain, indeed, he played
a great part in the political history of his time. George
III. restored him to his place in the Privy Council; he
held the post of Secretary of State for the Colonies in
the North Cabinet until its resignation in 1782, and
shared in the blunders which cost Great Britain her
American colonies. It was fitting, perhaps, that the
man whose conduct as a cavalry general marred the

glory of Minden should help by his policy as a minister of the Crown to rob England of her great inheritance in America. Yet George III., when the North Cabinet resigned, raised Lord George to the peerage as Viscount Sackville.

Minden was a great battle. The French lost 8000 men, thirty pieces of artillery, and thirteen flags. Their whole campaign in Germany was tumbled into wreck. They were driven back, broken and disordered, to the Rhine. But Minden will always be memorable as affording a supreme proof of the fighting quality of the British private. Its contribution to the glory of British generalship may be judged by the performance of Lord George Sackville.

RODNEY AND DE GRASSE AT THE BATTLE OF THE SAINTS

April 12, 1782

ALL through the night of April 7, 1782, a chain of British frigates was stretched across the thirty miles of sea betwixt Martinique and Santa Lucia, and every half-hour or so a flash of light ran as a signal from end to end of the line. Rodney, in his great flagship, the *Formidable*, with thirty-five ships of the line, was lying in Gros Ilot Bay; De Grasse, with the *Ville de Paris*, the biggest and most splendid ship of war then afloat, was lying in Fort Royal with thirty-four ships of the line, besides frigates and a convoy of 150 merchant vessels. That chain of watchful signalling frigates might be described as a huge living tentacle which the British admiral stretched across the thirty miles of sea, and by which, in spite of the darkness, he felt each move of his great antagonist.

Morning came, as it comes in the tropics, with glow and splendour, and while the stars were still shining, white and faint, in the sky, the look-outs on the mast-heads of the outermost British frigates, peering into Fort Royal itself, saw that the French ships were dropping their topsails. With stamp of innumerable feet on the resounding decks, and loud distracted clamour of

LORD RODNEY
From a mezzotint by J. WATSON, *after the portrait by* SIR JOSHUA REYNOLDS, P.R.A.

human voices, 250 ships at once—stately liners and smart frigates, and clumsy merchantmen—were heaving anchor. The French fleet was stirring, and, huge and confused — a forest of masts, acres of white swelling canvas—De Grasse led out his ships to what was his last battle. From masthead to masthead, in a flutter of tiny flags, the news sped down the line of British frigates to Rodney in Gros Ilot Bay, and with swift energy, but in characteristic silence, and with the ordered regular movements of a well-drilled regiment deploying, the British came out to what was the greatest sea-battle which, up to that date, the eighteenth century had witnessed.

The war growing out of the revolt of the British colonies in America was drawing to a close, and for Great Britain it was closing in disaster and gloom. Her troops had known defeat and surrender in America. There had been rebellion in Ireland; Spain demanded Gibraltar as the price of peace; France, in the accents of a conqueror, was proposing that Great Britain should give up all her possessions in India save Bengal. Only Rodney's sea victories saved the fame of England. He had relieved Gibraltar. He crushed the Spanish fleet off St. Vincent, and the fire of the pursuit with which, through tempest and darkness, he chased the flying Spaniards into Cadiz, had in it, to quote Hannay, "something of the Quiberon touch." It recalled Hawke's fierce and dashing chase of Conflans thirty years before.

But the greatest of Rodney's sea victories was that now in sight. De Grasse, with a fleet which represented the utmost naval power of France, and carrying, in addition, 5000 veteran troops, sailed for the West Indies to overthrow the British power there. A Spanish fleet of fourteen ships of the line, and 8000 troops, was to join De Grasse off Hayti. Thus an armada of fifty ships of the line, with 13,000 troops on board, would sweep down upon the British possessions from Barbados to Jamaica, in simply resistless strength. So confident of success were both French and Spaniards, that Don Galvez, who commanded the Spanish contingent, assumed the official title of "Governor of Jamaica" while yet lying in Havana. This was selling the bear's hide before the bear itself had been killed! Rodney, with Hood as his second in command, and a great fleet of thirty-six ships of the line, had to meet this threatening combination, and England at that moment possessed no sailor better fitted for the task. He was now sixty-four years of age, and his naval career had begun when he was a mere child. He was, therefore, as thorough a sailor as any salt in his forecastle, yet he was no mere "tarpaulin."

A man of brilliant parts, of aristocratic tastes and connections, he had been a member of the House of Commons, Governor of Newfoundland, Master of Greenwich Hospital. He was familiar with great men and great affairs. Few men ever knew more alternations of fortune than Rodney. He had led British fleets to victory, and afterwards himself had to flee before the terrors of a bailiff's warrant to France, and so escape the pursuit of his creditors. A story, which has some evidence in its favour, tells how he was there offered the command of a French fleet if he would take arms against his own country. Rodney replied to the offer by affecting to think that the bearer of it was temporarily insane. The Duc de Chartres—infamous afterwards as Philippe Egalité—asked Rodney what would happen if he met the British fleet off Brest. "In that case," said Rodney, "your Highness will have an opportunity of learning English." The generosity of a French nobleman, the Maréchal de Biron, enabled Rodney to settle with his English creditors, and in 1778 he returned to his native country to lead her fleet to the West Indies and destroy, only four years afterwards, the French naval power there. The sum lent by old De Biron to Rodney was 1000 louis, and that must be pronounced to be, for French interests, the very worst investment of French coin ever made.

A glance at Rodney's portrait while yet a young man, shows a curious resemblance to the younger Pitt. There are the same curved eyebrows and widely opened eyes, the same angle of forehead, the same challenging and haughty gaze. Rodney expended his life lavishly, drank deeply of what is called "pleasure," grew old quickly, was persecuted with gout, which gave impatient fire to his temper and scribbled his face with the characters of pain. Hence the sharpened gravity shown in his later portraits. Rodney was a man with many faults, but he had a great genius for battle. Green, the historian, describes him as "the greatest of English seamen save Nelson and Blake"; and it is certain that betwixt Blake's great defeat of Van Tromp in the Strait and Nelson's Titanic victory at Trafalgar, there is no sea battle which, for scale and far-reaching importance, can compare with Rodney's defeat of De Grasse.

Rodney, however, had not Blake's mingled simplicity and loftiness of character, and he lacked Nelson's electrical fire, and his faculty for knitting his officers to himself with a personal affection which made them, to use Nelson's own phrase, "a band of brothers." Rodney was too much of an aristocrat to try to win where he could command, and if he wrought his fleet into a perfect instrument of battle, flexible through all its parts to his every thought, he did this by mere force of imperious will. "I will be admiral," was his motto.

There were evil traditions at that moment in the naval service of Great Britain. Byng had been shot on his own quarter-deck for half-heartedness in battle. After Mathews's action off Toulon, in 1744, the admiral himself, his second in command, and eleven captains out of twenty-nine, were court-martialled. Mathews himself was cashiered because he had broken the line—an offence to the prim tactics of that day—and his captains because they did not follow him when he led down on to the enemy. Of the eleven captains, says Mahan, one died, one deserted, seven were dismissed, only two were acquitted. Rodney himself had been cheated of a great victory over Guichen, in 1780, by the deliberate disobedience of his own captains; and the story of how he created a new discipline in his fleet, and a new sense of duty and honour amongst his captains, is very stirring. He drilled his great fleet as a sharp-tempered sergeant drills a squad of recruits. "Every captain in this fleet," he said to a friend, "thinks himself fit to be prime-minister of Great Britain," and Rodney spared no pains to cure them of that delusion. The service, it must be added, was fissured by political divisions. A Whig captain was capable of remembering his politics even in the flaming stress of battle, and of refusing effective help to another British captain because he was guilty of being a

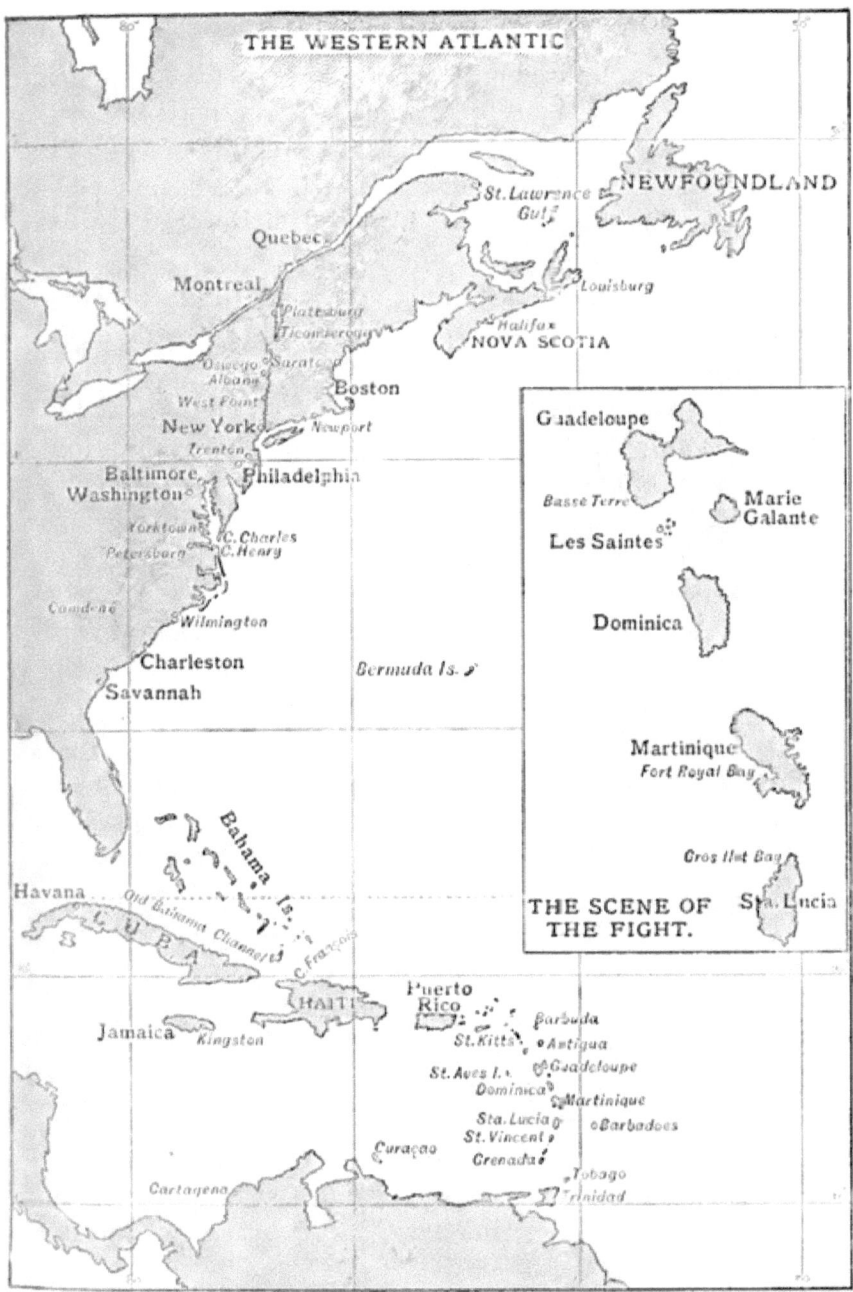

Copied by permission from Captain Mahan's work, "The Influence of Sea Power on History."

Tory. Rodney effaced all this. He put his fleet through drill manœuvres, scourging them into orders with angry signals and public rebukes until the captains of the old school, at least, were half-mad with wrath and perplexity. But he gave to his fleet that first condition of victory, an iron discipline.

The field upon which these two great fleets were now to manœuvre and contend for the next three days is a stretch of water, roughly 150 miles in extent from north to south, with a line of four islands—Guadeloupe, Dominica, Martinique, and Santa Lucia—running through it, of which the three first named were French, and the last English. The actual battle took place in the channel betwixt Guadeloupe and Dominica, some twenty-three miles wide. In the centre, slightly westward, is a group of islets called the Saints, which gives its name to the battle.

Of the four days' manœuvring which intervened betwixt the morning of April 8 and the great fight of the 12th, it is needless here to speak. Fleets in those sad days were governed by what may be called parade tactics, and their combats resembled the thrust and parry and flourish, the doubling, and the disengaging of a ceremonious duel, rather than the close and desperate fighting of Blake with his Dutchmen more than a century before, and of Nelson and his daring school twenty years afterwards. The ideal of an admiral in the early part of the eighteenth century was to keep his line intact, to manœuvre ingeniously for the advantage of the wind, to graze past his enemy's line from head to rear, each ship exchanging broadsides with each hostile ship as she passed. One fleet, more or less crippled, crawls up to windward, the other flutters down to leeward, and then the battle ceremoniously ends. There was no closing in fiery wrestle, no rush of boarders across the splintered bulwarks, no "ganging down into the middle o' it," to quote the words of the Scotch captain at Camperdown. So all the naval battles of that period were loitering and indecisive. De Grasse was of that school of tactics; and, though Rodney in the approaching battle was destined to bring this style of fighting to a peremptory close, yet even he had scarcely broken loose from the traditions of the school in which he had been reared.

For four days the two great fleets manœuvred and clawed at each other, like two hawks circling round each other in the empyrean with screams, and ruffled feathers, and outstretched talons. But on the night of the 11th came Rodney's chance. On the night of the 10th the *Zèle*, a clumsy French seventy-four, clumsily managed, clashed into a sister ship, the *Jason*, and on the morning of the 11th both ships were semi-disabled, De Grasse, who had got rid of his merchant ships, despatched the *Jason* into Guadeloupe, but the crippled *Zèle* greatly hampered the movements of his fleet, and on the night of the 11th that unfortunate ship managed to get in the track of De Grasse's own flagship, and was still more cruelly battered. De Grasse ordered a frigate, the *Astrée*—whose captain was the unfortunate La Pérouse, who afterwards flitted for a moment, like a ghost, across Australian history—to take the *Zèle* in tow.

But all this delayed the movements of the French fleet, and when the day broke De Grasse's fleet was sprawling over some fifteen miles of sea space, a little to the westward of the Saints, while the British fleet, in steadfast order, was on the horizon to windward. Sir Charles Douglas, Rodney's captain, hurried down to his admiral's cabin to report, with pious exultation, that "God had given him his enemy on the lee bow!" Rodney was quickly on deck, and a glance from his

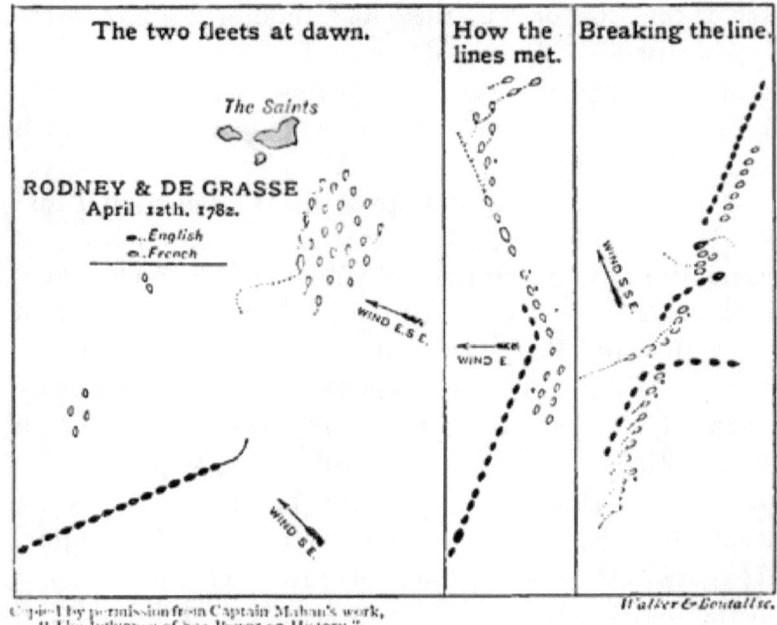

keen eyes, showed him that to-day, at least, De Grasse's wary tactics were in vain. To draw the Frenchmen still farther under his lee, Rodney signalled to four of his swiftest ships to make a dash at the unfortunate *Zèle*, straggling like a broken-winged sea-bird on De Grasse's rear. The French admiral could not abandon his crippled ship, and kept away to cover her with his line, and this gave Rodney the windward position. The choice of fighting or not fighting lay in his hand. He had thirty-six sail of the line, including five three-deckers, under his command, and he flung them with fierce energy into line of battle.

The wind was light, the sea smooth, and ship after ship of the British fleet glided on, a stately pile of canvas, each ship a cable's length, or about 200 yards, from her neighbour; and so perfect was the line, that a bucket dropped from the leading ship might have been picked up by almost every ship that followed. The stately British line had a northerly course; De Grasse, by this time formed into a somewhat straggling line, was standing to the south-east so as to cross the head of the British line, and, if possible, bar its entrance to the Strait. The two fleets, that is, formed the two moving sides of an obtuse angle. The French ships were the better sailers, and it remained to be seen whether they would scrape past the leading British ship, the *Marlborough*, and regain the position to windward. The crippled and lagging *Zèle*, however, held De Grasse fatally back.

Eight ships in the French line had crossed the line on which the British were moving, but it was clear that the head of the British column, like the point of a thrusting rapier, would smite the ninth ship—the *Brave* —in the French line, and the fate of the battle at this stage turned on the question of whether Rodney would push his thrust fiercely and resolutely home. If he followed the parade tactics of his day, he would play a game of long bowls; swing his column round, that is, parallel to the French line at long-shot distance, and fleet go sailing past fleet, with loud bellowing of cannon, and much rending of canvas, and no particular harm to anybody. But Rodney thrust the head of his column up within musket-shot distance of the French line; then his leading ships kept away in turn, and the two lines, moving in opposite directions, drifted slowly past each other. Each ship, as it drifted heavily past an enemy's ship, broke into the thunder of furious broadsides.

Nothing can be more dramatic than the pauses and the ear-shattering explosions of a fight of this character. A British ship moving steadily ahead sees through the smoke the tall masts of a French three-decker towering above her. A rift in the eddying smoke shows the black hull so near that the faces of the officers on the quarter-deck are recognisable, the black muzzles of the guns, the eager faces of the gunners behind them. Then comes the swift order to fire. Again, again, and yet again, as the two great ships glide slowly past each other, comes the curving line of flame, the deep-voiced roar of the broadside, the crash of the rending shot, the tumble of the falling spars. But in another minute the vision has faded, the choking smoke is swept away, the ship is crossing the gap in the enemy's line. But, wrapped in a cloud of smoke, comes on yet another huge three-decker, and once more with roar as of tropical thunder, and play of dancing flame as of tropical lightning, and tempest of splintering shot, the two contending ships float past each other.

The volume of battle-sound grew ever deeper and more terrible as ship after ship of the British line came slowly and majestically up till its bowsprit was almost thrust over the quarter of a French ship, then kept away, and added itself to that procession of deep-voiced giants who were thundering far ahead down the Frenchman's line. The captain of the *Hercules*, a gouty, hot-tempered old sailor, had a chair placed for himself in the waist of his ship, and sat there leaning over the bulwarks ironically saluting, it is to be feared with many salt forecastle expletives, the passing enemy. The British ships, in addition to their heavy guns, were armed with the newly-invented carronade, a gun very formidable at close quarters. The French ships were crowded with troops intended to capture Jamaica, and the slaughter amongst them was great.

Rodney, in the *Formidable*, held the exact centre of the British line, and eighteen British line-of-battle ships were growling and spluttering fire ahead of him down the French line, when he swung round parallel to a French ship at pistol-shot distance, and added the roar of his broadsides to the tumult of the battle. Eighteen French ships in succession were scorched with the flame of the *Formidable's* guns as they drifted past, and so menacing was the aspect of the British ship, as, edging ever closer, she broke into thunder and flame on each Frenchman's bow in turn, that, according to the testimony of an officer on the British flagship, "we could actually see the Frenchmen running from their guns, in spite of the frantic efforts of their officers to keep them steady." By nine o'clock the tumult of the great fight was at its climax. The two lines were wrapped in smoke and flame through their whole length.

De Grasse attempted one or two ineffective orders. He first signalled to his captains to wear in succession, but this also was impossible. By this time the leading British ships had drifted past the rear ship of the French line. Then came the crisis of the fight. In Hannay's words, "on emerging from the rolling masses of smoke, the captains looked eagerly back for the signals at the towering masthead of the *Formidable*. As they looked they saw a great three-decker heading north out of the cloud and the flame. For a moment they thought the French admiral had doubled back on them, but as the three-decker cleared the smoke they saw the cross of St. George, and knew that the *Formidable* had burst through the French line to windward." This is the stroke that made the battle famous. Rodney had broken the Frenchman's line.

A tempest of controversy has raged round this incident. Did Rodney learn the stroke from Clerk of Eldin, the Scotch laird who supplied Walter Scott with the original of Monkbarns in the "Antiquary," and who undertook to teach British admirals the art of victory? Or was the famous manœuvre owing to the swift insight and energy of Douglas, Rodney's captain of the fleet? A flaw in the wind threatened to take the French aback, and to keep their sails full the French ships had to throw their heads up into the wind, so that they formed what is called a "bow and quarter line." Each ship, that is, drifted past her particular antagonist, not parallel with her, but at an angle from her. At this moment a French ship, the *Glorieux*, drifted down on the *Formidable*, literally knocked out of the line by a broadside from the *Duke*, a British ninety-eight. The high bulwarks of the *Formidable*, and the hammocks stacked as a barricade across the break of the quarter-deck, made it difficult for Rodney to see the French line, and he stepped out on to the starboard gangway, and, leaning over its rail, saw the *Glorieux* drifting down upon him.

The drift of the *Glorieux*, and the flaw in the wind, combined to make a wide gap in the French line. Douglas, with a glance, saw the great opportunity. They might pierce the enemy's line, cut off the French rear, and put each ship betwixt two fires. He ran eagerly, hat in hand, to Rodney, and urged him to steer through the gap. Rodney was not in love with advice from anybody, and he replied, "I will not break my line, Sir Charles." But Douglas was so kindled by the opportunity he saw, that he pressed Rodney again, and even ventured to give the order to the quarter-master at the helm to port, a liberty which Rodney sternly checked. The evidence seems to show that Rodney himself saw the opportunity the gap in the French line offered, and rather resented Douglas's advice as unnecessary. The decisive step was taken, the wheel of the *Formidable* was sent flying round to port, the great ship slowly swung her bluff bows to starboard, and swept betwixt the *Diadème* and the *Glorieux*, pouring a tremendous broadside into each vessel as she did so. In breaking the line, says an eye-witness, "the *Formidable* passed so near the *Glorieux* that I could see the cannoneers throwing away their sponges and handspikes in order to save themselves by running below." "We passed," says another officer, "within pistol-shot of the *Glorieux*, which was so roughly handled that she was shorn of all her masts, bowsprit, and ensign-staff." It was this spectacle—the *Formidable* "heading north out of the cloud and the flames," which the captains of the British van, looking back, as they cleared the French rear, beheld.

But Rodney had no time to signal to the ships following him; signals, indeed, in the eddying smoke of the great fight were vain, and the question was whether his captains would understand the manœuvre and imitate it. The *Namur*, Captain Inglis, was next in the line to the *Formidable*. Inglis saw through the smoke the masts of his admiral's ship swing round till they were at right angles to the course, and then the great ship, with fire flashing out from both sides, swept across the enemy's track. The signal to engage to leeward was still flying, but the moment was one to disregard signals. Inglis never hesitated, but followed his admiral through the gap. Cornwallis in the *St. Albans*, Dumaresq in the *Canada*, Charrington in the *Repulse*, Fanshaw in the *Ajax* in turn came up to the fatal gap, swung to starboard, poured on the *Diadème* and the unfortunate *Glorieux* a destructive broadside, and swept triumphantly on to put the remaining ships of the French rear betwixt two fires.

Almost at the same moment Gardner, in the *Duke*, the ship ahead of Rodney, finding that the stoppage of the *Diadème* had thrown the French ships following her into a helpless cluster, ported his helm and passed through the gap just made at this point. In a word, the centre of the French line was hopelessly smashed. The *Bedford*, seventy-four, farther to rear, almost at the same moment had blundered in the smoke through the French line at the twelfth ship, and was followed through the gap by Hood's whole division of twelve ships. De

Grasse's line, in brief, was broken into three fragments. The British ships bearing up to windward in a very few minutes were clear of the smoke, and, looking back, saw such a spectacle as, to quote Hannay, "no British seaman had seen in this war so far." To west and south-west lay the great French fleet broken into three disconnected fragments. The clusters of ships which had formed De Grasse's rear and van were flying in opposite directions; in the centre towered the lofty masts of the great *Ville de Paris*, while round her clustered six sorely battered French ships.

The wind at this moment died away, the sea was calm, and victors and vanquished lay alike helpless for a space under the fierceness of the tropical noon. Hannay supplies a horrible detail of the scene. "On the surface of the water there was something which was pure horror to all whose eyes were compelled to see it. Shoals of sharks—which alone among God's creatures the sailor tortures without remorse, the loathsome brute which loiters to profit by his misfortune—had collected to feed on the corpses thrown overboard, or the living who had fallen with fragments of rigging. They were leaping over one another and ravening at their prey."

A little after midday the wind awoke, and with it reawoke the battle. The unfortunate De Grasse signalled in vain to his scattered squadrons for help, and the British ships, one after another, gathered round the central cluster of the broken French fleet. The *Glorieux* quickly surrendered; the *César*, the *Hector*, and the *Ardent* in turn struck, and the last was a peculiarly welcome conquest. She was a British ship, captured three years before by the French and Spanish fleet in the chops of the Channel, and when the white flag of France went fluttering down from her peak, great was the joy through all the British decks.

De Grasse fought his flagship like a gallant sailor. She was a magnificent vessel, copper-bottomed, carrying 106 guns and a crew of 1300 men. She was a present from the City of Paris to Louis XV., and was the proudest and most gallant ship afloat. For a long time the news of her capture in France was received with incredulity. "Not the whole British fleet," one distinguished French official declared, "would capture the *Ville de Paris.*" But the British ships came up slowly, one by one, and gathered round the stately French flagship like dogs round a bull. De Grasse's cartridges were exhausted; powder barrels had to be hoisted from the hold, and loose powder poured into the guns with a ladle. The light of a tropical sun lay on the sea outside, but so black and thick was the smoke betwixt the French ship's decks, where the crew, amid the wounded and dying, were toiling at their guns, that battle lanterns had to be lit to give the men light.

It was six o'clock, and still De Grasse fought. When the *Barfleur*, with Hood's flag as rear-admiral flying, came majestically into the fight, De Grasse, with something of the haughty courtesy of a knight in battle, fired a single gun by way of salute and challenge to Hood; Hood, the most gallant of sailors, replied with a like salute. Then, laying the *Barfleur* alongside the French flagship, he poured upon her a tempest of shot. There were but three unwounded men, of whom De Grasse himself was one, on the upper deck of the *Ville de Paris*. Her upper works were torn to splinters, her sails hung from the broken yards in shot-torn rags; more slain or wounded men lay around her guns than through Rodney's whole fleet. At six o'clock, with his own hands, the unfortunate De Grasse lowered his flag. A cutter pushed out from the stern of the *Barfleur*, and pulled to the shot-torn sides of the *Ville de Paris*, and De Grasse stepped into it a prisoner. He was the first French commander-in-chief, by land or sea, taken in conflict by the British since Marlborough packed Tallard and two other French generals into his coach at Blenheim.

The battle of the Saints abounds in picturesque incidents which cannot be told here. Thus, when the two giant ships of the battle, the *Formidable* and the *Ville de Paris*, were exchanging broadsides with each other at pistol-shot distance, a French shot smashed to pieces a coop of fowls on the British ship's deck. A little bantam cock, released by the shot, fluttered on to the poop railing, and with the roar of every British broadside flapped its wings in triumph, and crowed in notes so shrill as to be heard even through the crowded decks. That intelligent and patriotic fowl was, by Rodney's solemn orders, kept in fatness and ease till it died a natural death.

Rodney has been blamed for not pursuing the fragments of the broken French fleet with greater vigour. Douglas strongly urged him to pursue, and was rebuffed with the remark that he had offered advice once too often that day already. But the battle had raged thirteen hours with scarcely a moment's interval; Rodney was old and gouty and weary, and contented with his gains; and when night fell he signalled to his fleet to lie to. Six French ships were captured; but Rodney brought only two of his prizes—the *Ardent* and the *Jason*—into port. The *Glorieux*, according to an eye-witness, when boarded, "presented a scene of complete horror. The number of killed were so great that the surviving, either from want of leisure or through dismay, had not thrown the bodies of the killed overboard, so that the decks were covered with the bodies and mangled limbs of the dead as well as the wounded and the dying." The *Glorieux* foundered on its passage home; so did the *Hector*, and so did the great prize of the battle, the *Ville de Paris*. The *César* had a still more tragical ending. She took fire, by some accident, immediately after her capture, and burned to the water's edge. The English prize-crew perished in her, the lieutenant in command being "seen in the stern fighting the fire to the last. No boat dare approach; the sharks were swarming under the counter, and he staid to die in the flames at his post."

The French loss is reckoned at 3000 killed, whereas the loss of the British in killed and wounded together was less than 1000. The French refused to believe that the British loss was so slight, and Blanc tells the story of how he took an incredulous French officer round the *Formidable* and showed him how slight was the damage done by French shot before he could persuade him that the British returns were accurate. The French fire, one of the *Formidable's* officers wrote, "slackens as we approach, and is totally silent when we are close alongside"; whereas the British fire was fiercest when the ships were almost touching each other.

The battle brought great fame to Rodney. "It is

odd," he wrote to his wife the day after the battle, "but within two little years I have taken two Spanish, one French, and one Dutch admiral. Providence does it all, or how should I escape the shot of thirty-three sail of the line?" Rodney, it may be added, had taken a French admiral in the midst of the greatest French fleet then in existence, and on board the finest three-decker in the world. "More liners," says Hannay, "had struck to him than to any British admiral of his generation." But the public results of Rodney's great fight were of the highest character. As with the stroke of a thunderbolt, the whole prestige of French fleets in the New world was shattered. Jamaica was saved. Peace followed, and in the treaty Gibraltar remained a British possession, and the British power in India was acknowledged. Rodney's battle, too, stamped its fierce impress on the sea strategy of British ships in all future time "It marked," says Hannay, "the beginning of that fierce and headlong, yet well-calculated style of sea-fighting which led to Trafalgar and made England the undisputed mistress of the sea."

LORD HOWE AND THE FIRST OF JUNE

1794

> "So spake our fathers. Our flag, unfurled,
>   Blew brave to the north and south;
> An iron answer we gave the world,
>   For we spoke by the cannon's mouth."
>
> —NESBIT.

IN his "Autobiography," Prince Metternich tells how, on May 2, 1794, from the summit of a hill behind Cowes, he watched a great and historic spectacle. More than 400 ships—great three-deckers, smart frigates, bluff-bowed merchantmen—were setting sail at once. Their tall masts and widespread canvas seemed to fill the whole sea horizon. It was the Channel Fleet under Lord Howe, with a huge convoy of merchantmen. "I consider this," wrote Prince Metternich, "the most beautiful sight I have ever seen. I might say, indeed, the most beautiful that human eyes have ever beheld! At a signal from the admiral's ship the merchantmen unfurled their sails, the fleet for the West Indies turned to the west, the fleet for the East Indies passed to the east side of the island, each accompanied with a portion of the royal fleet. Hundreds of vessels and boats, filled with spectators, covered the two roads as far as the eye could reach, in the midst of which the great ships followed one another, in the same manner as we see great masses of troops moved on the parade ground."

LORD HOWE

From a mezzotint by R. DUNKARTON, *after the portrait by* J. S. COPLEY, R.A.

It would have added new and strange colours to that wonderful scene if Prince Metternich had realised that this stately fleet was sailing out to one of the most famous sea battles in history. If he could have looked, in imagination, beyond the sea-rim, and seen, only four weeks afterwards, this same gallant array of ships bearing down on the French line in that mighty combat off Ushant, which lives in British history as "the Glorious First of June." In the early days of June Prince Metternich saw that same fleet return to Portsmouth, with torn canvas and shot-battered sides, and he records how the stately *Queen Charlotte*, Howe's flagship, "presented the appearance of a ruin." But the British fleet brought with them six great French line-of-battle ships as prizes. France had lost her Mediterranean fleet only six weeks before; Hood had destroyed it at Toulon. And now Howe had broken the strength of her Channel fleet off Ushant; and in the long revolutionary war just beginning, Great Britain had scored the first and decisive success.

War betwixt Great Britain and Revolutionary France was inevitable. It was not merely that the wild scenes of the Reign of Terror had shocked the imagination and conscience of Great Britain. The French, in the intoxication of their new-found liberty, were eager to "sow the revolution" over the whole area of Europe. "All Governments are our enemies," said the President of the French Convention; "all peoples are our allies." Great Britain was threatened in common with all other European Powers. French agents nourished rebellion in Ireland, and supplied arms and soldiers to the native princes in India against England. Holland was the ally of England; and a French army overran the Netherlands and seized the Scheldt, and England had to face the prospect of seeing a French fleet at Antwerp. In 1793 France declared war.

In France itself the harvest had failed. Famine threatened, and in May 1794 a great American convoy of 160 sail, chiefly laden with flour—its cargoes valued at £5,000,000—was on its way to France, and was most eagerly expected. The French Government despatched a great fleet under its ablest admiral, Villaret-Joyeuse, to bring the merchant ships safely into Brest. The British fleet which Prince Metternich had watched on May 2 put out from Portsmouth, was intended, first to convoy through the narrow seas some 148 merchantmen bound to Newfoundland and the Indies, and then to go in pursuit of Villaret-Joyeuse, crush his fleet, and capture the American convoy.

On May 28 Howe fell in with the French fleet in wild weather some 400 miles to the westward of Ushant. It is unnecessary to describe in detail the far-stretching evolutions, the partial combats, the retreats and advances, of the five days which preceded the great fight, though the sea has seldom witnessed a more picturesque spectacle. The sea ran high; a gale blew from the south-west. Villaret-Joyeuse was an admirable tactician; his ships were quicker and more weatherly than those of the British, and his aim was not to fight Howe, but to evade him, to decoy him off the line by which the American convoy was approaching, and so enable it to reach Brest safely—a feat on which, as the French Convention had bluntly warned him, depended the safety of his own head. On the tossing floor of that wild sea, scourged with angry south-west gales, for five days these two mighty fleets struck at each other, and circled round each other like two sea-birds contending, with ruffled feathers and slanting wings, in the sky. Villaret-Joyeuse clung to the weather-gage, evaded a general action, and strove to draw his stubborn antagonist off the track of the coming convoy. Howe could not overtake the main body of the French fleet, but with his faster ships he clung desperately to the more laggard ships in the rear of the French line—clinging, in a word, to Villaret-Joyeuse's tail—and watched every flaw of the wind that might give him the weather-gage. One of the most gallant episodes in naval history is the story of how the *Audacious*—a stumpy, short-bodied seventy-four, the smallest of her class in Howe's fleet—hung for a long day on the quarter of the *Révolutionnaire*, a huge three-decker of 120 guns, and with the occasional help of the *Russell*, another seventy-four, actually compelled her giant antagonist to strike—though a dash of the French van for the rescue of the *Révolutionnaire* prevented the *Audacious* from actually putting a prize crew on board the Frenchman.

On May 30 a dense fog swept over the field of action, and for thirty-six hours the two fleets were absolutely invisible to each other, though the sound of the bells struck on the French ships was distinctly audible to the British. Sometimes through a sudden lane in the fog the huge heavily-rolling black hulls of the hostile ships would become for a moment visible; or a look-out perched on some British topmast would see above the low, drifting fog, like spars thrust through some continent of snow, the top-masts of a dozen French battleships. At mid-day on the 31st the fog had cleared, and the French fleet—thirty-two vessels, twenty-six of them line-of-battle ships—was on the lee bow of the British fleet. Howe, that is, by his patient tactics and fine seamanship, was getting the weather-gage of Villaret-Joyeuse, and would be able to compel an engagement. Night fell, however, and still the French admiral was able to evade his stubborn antagonist, and Villaret-Joyeuse, with lights concealed so as to give no clue to his movements, spread every inch of canvas, and pressed on, hoping in the morning to be to windward of his foe. Howe, however, guessed his enemy's tactics. He thrust out his swiftest frigates as tentacles, so as to keep touch with the French fleet, and held a westerly course under full sail all night.

Morning broke clear and dazzling, and full of summer light. It was Sunday. A soft south-west wind blew; an easy sea was running, and about four miles on the starboard or lee bow, stretched the long line of the French fleets—a procession of giants! Howe at last was able to force his adroit antagonist to a fight on something like equal terms. His crews, however, were almost worn out with the toils of the five stormy days and nights, flavoured with intervals of battle, through which they had passed. Howe himself, nearly seventy years of age, had taken no sleep for that period except in a chair, and with cool judgment, before running down to engage, he first sent his fleet to breakfast. The French captains, who expected to see the British ships bear down upon them with all sails spread, misunderstood that pause. Troubridge, who afterwards commanded the *Culloden* at the battle of the Nile, was, as it happened, a prisoner of war on board the *Sans Pareil*, and its captain made some sneering remark to him about the reluctance of the British to engage. "There will be no fight to-day," he said, "your admiral will not venture down." Troubridge, however, perfectly understood Howe's tactics. "English sailors," he replied, "never like to fight on empty stomachs. The signal is flying for all hands to breakfast, after which, be quite sure, they will pay you a visit!" Less than six hours afterwards the captain of the *Sans Pareil*, with his masts gone by the board, his bulwarks torn to splinters, and one-third of his crew struck down, was inviting Troubridge to pull down the colours of his ship in token of surrender!

The two fleets just about to close in the fiery wrestle of battle, made up a stately spectacle. The French admiral's flagship, the *Montagne*, was, perhaps, the finest battleship then afloat. She carried 120 guns and a crew of nearly 1200 men. In addition, Villaret-Joyeuse had under his command two three-deckers of 110 guns each, four of eighty guns, and nineteen seventy-fours. This formed a fleet of twenty-six line-of-battle ships, which, with some frigates and one fifty-gun ship, brought the total up to thirty-two vessels. The British had only twenty-five line-of-battle ships to oppose this force, and no one of them, in tonnage or weight of fire, could compare with the French flagship. The French, in fact, had a decisive, though not an overwhelming, advantage at every point. A French ship of that period had almost invariably a heavier tonnage and weight of fire than a British ship of the same class. Thus, the broadside of a British

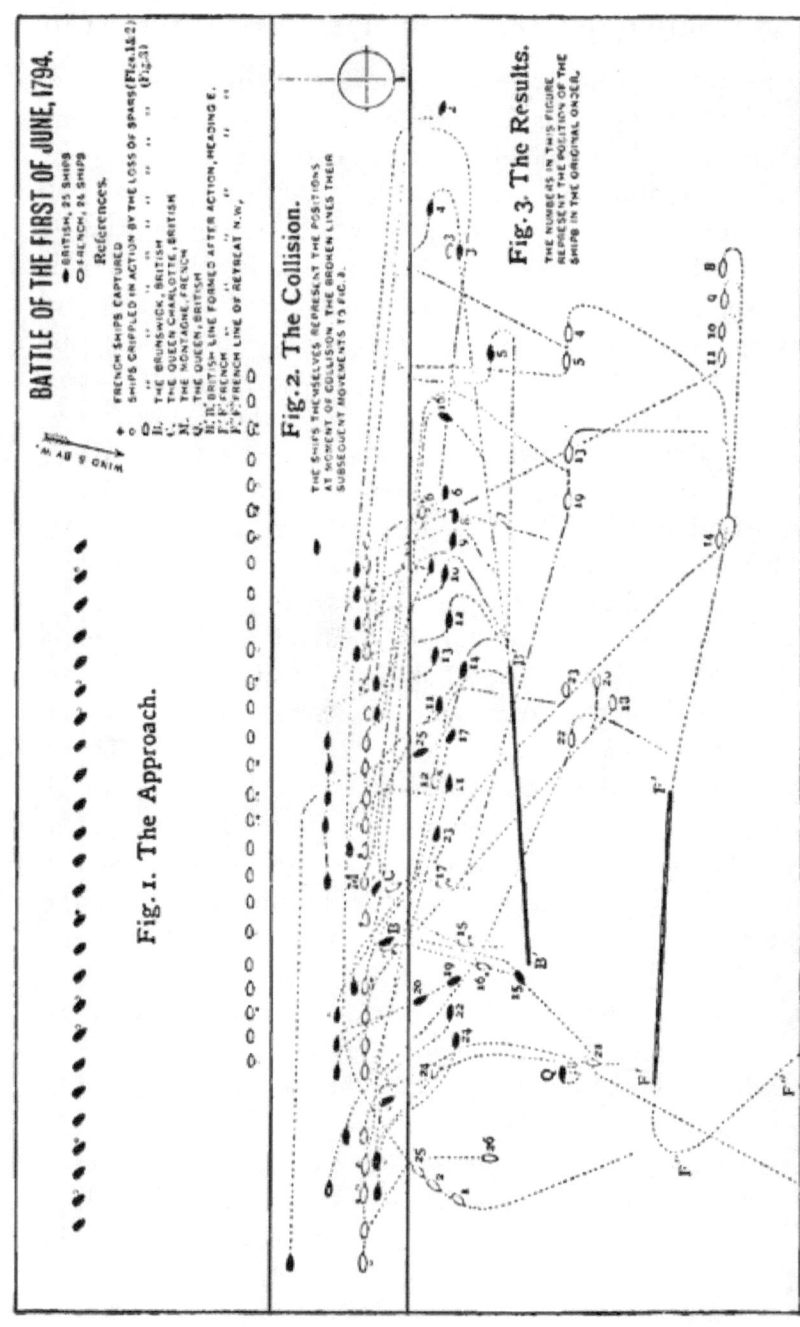

ninety-eight weighed 958 lbs.; that of a French second-class eighty-gun ship weighed 1079 lbs. A French 110-gun ship threw a broadside of 1278 lbs.; the *Queen Charlotte's* broadside weighed only 1158 lbs., and the *Montagne* was 800 tons bigger than the *Queen Charlotte!* The French fleet was manned by 20,000 men, the British by about 17,000.

The advantage was thus with the French at every point, and the French Convention had taken special steps to harden the courage of its admirals and sailors. It had passed a motion directing that every officer should be adjudged a traitor who struck his colours to a superior force until his ship was actually sinking. A member of the Convention, Jean Bon Saint-André, was present as commissioner on board the *Montagne*, to remind the French admirals that defeat would cost them their heads. It is interesting to learn that Jean Bon Saint-André, whose business it was to keep the courage of the fleet up to the heroic standard, proved, on actual trial, not to have a stock of courage sufficient for his own consumption! When the tall masts of the *Queen Charlotte* threw their menacing shadow over the quarter of the *Montagne*, and the blast of its terrific broadside swept like a tempest of flame along the decks of that great ship, M. Jean Bon Saint-André, with all the authority and heroism of the Convention under his cocked hat, fled in mere terror to the safe and ignoble seclusion of the cockpit, and never emerged till the battle was over.

Howe's plan of action was simple and bold. He spent some time in changing the order of his ships, so as to pit against each French vessel one of reasonably equal strength; then he signalled to his captains to bear down on the enemy. The two lines were approaching obliquely, and each British captain was directed, on nearing the French line, to put his helm down, run through an interval betwixt two French ships, then bear up and engage his special antagonist to leeward. In this way the line would be pierced simultaneously at twenty points; the British ships as they passed through the intervals in the French line, would rake the ships to larboard and starboard; and, fighting to leeward, each ship would make the escape of her crippled antagonist impossible.

It was a pretty scheme, implying a haughty confidence in the superiority of each British ship to each French ship, and involving much hard fighting; but if successful it meant the destruction of Villaret-Joyeuse's whole force.

Howe brought his fleet up in perfect order, and, at 9.20 A.M., he closed his signal-book with a sigh of relief and satisfaction. His functions as admiral had ceased. Further "tactics" were unnecessary; nothing remained but that in which British sailors seldom fail—plain, straightforward combat. But Howe closed his signal-book prematurely. Two circumstances suddenly threatened to spoil his whole plan. One was the fact that, in some cases, the intervals betwixt the French ships were too narrow to permit the passage of an English ship. The other was of an uglier quality. The ship that led the British van, the *Cæsar*, instead of leading boldly on and running down through its assigned interval in the French line, threw its main topsail aback, hauled to the wind, and opened a somewhat useless fire on the enemy 500 yards distant. This checked the advance of the British line, and was a conspicuous example of disobedience to orders. The captain of the *Cæsar*, Molloy, had shown courage in many engagements, but Howe had been dissatisfied with him during the sparring betwixt the fleets on the previous days, and proposed to displace the *Cæsar* from its place of honour at the head of the British line. The captain of the fleet, Sir Roger Curtis, who was Molloy's friend, persuaded the admiral to abandon that intention; but when Howe saw the *Cæsar*, with her topsails aback, checking the British line, and failing to close with decision on the enemy, he put his hand on his captain's shoulder and said, " Look, Curtis! there goes your friend. Who is mistaken now?" It was found afterwards that a French shot had damaged the rudder of the *Cæsar* and almost rendered her unmanageable; but Molloy, who himself after the fight demanded a court-martial, was dismissed his ship. The truth is, this was the first great naval engagement of the war, and British captains had not developed that habit of fierce and close fighting which Jervis and Nelson afterwards made their characteristic.

Howe himself, however, moved steadily on his path, grimly silent. He had chosen the French flagship, the huge *Montagne*, with her 120 guns, as his special antagonist. As the *Queen Charlotte*, in perfect fighting order, came majestically along the French line, the *Vengeur*, a heavy seventy-four-gun ship, smote her with a fierce broadside, to which Howe deigned no answer. Still moving onward, and now approaching very close to the French flagship, the *Achille*, a sister ship to the

Vengeur, joined in the tempest of fire being poured on the silent *Queen Charlotte*. Howe blasted that unfortunate ship with one terrific broadside, then, being within two ship's lengths of the *Montagne*, he swung his ship round and pointed her stem towards the interval betwixt the flagship and the ship to the rearward of her in the French line, the *Jacobin*, a fine vessel of eighty guns. Both the *Montagne* and the *Jacobin* tried to cheat Howe of his purpose. The captain of the *Montagne* threw his sails aback, so that the ship began to drift astern; the captain of the *Jacobin*, on the other hand, shook out some of her sails so as to move ahead, and thus close the interval. Howe held on his course unswervingly. The stems of the *Jacobin* and the *Queen Charlotte*, and the stern of the *Montagne* threatened to meet in ruinous collision.

But the nerve of the captain of the *Jacobin* at the critical instant failed. The triple lines of silent guns that looked grimly out from the tall sides of the *Queen Charlotte* wore a very menacing aspect. If they broke into flame across his bows, the *Jacobin* would be half destroyed at a blow. The *Jacobin's* captain put down his helm, the bow of his ship fell off, and that vessel shot ahead, and to the leeward of the *Montagne*. At the same moment the helm of the *Queen Charlotte* was put hard over, and she swept under the stern of the French flagship. The two ships were so close, indeed, that the French ensign, as it waved from the *Montagne's* flagstaff, brushed the main and mizzen shrouds of the *Queen Charlotte*. Howe had held his fire up to that moment, but just as the French flag was scraping the shrouds of the *Queen Charlotte*, her fifty guns poured their iron hail through the sides and across the decks of the Frenchman. A more destructive broadside has, perhaps, seldom been fired. It slew, or struck down, or wounded, more than 300 men, including the captain. The sailors afterwards declared that a coach might have been driven in the huge rent made in the stern of the *Montagne* by that one broadside! So staggering was the blow, indeed, that the *Montagne* did not fire a gun by way of reply.

Codrington, who afterwards commanded at Navarino, was lieutenant on the *Queen Charlotte*, Howe's flagship, and had charge of seven guns on the lower deck. He tells how the first guns were fired in very realistic fashion. "I," says Codrington, "was on the lower deck. The ports were lowered to prevent the sea washing in. On going through the smoke I hauled up a port, and could just see it was a French ship we were passing." Codrington was without orders; he was a young lieutenant in his first battle, but the sight of the Frenchman's stern was enough for him, and he instantly acted. "I successively hauled up the ports," he says, "and myself fired the whole of my seven weather guns into her; then ran to leeward and fired the lee guns into the other ship. The weather guns bore first as we went through on a slant, therefore I had time for the lee guns." When the ports were lifted the sea broke in, and as the guns were fired the breechings were, in most instances, carried away. The scene, in brief, was one of the wildest confusion; but nothing shook Codrington's steady nerve. "In passing under the *Montagne's* stern," he says, "I myself waited at the bow port till I saw the Frenchman's rudder guns (thirty-two pounders, double-shotted), and then I pulled the trigger, the same sea splashing us both, and the fly of her ensign brushed our shrouds. I pulled the trigger of the whole seven guns in the same way, as I saw the rudder just above the gun-room ports. On going on deck Bowen (Howe's flag-captain), in answer to my asking if I had done wrong in firing without any immediate orders, said, 'I could have kissed you for it!' He added, 'In going through, the helm was hard up, and we were thinking we should not clear her, and we quite forgot to send you any orders.'"

The *Queen Charlotte* should now have rounded the stern of the *Montagne* and engaged her to starboard, but the *Jacobin* occupied the exact position the *Queen Charlotte* desired to take. Howe was about to take his position outside the *Jacobin*, when his master, Bowen, a cool and quick-eyed sailor, saw that the *Jacobin's* rudder was swinging to port. That ship, in a word, was about herself to move off to leeward. Instantly the helm of the *Queen Charlotte* was shifted, her stem swung round. So close was she to the *Jacobin* that her jib-boom was drawn roughly across the mizzen-shrouds of that vessel, and through the narrow lane betwixt the two ships the *Queen Charlotte* moved, while her guns broke into angry speech along her whole length on both sides.

Had the *Jacobin*, indeed, kept her position, the *Queen Charlotte*, with a ship of eighty guns to leeward, and one of 120 guns to windward of her, would have fared ill. She might well have been blown into mere chips! But the *Jacobin* had no intention of staying near an antagonist with such a fury and weight of fire, and she ran down to leeward out of the fight, firing as she went. Howe, meanwhile, was thundering on the *Montagne* with broadsides so close and deadly, that the great ship, as though bewildered by strokes that followed each other in such breathless haste, scarcely made any reply. She found a door of escape, however. A chance shot from the *Jacobin* carried away the *Queen Charlotte's* fore-topmast, and checked her progress, and the French flagship, moving ahead, passed out of the range of the British ship's fire. But her decks were strewn thick with the dead, many of her guns were dismounted, her stern frame and starboard quarter were wrecked.

The spectacle of the *Jacobin* running to leeward, and of the flagship herself quitting the line, moved many of the French ships to imitation. Their line crumbled into shapelessness, and Howe threw out the signal for a general chase. The *Queen Charlotte*, meanwhile, was engaged in fierce duel with a French eighty-four, the *Juste*, which ship at last struggled out of the whirlwind of fire with which the *Queen Charlotte* encompassed her, in a very wrecked condition, and the *Queen Charlotte* herself—which by this time could barely keep steerage way—was left to point her battered nose towards some new antagonist.

The story of the First of June is a catalogue of duels betwixt individual ships under the rival flags, and the most gallant—perhaps the most gallant single fight ever fought at sea—is that betwixt the *Vengeur*, a French seventy-four, and the *Brunswick*, a ship of the same class, but with a lighter weight of fire, and a crew of only 600 men against the *Vengeur's* 700.

The *Brunswick* was Lord Howe's second astern, and

was to have cut through the line behind the *Jacobin*, the ship next to the French admiral. Both the *Achille* and the *Vengeur*, however—the ships next in succession—moved up and closed the interval, and Harvey, who commanded the *Brunswick*, impatient of further delay, put his helm aport and ran fairly on the *Vengeur*, the *Brunswick's* anchors hooking into the *Vengeur's* foreshrouds and channels. The master of the *Brunswick* asked Harvey if he should cut the ship clear of the *Vengeur*. "No," was the reply; "we've got her, and we'll keep her!" and both ships, paying off before the wind, drifted to leeward wrapped in a whirlwind of flame. The crew of the *Brunswick* were unable to open their lower-deck starboard ports, as the sides of the two ships were grinding together, and they coolly fired through the closed ports; and, as far as the fire from the lower decks was concerned, the British had all the advantage. As the great ships rolled in the trough of the sea, the British seamen alternately withdrew the coins from their guns, and drove them home; thus one broadside was fired with muzzles depressed so that the shot pierced through the enemy's hull below the waterline, the next broadside was fired with muzzles elevated so as to rip up the decks.

On the upper deck, however, the *Vengeur* had the advantage. She had thirty six-pounder carronades on her poop deck, and with these she swept the poop and forecastle and main deck of the *Brunswick* as with a besom of fire. The gallant Harvey himself was thrice wounded, and carried a dying man off the deck. After this dreadful combat had lasted nearly an hour, a French three-decker, the *Achille*, was seen bearing down on the *Brunswick*. Her mizzen and main masts were gone, but the foremast still stood. The *Brunswick's* larboard broadside was opened on the *Achille* when that ship was within musket-shot distance, with such effect, that her sole remaining mast, with its pile of canvas, came tumbling down. She swung round parallel with the *Brunswick*, and after exchanging half-a-dozen broadsides with that ship, struck her colours! Thus the *Brunswick*, while fighting the *Vengeur* to leeward, compelled the *Achille*, to windward, to strike. The *Brunswick*, however, still engaged in deadly wrestle with the *Vengeur*, could not launch a boat to take possession of the *Achille*, and that ship, at last, hoisting up a spritsail, crept out of fire with re-hoisted colours.

At 12.45 P.M. a heavy roll of the two ships tore the *Brunswick's* anchors loose from the *Vengeur*, and the dismasted and shattered hulls, still sullenly firing at each other, swung apart. The *Ramilies*, an English seventy-four, commanded, as it happened, by the brother of the *Brunswick's* captain, at this moment swept through the zone of smoke which encircled the two ships, in pursuit of the *Achille*, and fired one deadly broadside as it passed into the stern of the *Vengeur*. At one o'clock the *Vengeur* struck, a Union Jack being hung out over her quarter as a sign of surrender; but the *Brunswick* was in no condition to take possession of her beaten foe. The much-battered *Vengeur* sank lower and still lower in the sea; at each roll the water swept in through her ports. Late in the afternoon the boats of the *Alfred*, the *Culloden*, and of a British cutter, the *Rattler*, took off the captain and crew of the *Vengeur*, and the great ship, with splintered bulwarks, dismounted guns, and decks splashed red with slaughter, sank. Four hundred of her crew had been taken off by the boats of the British, but some remained. They had broken, it was said, into the spirit-room, and were drunk, and, just as the great ship made her final plunge, a few of them were visible on deck, shouting, in drunken defiance, "Vive la République!"

By noon the firing had died down. Eleven of the British ships were more or less nearly dismasted, twelve of the French were in yet more evil case, and were drifting helplessly to leeward. Villaret-Joyeuse gathered by signal his uninjured, or slightly injured ships around him, and bore down to cover the shattered, drifting hulks which formed the rest of his fleet. It was a gallant stroke, both of tactics and of seamanship, and actually saved at least five French ships from becoming prizes. Howe met the attempt by a counter-stroke, and Villaret-Joyeuse drew off, leaving seven great line-of-battle ships to become British prizes. Of these one, the *Vengeur*, sank; the other six were carried in triumph into Portsmouth.

The battle of the First of June, in one sense, failed of its strategic object. The great American convoy was not intercepted; afterwards, indeed, it crossed the waters where the great fight had raged, and found them strewn with the wrecks of the fight, and reached Brest in safety. Howe, too, has been blamed for not making the most of his victory. He had at least one-third of his fleet in perfect fighting condition, yet he allowed Villaret-Joyeuse to carry off five dismantled ships in safety. The truth is, Howe himself, a man nearly seventy years of age, was physically prostrate with the long strain of the fight and of the manœuvres of the preceding days; and he had reason to complain of some of his captains. But the First of June was a great and memorable victory. The total loss of the British in killed and wounded was less than 1200, that of the French was not less than 7000. The moral effect of the victory, too, was immense. It was the first great naval engagement of the revolutionary war, and it gave to British fleets a confidence and prestige which powerfully influenced the whole history of that war.

The battle abounded in picturesque and even amusing incidents. Pakenham, for example, who commanded the *Invincible*, was a daring but somewhat reckless Irishman. He drifted through the smoke on a French ship, and opened fire upon her with great energy. After a time, the fire of the Frenchman died away, while that of the *Invincible* grew yet more furious. Pakenham, however, was dissatisfied with the circumstance that the Frenchman made no reply, and he hailed her to know if she surrendered. The Frenchman replied, energetically, "No!" whereupon the gallant Irishman inquired in tones of disgust, "Then, —— you, why don't you fire!" Gambier, another of Howe's captains, was the exact opposite of the hare-brained Pakenham; a fine sailor, a brave fighter, and of sober and puritanic temper. His ship, the *Defence*, of seventy-four guns, fought gallantly, and had two of her masts shot away; when, through the smoke, the tall masts of a French three-decker were visible bearing down upon her. A lieutenant hurried to the quarter-deck and cried to Gambier, "—— my eyes, sir, but here's a whole mountain coming down upon us! What shall we do?" To which the unmoved Gambier answered by asking how his officer dared at such a moment as that to come to him with an oath in his mouth. "Go down to your guns, sir," he added, "and encourage your men to stick to their guns like British tars!"

Perhaps the most humorous story in connection with the First of June is the amazing fable of the *Vengeur*, which is due to the patriotic imagination, unrestrained by any regard for prosaic accuracy, of Barrère. Barrère reported to the Convention that the *Vengeur* went down with all her colours flying, scorning to surrender; "Vive la République, and a universal volley from the upper deck being the last sound she made." "Glorieuse affaire du *Vengeur*" became, for the French, a national myth. It has inspired innumerable French songs. A wooden model of the *Vengeur* was solemnly consecrated, and placed in the Pantheon. Carlyle embodied the story in his "French Revolution." "Lo!" he wrote, "all flags, streamers, jacks, every rag of tricolour that will yet run on rope flies rustling aloft. The whole crew crowds to the upper deck; and with universal soul-maddening yell, shouts, 'Vive la République,' sinking, sinking." Carlyle later on discovered how wild a flight of fiction the whole story was. Barrère was a liar of Titanic scale; but the *Vengeur* myth, Carlyle declared, must be pronounced "Barrère's masterpiece; the largest, most inspiring piece of blague manufactured for some centuries by any man or nation." At the time the *Vengeur* went down, the battle had ceased for some hours; her captain was peacefully getting his lunch in one of the cabins of the *Culloden*, and some 400 of her crew had been rescued, much to their own satisfaction, by the boats of the various British ships!

Howe, the victor of the First of June, does not stand in the first rank of British admirals. He had no touch of Nelson's electric genius for war, or of Jervis's iron will. It may be doubted whether he could have followed an enemy's fleet through tempest and darkness and unknown reefs, with the cool and masterful daring with which Hawke followed Conflans into the tangle of reefs off Quiberon. But Howe belongs to the type of men who are the strength of the State. Unselfish, loyal, single-minded, putting duty before glory and the State before self. He was known as " Black Dick " amongst his crews, from his dark complexion and hair, and he was loved as few British leaders, by either sea or land, have ever been loved. And the secret of the affection he awakened lay not so much in his patience and gentleness of temper, or his keen regard for the health and comfort of his men—it was found in the crystalline simplicity and sincerity of his character; his calm indifference to either gain or fame; and his self-forgetting patriotism.

SIR JOHN MOORE AT CORUNNA

January 16, 1809

"Not a drum was heard, not a funeral note,
    As his corse to the rampart we hurried;
Not a soldier discharged his farewell shot
    O'er the grave where our hero we buried.

We buried him darkly at dead of night,
    The sods with our bayonets turning;
By the struggling moonbeam's misty light,
    And the lantern dimly burning.
    .   .   .   .   .

Slowly and sadly we laid him down,
    From the field of his fame fresh and gory;
We carved not a line, and we raised not a stone—
    But we left him alone with his glory."

—Wolfe.

"AS to the English armies, I will chase them from the Peninsula!" Into that sentence, spoken to a great assemblage of the notables of Spain at Charmartin, Napoleon compressed the wrathful purpose which led to the fierce, swift, sure, and bloody campaign ended at Corunna.

It may be admitted that, at that particular moment, Napoleon had good reasons for turning in warlike wrath upon the British. Some two months before, in a proclamation to his armies, Napoleon wrote: "Soldiers, I have need of you. The hideous presence of the leopard contaminates the Peninsula of Spain and Portugal. In

SIR JOHN MOORE

From a mezzotint by Charles Turner, after the portrait by Sir Thomas Lawrence, P.R.A.

terror he must fly before you. Let us bear our triumphal eagles to the pillars of Hercules!" In an address, too, published in the *Moniteur* of October 26, 1808, Napoleon wrote: "In a few days I shall set out to place myself at the head of my army; shall crown at Madrid the King of Spain, and plant my eagles on the towers of Lisbon." Napoleon, in a word, was determined to grasp "the Spanish nettle." French arms had not prospered in the Peninsula. The Emperor's marshals were in nominal possession of the country; but one French force had been beaten, and had surrendered at Baylen; and Vimieiro, won by British bayonets, had driven the French eagles out of Portugal. Napoleon, taking advantage of the pause in the great wars of the Continent, which followed the conference at Erfurt, determined to overthrow all opposition in the Peninsula, as with the stroke of a thunderbolt.

Some 70,000 Spanish soldiers were in arms against him. But they were scattered along the line of the Ebro, over a distance of 200 miles and under three independent commanders. They were badly armed and worse drilled. Their generals had no warlike knowledge, and hated each other almost more than they hated the French. Wild ravines and swift and bridgeless rivers broke these forces up into disconnected fragments. Napoleon himself years afterwards, at St. Helena, in a spasm of bitter frankness, said, "The Spanish ulcer destroyed me"; and British statesmen, in some dim, blundering fashion, realising what an entanglement Spain might prove to Napoleon, had begun to feed the war in Spain. But their methods were of almost incredible stupidity. In the early days of November 1808, there were 30,000 British troops in Spain; but they were broken up into three independent divisions, separated by nearly a hundred miles from each other, without any common base, and in touch neither with each other nor with the Spanish armies. The three British divisions, in brief, and the three Spanish armies—not 100,000 strong taken altogether—were scattered, like fragments from some exploded planet, across the north of Spain, from the Asturian mountains to Saragossa. No one brain shaped their plans; no single will controlled them.

And upon this military chain, of which each link was already broken, Napoleon suddenly poured, like a tempest, the whole warlike strength of France. All through the month of October he was hurrying through the wet passes of the Eastern and Western Pyrenees his choicest troops, the fierce warriors who had struck down one after another the great Powers of the Continent, the veterans of Jena and Austerlitz and Friedland. The eight corps which formed the army now flowing like a deluge through the Pyrenees were under the command of generals into the syllables of whose very names the echoes of a hundred victories were packed: Soult and Lannes, Mortier and Ney, St. Cyr and Bessières. And the fiercest and most splendid intellect ever employed in the service of war since the days of Hannibal—that of Napoleon himself—governed the whole movement. For nearly four weeks the road from Bayonne to Vittoria was crowded with infantry and cavalry and guns. The Imperial Guard itself, with the halo of a hundred victories on its bayonets, formed part of the great host pouring southward into Spain.

As the French forces deployed from the passes they formed a mighty host more than 300,000 strong, of whom 40,000 were cavalry, while in equipment, in discipline, in martial ardour, in that gay and reckless valour which is the note of the French character, they formed one of the most terrible fighting instruments known to history.

There is no space to describe here the sudden and terrible fashion in which the tempestuous strategy of Napoleon struck down the Spanish forces. Napoleon swept over them, in fact, with something of the breathless speed and resistless fury of a tropical whirlwind. The Emperor reached Bayonne on November 3; within three weeks three Spanish armies were not so much overthrown as annihilated. They had been smitten at Espinosa, at Burgos, at Tudela; and scattered fugitives, without artillery, supplies, or ammunition, had taken refuge in the rugged mountains at the head-waters of the Ebro, or amongst the Guadarrama Hills, or behind the walls of Saragossa. On December 2 the cavalry of the French Guard were gathered like a threatening cloud on the hills which overlook Madrid from the north-west; and on December 4 the French eagles flew over Retiro, and Madrid was captured!

Spain lay, in a word, at Napoleon's mercy. His cavalry could swoop, almost without check, over the fertile southern provinces. On December 20 the sixth corps under Ney, the Imperial Guard, and the reserve, under the personal command of Napoleon, stood ready to begin that great triumphant march to the south-west, which was to end at Lisbon. The Imperial muster-roll showed at that moment that the French forces in Spain numbered more than 330,000 men, with 60,000 horses and 400 guns; and Spain was, in Sir John Moore's terse phrase, "without generals, without armies, without a government." What human force could arrest a strategy framed by what Napier calls "the mightiest

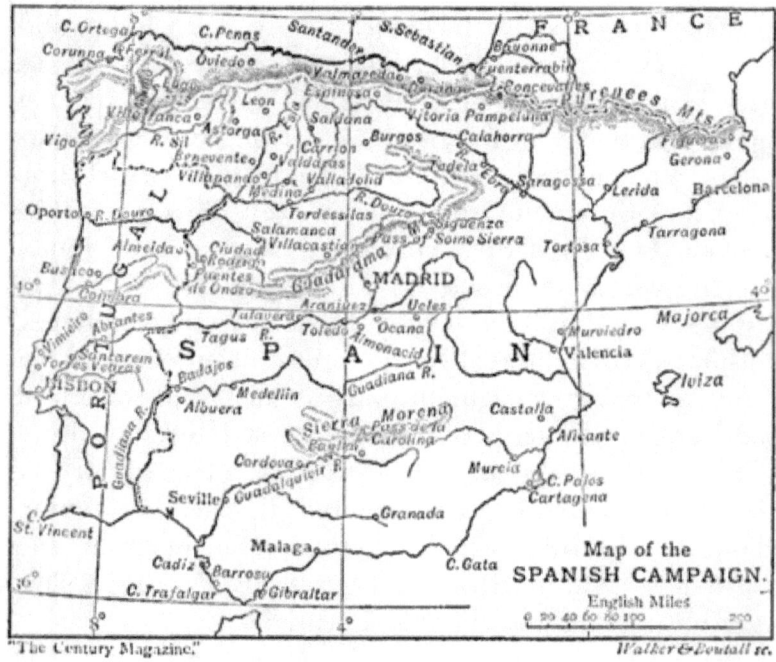

genius of two thousand years," and carried out by more than 300,000 of the finest soldiers of that period, with a glow of victory in their very blood?

It is a matter of sober history that the daring resolve of a single British soldier arrested the whole of Napoleon's designs, diverted the march of all his mighty and crowded battalions, and, in the darkest hour of its fortunes, saved Spain! "I will sweep the English armies from the Peninsula," said Napoleon, as, from under the walls of Madrid, he set out on what he meant to be the swiftest and most dazzling campaign of his life. Terrible is the irony of history! As a matter of fact, the British armies chased the French from the Peninsula, and in turn poured through the passes of the Pyrenees on France; and defeat in Spain finally overthrew Napoleon's throne. "It was the Spanish ulcer," as he himself said in wrathful anguish, "that destroyed me." But there would have been no "Spanish ulcer" —there might have been no storming of Badajos, no Vittoria, no Salamanca, and perhaps no Waterloo and no St. Helena—if, at the moment when Napoleon was about to set out on his march to Lisbon at the head of what seemed resistless forces, Sir John Moore, with 20,000 British soldiers, had not made that famous march—a thrust as with the point of a glittering rapier at Napoleon's flank—which threatened the Emperor's communications. That audacious stroke made him stay his march through Spain—a march never to be resumed—while he swung round to crush the tiny but daring foe that menaced him.

Moore's strategy was, indeed, of a singularly daring quality. The Spanish armies with whom he was directed to co-operate, had simply vanished, like a cluster of eddying wind-driven leaves before a tempest. Napoleon, at the head of an apparently overwhelming force, was about to invade the rich provinces to the south, and the march of his victorious columns would not cease till their feet were wet with the waves of the

Atlantic beyond Lisbon. Moore by this time had partially concentrated the scattered divisions of the British army, but his total force numbered not more than 26,000 men, of which 2000 were cavalry, with sixty guns. Moore's position was in the angle that forms the north-west shoulder, so to speak, of Spain, on Napoleon's right flank. Napoleon never doubted that Moore, when he learned the disasters which had overtaken the Spanish armies, and knew the resistless tide of war which was about to sweep across Spain to Lisbon, would instantly fall back to Corunna, or Vigo, on the sea-coast, and take ship to Lisbon. He would thus pluck his army out of deadly peril, and transport it south in readiness to meet Napoleon in front of Lisbon; if, indeed, the British Government had the courage to face the French standards there.

Moore himself, at first, resolved on that plan, but a bolder strategy took shape in his brain. He had the power of striking at Napoleon's communications with France. If he thrust boldly eastward, and menaced Napoleon's communications on the side of Burgos, he made no doubt that the Emperor would instantly swing round upon him, and a force outnumbering his by ten to one, and urged by the fiery genius of the greatest soldier of the century, would be hurled upon him. But Moore believed that he could strike at Napoleon's communications sufficiently to arrest the southward march of his columns, and so secure for Spain a breathing space, and yet pluck back his tiny army in safety before Napoleon's counter-stroke could crush it. He would draw, that is, Napoleon's whole power upon himself, would thrust his head, so to speak, into the lion's very jaws, and yet cheat the lion's fury. As Napier puts it, he saw the peril for his own army. He knew that "it must glide along the edge of a precipice: must cross a gulf on a rotten plank; but he also knew the martial quality of his soldiers, felt the pulsation of his own genius; and, the object being worth the deed, he dared essay it even against Napoleon."

Moore was indeed a great soldier, and with better fortune might have anticipated and outshone even the fame of Wellington. He was of Scottish birth, and was one of the very finest soldiers that martial race has in modern times produced. He had a vivid, commanding personality that made him a sort of king amongst men. His eyes were dark and searching, and were set beneath a forehead of singular breadth and aspect of power His mouth had a womanly sweetness about it, while the curve of his chin and the general contour of his face gave an extraordinary expression of energy. He lacked, perhaps, that iron quality of blood and will which augmented Wellington's capacity as a general, while it won for him an unpleasant reputation for cold-bloodedness as a friend. Moore, in fact, had a strain of gentleness in him that made him adored by his own circle. He was generous, high-minded, with a passionate scorn of base things and of base men—a quality which made mean men hate him, and evil men afraid of him. Of his signal capacity for war there is no room to doubt. His ideal of soldiership was very noble, and he had the art of stamping it on all those around him. "No man with a spark of enthusiasm," says Charles Napier, afterwards the conqueror of Scinde, "could resist the influence of Moore's great aspirings, his fine presence, his ardent penetrating genius." Moore did more, perhaps, to create the modern British soldier than any other British general that can be named. At Shorncliffe Camp three regiments—the 43rd, the 52nd, and the Rifles—were under his hands. Up to that point they were commonplace regiments with no gleam of special fame about them. Moore so kindled and fashioned them that afterwards, as Wellington's famous Light Division, they were found to be "soldiers unsurpassable, perhaps never equalled." From the officers of these three regiments, who felt the breath of Moore's quickening genius, there came a longer list of notable men than has ever been yielded by any other three regiments of any service in the world. Napier says that in the list were four who afterwards commanded armies—three being celebrated as conquerors—above ninety who attained the rank of field officer; sixteen governors of colonies, many generals who commanded districts, &c. &c. Half-a-dozen Moores, in a word, might well have transmuted to gold the whole clay of the British army!

Napoleon himself recognised Moore's genius, when he learnt that the British commander, instead of falling back to the sea-coast, was actually striking at his communications. "Moore," he said, "is the only general now fit to contend with me; I shall advance against him in person."

Nothing could surpass the speed and energy with which Napoleon instantly changed his plans, arrested the southward march of his columns, and swung round on his daring foe. Moore on December 23 had reached Carrion, purposing to leap on Soult, who held Saldaña. To beat Soult, however, was a secondary object. His real purpose was to draw Napoleon from the south, and, as Napier expresses it, "it behove the man to be alert who interposed between the lion and his prey." On December 19, 60,000 men and 150 guns were reviewed by Napoleon at the gates of Madrid, and were just being launched on that long march which was to end at Lisbon. The French light cavalry were already riding on the borders of Andalusia, the first French corps was holding Toledo. But on December 21, Napoleon heard of Moore's daring march, and within twenty-four hours his southward-moving columns were all arrested; within forty-eight hours, 50,000 French troops were at the foot of the Guadarrama Hills, the range to the northwest of Madrid, across which Napoleon must lead his troops to cut off Moore from the sea-coast.

It was winter-time. The passes were choked with snow, the cliffs were slippery with ice. Furious tempests, heavy with rain or sword-edged with sleet, howled through the ravines. Twelve hours' toil left the halffrozen French columns still on the Madrid side of the mountain range, and the generals reported the passage "impossible." The leader who had crossed the St. Bernard, however, was not to be stopped by Spanish hills and snows. Napoleon, with his staff, joined the advance-guard, and, with fiery gestures and fiery speech, urged on the soldiers. Many men and many beasts perished; the struggle across the snow-filled passes lasted for two days. But Napoleon's vehemence swept all before it, and on the 24th the army had reached Villacastin, sixty miles from Madrid. On the 26th, Napoleon was at Tordesillas with the Guard, and he wrote to Soult: "Our cavalry scouts are already at

Benavente. If the English pass to-day in their position, they are lost."

Napoleon, in brief, was paying back Moore with his own tactics. The British general had only to loiter on the Esla for twelve hours longer, and Napoleon would have swept like a whirlwind across his communications; and, betwixt Soult and Napoleon, the British army would have been crushed like a nut betwixt the hammer and the anvil. The speed of Napoleon's march, too, had been little less than marvellous. In the depth of winter he had executed a march of 200 miles with 50,000 men, with the energy, and something of the speed, of a thunderbolt. On December 22 he was at Madrid; on the 28th he was at Villalpando, having performed a march on bad roads, and in wild weather, of 164 miles in six days.

And yet Moore evaded him! When Napoleon reached Valdaras, the British were across the Esla; but so nicely did Moore time his movements, and with such daring did he hold on to his position in front of the converging French armies, to the very last moment, that Napoleon only missed his stroke by twelve hours, and the French cavalry scouts cut off some of the British baggage as it crossed the Esla!

Nor did Moore, indeed, begin his retreat without a brisk counter-stroke on his too eager pursuers. Thus, at Mayorga, Paget, who commanded the British cavalry, and was watching Soult, was cut off from the main body of the British by a sort of horn of cavalry thrown out from Napoleon's columns. The force falling back before Soult, that is, found solid squadrons of French horse drawn up on a hill, wet with rain, and thick with snow, on the line of its retreat. Paget led two squadrons of the 10th Hussars straight up the hill. It was stiff riding up the wet slope, and Paget halted his squadrons a few yards from the summit to give them breathing time, and then led them furiously at the enemy. With such daring did the Hussars drive their charge home that the French cavalry were smitten into fragments, and more than 100 captured. The British cavalry, it may be explained, had been for twelve days in almost hourly combat with the French outposts, and had established such a superiority over their enemies that they rode cheerfully at any odds, with an exultant certainty of success!

Napoleon urged his pursuit with amazing vehemence till he reached Astorga on January 1. His vehement will carried his troops the whole distance, from Benavente to Astorga, a distance of over thirty miles, during the brief span of a single winter's day. An icy rain beat upon the troops during the whole day, and no less than five times the infantry had to strip, and wade through the rain-swollen and snow-chilled streams. And yet they never halted. But, eagerly as Napoleon pressed on, Moore still outmarched and evaded him. At Astorga, Soult joined Napoleon, and 70,000 French infantry, 10,000 cavalry, and 200 guns were thus assembled under one command. It was an amazing proof of Napoleon's energy that, in the brief space of seven days, he should thus have flung on Moore so mighty a force. Napoleon, to quote Napier, "had transported 50,000 men from Madrid to Astorga in less time than a Spanish courier would have taken to travel the same distance." But it was also a justifica-

K

tion of Moore's strategy that he had thus diverted the very flower of Napoleon's forces from their march southward, to the north-west corner of Spain.

At Astorga, Napoleon was overtaken by a courier with despatches. He was galloping with the advanced posts on Moore's track, when the courier overtook him. He dismounted, ordered a bivouac fire to be lit, and cast himself down on the ground beside it to read his despatches. The snow fell heavily upon him as he read, but left him unmoved. His despatches told the Emperor that Austria had joined the league of his enemies, and that France was menaced. Napoleon's decision was swift and instant. He left Soult and Ney, with 60,000 men, to push Moore back to the sea, and, if possible, destroy him. He turned the faces of the Imperial Guard once more towards the Pyrenees, and himself rode at furious speed, and almost without escort, to Paris.

Soult, the ablest of Napoleon's marshals, pressed hard on Moore's tracks, Ney marching by a parallel route and endeavouring to turn Moore's flank. The three armies, pursuers and pursued, passed through the mountains of Galicia; but Moore, riding always with his rear-guard, kept a front of steel against his enemies, and continually evaded them.

His troops were young and inexperienced, and British soldiers at their best, do not shine in retreat. Discipline is apt to vanish. The men grow sulky and desperate. The ordered battalions, somehow, dissolve into reckless units. And it cannot be denied that in the speed and hardship of Moore's retreat, with inexperienced officers and raw troops, the British army went sadly to pieces. The rear-guard, it is true, on which perpetual combat acted as a tonic, kept magnificently together. Discipline in it was perfect, and, as a matter of fact, it suffered less loss than the main body. For twelve days, says Napier, these hardy soldiers had covered the retreat, during which time they traversed eighty miles of road in two marches, passed several nights under arms in the snow of the mountains, and were seven times engaged. Yet they lost fewer men than any other division in the army! At Lugo, on January 7, Moore halted, and offered battle to his pursuers, and that gallant challenge, as with a touch of magic, restored discipline and cheerfulness to the British army. The stragglers, as by an electric shock, were transfigured once more into soldiers. Grumbling was silenced; battalions grew close-packed and orderly. The British soldier, at his worst, grows cheerful at the prospect of a fight, while a retreat is hateful to him. Wellington's veterans, in their famous retreat from Burgos two years afterwards, did no better than Moore's young soldiers. Soult, however, would not accept Moore's challenge of battle, and the retreat was resumed, and the pursuit urged afresh. On January 11 Corunna was reached. Moore's plan was to embark at Corunna and carry his troops to Cadiz, there to assist the Spaniards in defending the southern provinces. But when the troops reached the summit of the hills that looked down on Corunna the bay was empty! The transports were wind-bound at Vigo.

It was a marvellous retreat. Moore's marches, in all, extended over 500 miles. At one time he had no less than two great armies thundering in pursuit of him,

Napoleon himself striking at his flank. Yet the English general never lost a gun, nor suffered his rear-guard to be broken; and his total losses, in spite of the temporary breakdown of the discipline of his army, were not more than 4000 men. His retreat, too, was marked with a hundred acts of daring. Again and again he turned on his pursuers, and sent their too eager squadrons staggering back with the vehemence of his counter-stroke. A charge of the 10th Hussars broke the Imperial Guard itself, slew 130, and took seventy prisoners, including their commander, General Lefebvre Desnouettes. At Villafranca, the French general, Colbert, one of Napoleon's favourite officers, was slain and his men roughly overthrown when pressing too sharply on Moore's rear. At Valladolid, Major Otway, with some British dragoons not only overthrew a French cavalry force much superior to his own, but took a colonel and more prisoners than he had men to guard.

As an example of the soldierly quality of the men who marched and fought under Moore, a single incident may be taken from Napier. At Castro Gonzalo, two privates of the 43rd, John Walton and Richard Jackson, were posted beyond the bridge, with orders that, if a force of the enemy approached, one should fire and run back to give the alarm, the other stand firm. In the grey, bitter dawn, a squadron of French cavalry, who had crept up unperceived, dashed at the two men. Jackson fired and ran, as ordered, to give the alarm. A score of horsemen in a moment were round him, slashing at him as he ran. He received fourteen sabre cuts, but, staggering, and with uniform drenched in blood, he yet ran on and gave the alarm. Walton, in turn, obeying his orders, stood at his post, a sturdy, red-coated figure, standing steadfast in a whirlwind of galloping horses and gleaming, hissing sword-strokes. Walton parried each flashing stroke as well as he could, and answered them, when possible, with a vengeful bayonet-thrust. The combat lasted for some breathless, desperate minutes; then, the British infantry coming running up, the French horsemen galloped off, leaving Walton still standing, with iron loyalty, at his post. His cap, his knapsack, his belt and musket were cut in a score of places, his bayonet was bent double, was bloody to the hilt, and notched like a saw, yet he himself was unhurt!

On January 11, as we have said, Moore reached Corunna, and faced swiftly round to meet his pursuers. He was twelve hours in advance of Soult, and the French general lingered till the 15th before joining in the shock of battle—a delay which was, in part, necessary to allow his straggling rear-guard to close up, but in part, also, it was due to a doubt as to what might be the result of closing on a foe so hardy and stubborn. Moore employed this breathing time in preparing for embarkation. He blew up on the 13th two outlying powder magazines; in one were piled 4000 barrels of powder, and its explosion was like the crash of a volcano. The earth trembled for miles, a tidal wave rolled across the harbour, a column of smoke and dust, with flames leaping from its back flanks, rose slowly into the sky, and then burst, pouring a roaring tempest of stones and earth over a vast area, and destroying many lives.

Moore next shot all his foundered horses, to the mingled grief and wrath of his cavalry. The 15th

Hussars alone brought 400 horses into Spain, and took thirty-one back to England! The horses, it seems, were ruined, not for the want of shoes, but "for want of hammers and nails to put them on." Having embarked his dismounted cavalry, his stores, his wounded, his heavy artillery, and armed his men with new muskets, Moore quietly waited Soult's onfall. His force was only 14,000 strong, without cavalry, and with only nine six-pounders, and he could not occupy the true defence of Corunna, the great rocky range which runs at right angles to the Mero. He had to abandon this to the French, and content himself with holding an inferior ridge nearer the town.

Hope's division held the left of this ridge; Baird's the right. Paget's division was in reserve, covering the valley which curved round the western extremity of the ridge, and ran up to Corunna. Still farther to the west Fraser's division guarded the main road to Corunna. Paget's division thrust forward a battalion to the lower ranges of the hills on the western side of the valley, and then stretched a line of skirmishers across the mouth of the valley itself. Soult thus could only cross the ridge by breaking through Hope's or Baird's division. If he came up the valley he would expose his flank to Baird, and find his march barred by Paget. Moore, as a matter of fact, reckoned on his left and centre repulsing the main attack of the French; then Paget and Fraser would move up the valley and complete the French overthrow. Soult had 20,000 veteran troops and a strong artillery; and, with great skill, he planted eleven heavy guns on a rocky eminence on his left, whence they could search the whole right

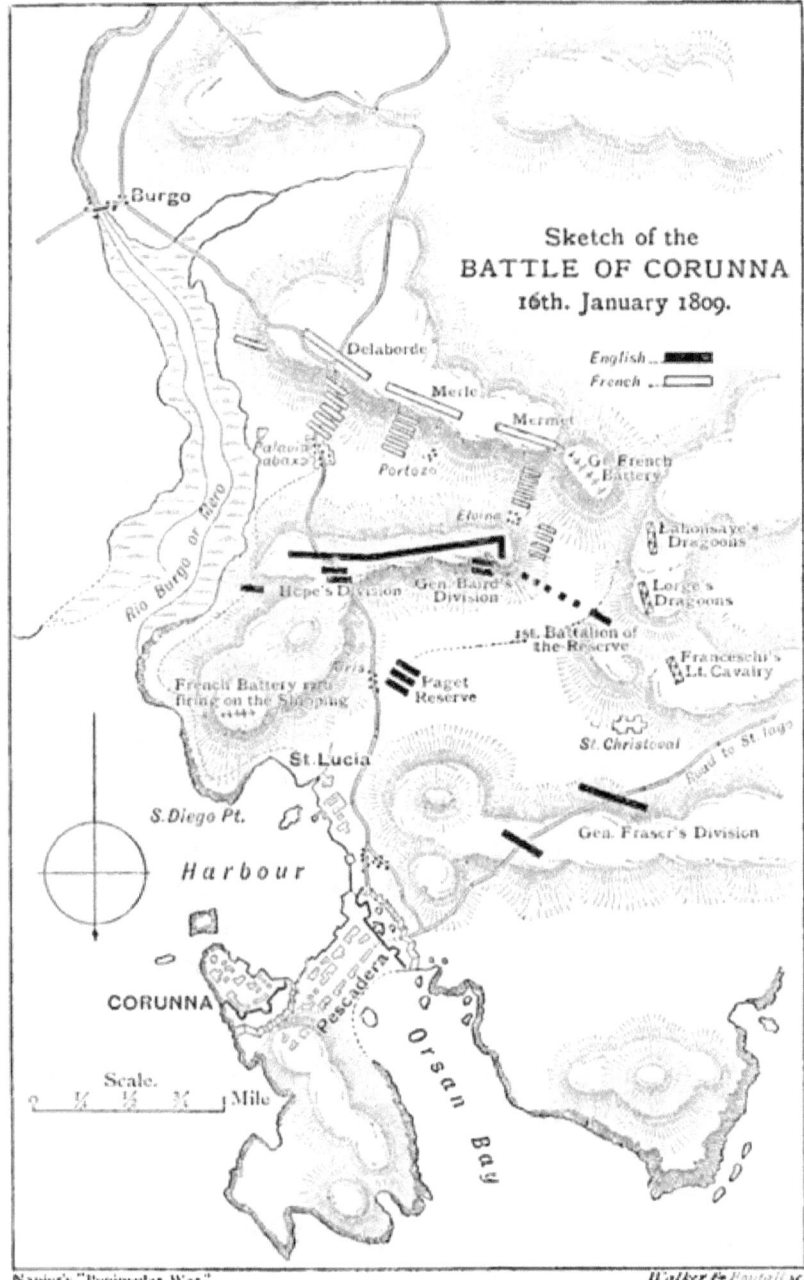

and centre of the British. He launched his attack in three columns—the strongest, under Mermet, being intended to carry the village of Elvina, which served as an outpost to the extreme British right, and then to sweep round the right flank of Moore's position.

The onfall of the French was swift and vehement. The eleven great guns from the crags poured a tempest of shot on the British ridge, the skirmishers of Mermet's column ran forward, and drove back the British pickets with a heavy fire, while the solid column, coming on at the double after them, carried the village.

Moore, with his swift soldierly glance, instantly saw that this was the pivot of the battle, and he galloped to the spot. The 50th and the 62nd were stationed here, and Charles Napier, who as senior Major commanded the 50th, has left a most vivid word-picture of Moore's bearing on the field of battle:—

"I stood in front of my left wing on a knoll, from whence the greatest part of the field could be seen, and my pickets were fifty yards below, disputing the ground with the French skirmishers, but a heavy French column, which had descended the mountain at a run, was coming on behind with great rapidity, and shouting —'En avant, tue, tue, en avant, tue!' their cannon, at the same time, plunging from above, ploughed the ground, and tore our ranks. Suddenly I heard the gallop of horses, and, turning, saw Moore. He came at speed, and pulled up so sharp and close, he seemed to have alighted from the air, man and horse looking at the approaching foe with an intentness that seemed to concentrate all feeling in their eyes. The sudden stop of the animal—a cream-coloured one, with black tail and mane—had cast the latter streaming forward, its ears were pushed out like horns, while it eyes flashed fire, and it snorted loudly with expanded nostrils. My first thought was, it will be away like the wind; but then I looked at the rider, and the horse was forgotten. Thrown on its haunches, the animal came sliding and dashing the dirt up with its fore-feet, thus bending the General forward almost to its neck; but his head was thrown back, and his look more keenly piercing than I ever before saw it. He glanced to the right and left, and then fixed his eyes intently on the enemy's advancing column, at the same time grasping the reins with both his hands, and pressing the horse firmly with his knees; his body thus seemed to deal with the animal while his mind was intent on the enemy, and his aspect was one of searching intenseness beyond the power of words to describe. For a while he looked, and then galloped to the left, without uttering a word!"

Moore's tactics were both daring and skilful. He swung round the 4th Regiment, so as to smite with a flank fire that section of the French column moving with unwise daring round his right. He ordered up Paget, and after him Fraser, so as to make a counter-stroke at the French left, and meanwhile he launched the 42nd and 50th against the French column which had carried the village in the front. Napier, who commanded the 50th, has painted a most graphic picture of the struggle. "Clunes," he said to the captain of the Grenadier company, "take your Grenadiers and open the ball!" "He stalked forward alone, like Goliath before the Philistines, for six feet five he was in height, and of proportionate bulk and strength; and thus the battle began on our side."

Napier sternly forbade any firing, and to prevent it, and to occupy the men's attention, made them slope and carry arms by word of command. "Many of them," he says, "cried out 'Major, let us fire!' 'Not yet,' was my answer." The 42nd had checked a short distance from a wall, but Napier led his men right up to the wall, and then said, "Do you see your enemies plainly enough to hit them?" "Many voices shouted, 'By —— we do!' 'Then blaze away,' said I; and such a rolling fire broke out as I hardly ever heard since." The wall was breast-high. Napier, followed by the officers, leaped over, and called on the men to follow. About a hundred did so at once, and, finding the others not quick enough for his impatience, Napier leaped back, and holding a halberd horizontally pushed the men quickly over. He then leaped over himself, and the instant he did so five French soldiers suddenly rose from the ground, levelled their muskets at him, and fired! The muskets were so near as to almost touch him, but his orderly sergeant, running at his side, struck them up with his pike, and saved Napier's life.

Napier dressed his line; and, as he says, remembering the story of how the officers of the English guards at Fontenoy laid their swords over the men's firelocks to prevent them firing too high, he did the same with a halberd—a curious example of how one brave act, across a hundred years, will inspire another. How Napier, with the hope of carrying the great battery, afterwards led part of his regiment up a lane lined on either side by French infantry, and so turned into a mere track of fire; how some unhappy counter-order prevented the 50th supporting him, and how Napier himself was wounded and taken prisoner cannot be told here. The story will be found, related with inimitable fire and humour, in Napier's own life.

Meanwhile, at every point, the British were victorious. The Guards and the Black Watch carried the village; Baird and Hope drove back with confusion and loss the columns that assailed them, and Moore, eagerly watching the whole line of battle from the right of his position, was about to hurl Paget, supported by Fraser, on the French left.

At that moment Moore was struck on the left breast by a cannon-ball, and dashed violently on the ground. It was a dreadful wound. The shoulder was smashed, the arm hung by a piece of skin, the ribs over the heart were stripped of flesh and broken, and the muscles that covered them hung in long rags. But Moore, absorbed in the great struggle before him, sat up in an instant, his eyes still eagerly watching Paget's advance. His staff gathered round him, and he was placed in a blanket, and some soldiers proceeded to carry him from the field. One of his staff, Hardinge, tried to unbuckle his sword, as the hilt was entangled in the strips of flesh hanging from his wound, but the dying soldier stopped him. "I had rather," he said, "it should go out of the field with me!" One of his officers, taking courage from Moore's unshaken countenance, expressed a hope of his recovery. Moore looked steadfastly at his own shattered breast for an instant, and calmly answered, "No, I feel that to be impossible." Again and again, as they carried the dying general from the field, he made his bearers halt, and turn round, that he might watch the fight. It was the scene of Wolfe on the Heights of

Abraham repeated! And the spectacle was such as might well gladden the eyes of Moore. On the left, and at the centre, the British were everywhere advancing. Paget's column was overthrowing everything before it in the valley.

Had Fraser's division, as Moore intended, been brought up and frankly thrown into the fight, it can hardly be doubted that Soult would have been not merely overthrown, but destroyed. His ammunition was almost exhausted. His troops were in the mood of retreat. The Mero, a fordless river, crossed by a single bridge, was in his rear. He had lost 3000 men; the British less than 1000; and the British, it may be added, were full of proud and eager courage.

But Moore was dying. Baird was severely wounded. The early winter night was creeping over the field of battle, and Hope, gallant soldier though he was, judged it prudent to stay his hand. Soult had been roughly driven back; the transports were crowding into the harbour. It was enough to have ended a long retreat with the halo of victory, and to have secured an undisturbed embarkation.

Meanwhile Moore had been carried into his quarters at Corunna. A much-attached servant stood with tears running down his face as the dying man was carried into the house. "My friend," said Moore, "it is nothing!" Then, turning to a member of his staff, Colonel Anderson, he said, "Anderson, you know I have always wished to die in this way. I hope my country will do me justice." Only once his lips quivered, and his voice shook, as he said, "Say to my mother—" and then stopped, while he struggled to regain composure. "Stanhope," he said, as his eye fell on his aide-de-camp's face, "remember me to your sister"—the famous Hester Stanhope, Pitt's niece, to whom Moore was engaged. Life was fast and visibly sinking, but he said, "I feel myself so strong, I fear I shall be long dying."

But he was not: death came swiftly and almost painlessly. Wrapped in a soldier's cloak he was carried by the light of torches to a grave hastily dug in the citadel at Corunna; and far off to the south, as the sorrowing officers stood round the grave of their dead chief, could be heard from time to time the sound of Soult's guns, yet in sullen retreat. The scene is made immortal in Wolfe's noble lines:—

> "Few and short were the prayers we said,
>   And we spoke not a word of sorrow,
> But we steadfastly gazed on the face that was dead,
>   And we bitterly thought of the morrow.
>
> "We thought as we hollowed his narrow bed,
>   And smoothed down his lonely pillow,
> That the foe and the stranger would tread o'er his head,
>   And we far away on the billow."

Borrow, in his "Bible in Spain," says that in the Spanish imagination strange legends gather round that lonely tomb. The peasants speak of it with awe. A great soldier of foreign speech and blood lies there. Great treasures, they whisper, were buried in it! Strange demons keep watch over it! "Yes, even in Spain, immortality has already crowned the head of Moore—Spain, the land of oblivion, where the Guadalete flows."

WELLINGTON AT SALAMANCA

July 22, 1812

"Salamanca was the first decided victory gained by the allies in the Peninsula. In former actions the French had been repulsed; here they were driven headlong, as it were, before a mighty wind without help or stay. . . . And the shock, reaching even to Moscow, heaved and shook the colossal structure of Napoleon's power to its very base."—NAPIER.

"I saw him [Wellington] late in the evening of that great day, when the advancing flashes of cannon and musketry, stretching as far as the eye could command in the darkness, showed how well the field was won; he was alone, the flush of victory was on his brow, his eyes were eager and watchful, but his voice was calm and even gentle. More than the rival of Marlborough, for he had defeated greater generals than Marlborough ever encountered, with a prescient pride he seemed only to accept this glory as an earnest of greater things."—*Idem.*

IT was a French officer who condensed the story of Salamanca into the epigram that it was "the battle in which 40,000 men had been beaten in forty minutes." In an epigram, truth is usually sacrificed to picturesqueness, and this oft-quoted saying is in open quarrel with fact. The battle of Salamanca lasted, not forty minutes, but six hours. Yet, in dramatic quality, it is one of the most remarkable fights in modern history; and the tactics of the three or four weeks which preceded it—the marches and counter-marches, the tangled manœuvring, the swift thrust and swifter parry of two great masters in the art of war—are almost as dramatic in their features as the battle itself.

WELLINGTON

From a mezzotint, after the portrait by Sir Thomas Lawrence, P.R.A.

Salamanca was fought on July 22, 1812. A little more than a month earlier—on June 13—Wellington crossed the Portuguese border, and began the movement designed to drive the French out of Spain. It was a step of singular daring. Wellington had under his nominal command some 90,000 men, but they were widely scattered, composed of four different nationalities, were ill supplied and worse paid, and the number under his immediate command did not reach 50,000. The French, on the other hand, had 300,000 soldiers in Spain, of one blood and discipline, veterans in war, and led by generals trained in Napoleon's school and familiar with victory. Marmont, who directly confronted Wellington on the east, had 70,000 men under his standard; but the French system of "making war sustain war"—of feeding an army, that is, by supplies taken from the enemy—caused Marmont's troops to be widely scattered. Yet he had 52,000 present with the eagles. Marmont, too, had Madrid, strongly held by Napoleon's brother Joseph, behind him. Soult, to the south, held Andalusia with 56,000 men; Souham held the Asturias to the north with 38,000; Suchet had 76,000 men in Catalonia and Valencia.

Wellington's plan was to leap on Salamanca, capture it, and, if possible, crush or defeat Marmont before reinforcements could reach him. He thrust hard and fiercely, that is, at the French centre, and calculated that the thrust would draw the widely-scattered French armies from the extremities, and so, with one stroke, clear northern and southern Spain. In any case, the march to Salamanca and Madrid must bring Soult hurrying up from the south, as otherwise his communications with France would be cut off. To advance with 50,000 troops against forces numbering in all 300,000 was an act of signal hardihood. Wellington was thrusting his head, in brief, into the lion's mouth; and if, while engaged in deadly wrestle with Marmont at the centre, the French armies on either flank closed in upon him, he must be destroyed.

Wellington, however, measured with ice-clear intellect, and faced with ice-cool courage, the risks of this daring stategy, and made his historic dash at Salamanca. There were two circumstances in his favour. First, the French quite misread his strategy. Soult, on March 26, wrote he "was certain Wellington would march upon Andalusia to raise the siege of Cadiz." But Wellington, with more subtle strategy, proposed to raise the siege of Cadiz by striking at Salamanca! The other circumstance in Wellington's favour was the total want of concert betwixt the French generals. Napoleon, whose genius alone could control their fierce jealousies of each other, was far off in Russia. Joseph lacked the skill and daring of a great soldier. His more famous brother had put the crown of Spain upon his head, but he could not put within that head the brains necessary to sustain it; and his generals were loyal neither to him nor to each other. Napoleon himself attributed the loss of Salamanca to the "vanity" of Marmont, eager rather to win personal fame than to serve France. But that same flame of restless and selfish vanity burned in the breasts of all the French marshals. They cared more to outshine each other than even to beat the common enemy.

Wellington reached Salamanca on June 17, and

Marmont, who could assemble only 25,000 troops, fell back before him. But he left Salamanca strongly fortified. No less than thirteen convents and twenty-two colleges, it was said, had been pulled down to yield material for the French forts; and these were heavily armed with artillery, while Wellington had only four heavy guns and three 24-pounders, and a very scanty supply of ammunition for even these. Marmont reckoned that the forts would hold out for at least fifteen days; and in less than that time he would be heavily reinforced from Madrid and from the north, and could then advance and crush Wellington. Wellington's attack, however, was fierce. The men who had stormed Badajos and Ciudad Rodrigo were not to be denied at Salamanca, and the forts would have fallen in five days, but that ammunition failed and gave the garrison a brief respite.

Marmont found he must do something to divert the fierceness with which the British pressed on his forts. He was a gallant soldier, a fine tactician, full of French *élan*, and of a half-scornful eagerness to overthrow the mere "sepoy general" opposed to him, and drive the British into the sea; and with a force of 30,000 he advanced in very tempestuous fashion against the force covering the attacked forts. Wellington knew that a barren victory would be hardly less disastrous than a defeat, and was determined to fight only when he could destroy his enemy. He was content with barring Marmont's advance, day after day, by positions skilfully taken up, until on June 29 the forts surrendered. Marmont then fell back with shrewish wrath to the Duero, holding the northern bank of it from Tordesillas to

L

Toro—a distance of less than fourteen miles—there to await the reinforcements pressing to join him. Wellington followed him in the expectation that either the difficulties of gathering supplies would compel Marmont to fall back, or his impatient and eager genius would make him attempt some rash stroke.

Marmont, however, was a tactician of the first order. His troops were hardy and quick of foot. The country, a series of open rolling downs seamed with shallow rivers, lent itself to rapid movements, and was perfectly familiar to him; and he commenced a series of swift movements in which, again and again, he out-marched and out-generalled Wellington. His aim, in brief, was to march round Wellington's flank, and strike at the Ciudad Rodrigo road on his rear, which formed his only line of retreat to Portugal. And the feints and movements on his part to accomplish, and on Wellington's part to prevent, this, form one of the most brilliant chapters of tactics in the history of war. The movements of the armies resembled the quick and gleaming thrusts and parries of two accomplished fencers engaged in fierce and close duel; or, to vary the figure, the armies circled round and dashed at each other with breathless attack and recoil, like two contending hawks in mid-air, swooping on each other in airy curves that grow ever closer. There is no space here to tell the story of this struggle, which lasted more than a week, and in which the weapons were not so much bayonet and sabre, as the brains of the general and the legs of the soldier. But some of the picturesque incidents yielded by that struggle in generalship are worth describing.

Marmont, on July 16, made a show of crossing the Duero at Toro, and so marching past Wellington's left to Salamanca. Wellington moved to his left to block this road, but yet, as a precaution, left the fourth and light divisions and Anson's cavalry, under Sir Stapleton Cotton, on the Trabancos, so as to guard against any advance past his right from Tordesillas. As soon as Marmont saw the bulk of the British forces drawn to his right, he countermarched his troops, pressed on at the utmost speed back to Tordesillas, crossed the Duero there without pause, and came rushing down past Wellington's right towards Salamanca. Some of his men actually marched forty miles, some fifty, without a halt!

It was a brilliant stroke of generalship, and on the evening of the 17th, Cotton, with two divisions and some cavalry, was, without support, in the presence of the whole French army. Cotton had the obstinate courage that grows yet more stubborn in actual combat, characteristic of his race, and he clung to his position. In the deep folds of the treeless downs the full strength of the French was hidden, and Cotton, with cheerful confidence, drove back the skirmishers as they crossed the stream. But the columns of the French became denser, their fire heavier; and soon the deep sound of heavy guns was added to the sharp crackle of musketry.

It was early morning, and the black masses of powder-smoke mingled with the light mists rising from the river. Here is a vivid battle-picture, taken from Napier:—

"The cannonade became heavy, and the spectacle surprisingly beautiful, for the lighter smoke and mist, mingling and curling in fantastic pillars, formed a huge and glittering dome tinged with many colours by the rising sun; and through the grosser vapour below the restless horsemen were seen or lost, as the fume thickened from the rapid play of the artillery, while the bluff head of land beyond the Trabancos, covered with French troops, appeared by an optical deception close at hand, dilated to the size of a mountain, and crowned with gigantic soldiers, who were continually breaking off and sliding down into the fight. Suddenly a dismounted English cavalry officer stalked from the midst of the smoke towards the line of infantry; his gait was peculiarly rigid, and he appeared to hold a bloody handkerchief to his heart; but that which seemed a cloth was a broad and dreadful wound; a bullet had entirely effaced the flesh from his left shoulder and breast, and carried away part of his ribs, his heart was bared, and its movement plainly discerned. It was a piteous and yet a noble sight; for his countenance, though ghastly, was firm, his step scarcely indicated weakness, and his voice never faltered. This unyielding man's name was Williams; he died a short distance from the field of battle—it was said, in the arms of his son, a youth of fourteen, who had followed his father to the Peninsula in hopes of obtaining a commission, for they were not in affluent circumstances."

By seven o'clock Wellington, accompanied by Beresford, drawn by the sound of the firing, had reached the scene of the conflict, and was almost at once in great personal peril.

A couple of squadrons of French cavalry, gallantly

led by their officer, swept down the farther bank of the river, splashed through the current, and galloped up the steep slope beyond. As they reached the crest, disordered and breathless, they found themselves confronted with a squadron of British dragoons. The Frenchmen were heavy cavalry, splendidly mounted, in gay uniform, with high fur caps. Their officer halted his men within a hundred yards of the British cavalry, thrown out in skirmishing order, held his sword high in air, and, with a shout of "Vive l'Empereur! En avant, Français!" dashed on the British, who were carried away in a moment by the rush of the heavier horses of the French. The whole mass, French and British, struggling together, and smiting furiously at each other, went tumbling down the reverse slope.

In the valley below were two guns, covered by some infantry pickets and another squadron of light cavalry; and without a pause the French officer rode at these, his men following, and swept through them like a whirlwind, the artillerymen stooping with heads bent, spurring their horses to save their guns, while the Frenchmen slashed at them with their sabres. Wellington and Beresford were caught in the *mêlée*; and Maxwell tells how he saw the British general as he crossed the ford "with his straight sword drawn, at full speed, and smiling." At this moment a squadron of heavy British dragoons charged the furious French swordsmen, and the latter were destroyed almost to a man; but "their invincible leader," says Napier, "assaulted by three enemies at once, struck one dead from his horse, and, with surprising exertions, saved himself from the other two, though they rode hewing at him from each side for a quarter of a mile."

Meanwhile Marmont, having discovered how small was the force opposed to him, crossed the Trabancos, and pushed on straight for the Guareña. If he could throw himself across it before the British, Wellington would be cut off from Salamanca.

Ten miles of dusty soil had to be crossed under a blazing sun and at high speed. The troops that could march fastest would win. And, urged by their officers to the utmost exertions, the rival columns pressed on. It was one of the strangest scenes ever witnessed in war, and only Napier's resonant prose can do justice to it:—

"The British retired in three columns, the light division being between the fifth division and the French, close to the latter, the cavalry on the flanks and rear. The air was extremely sultry, the dust rose in clouds, and the close order of the troops was rendered very oppressive by a siroc wind; but where the light division marched the military spectacle was strange and grand. Hostile columns of infantry, only half musket-shot from each other, were marching impetuously towards a common goal, the officers on each side pointing forward with their swords, or touching their caps and waving their hands in courtesy, while the German cavalry, huge men on huge horses, rode between in a close compact body, as if to prevent a collision: at times the loud tones of command to hasten the march were heard passing from the front to the rear on both sides, and now and then the rush of French bullets came sweeping over the columns, whose violent pace was continually accelerated.

"Thus moving for ten miles, yet keeping the most perfect order, both parties approached the Guareña, and the enemy, seeing the light division, although more in their power than the others, was yet outstripping them in the march, increased the fire of their guns and menaced an attack with infantry: the German cavalry instantly drew close round, the column plunged suddenly into a hollow dip of ground on the left, and ten minutes after the head of the division was in the stream of the Guareña between Osmo and Castrillo. The fifth division entered it at the same time higher up on the left, and the fourth division passed on the right. The soldiers of the light division, tormented with thirst, yet long used to their enemy's mode of warfare, drank as they marched; those of the fifth division, less experienced, stopped a few moments, and on the instant forty French guns, gathering on the heights above, sent a tempest of bullets amongst them. So nicely timed was the operation."

Maxwell describes the scene as the river was reached. "A buzz," he says, "ran through the ranks that water was at hand; and the soldiers were impelled forward with eyes staring and mouths open; and when within fifty yards of the stream a general rush was made."

The French general had accomplished much. He had crossed a great river, surprised Wellington's right, and driven it back for ten miles. Nevertheless, a glance at the map shows how Wellington had thwarted the attempt to sweep past his flank and get between him and Salamanca. Marmont's troops, too, had been marching for two days and nights, and were exhausted, and a brief pause followed. The two great hosts bivouacked on the opposite slopes of a narrow valley, and the outposts were placed so near each other that, to quote Maxwell, "the fixed sentinels almost received the secret whispers of each other's watch!"

On the morning of the 20th, Marmont was moving again. His light-footed battalions, while the stars were yet burning in the Spanish night skies, were pushing past Wellington's right up the Guareña. Parallel lines of hills, with a very narrow and shallow valley betwixt, run curving to the south-west towards the Tormes, on which river stands Salamanca; and along the crest of the outer range Marmont pushed at fiercest speed. On the inner ridge, and within easy musket-shot, marched the British, the eager columns trying to head each other. Wherever the ground favoured the movement, the guns on either side wheeled round, and smote the hostile flank opposite them with grape and round shot. But the dusty panting soldiers, with sloping muskets and shoulders thrown forward, never halted; while, to quote Napier, "the officers, like gallant gentlemen, who bore no malice and knew no fear, made their military recognitions, and the horsemen on each side watched with eager eyes for an opening to charge." At one point the swiftly moving lines, for a moment, so to speak, jostled, and two dust-covered brigades on either side clashed fiercely together. The British, however — a brigade of the fourth division — swung round, poured in a deadly volley, charged home with bayonet, dashed their opponents into mere fragments, then wheeled back, and pressed on their scarcely interrupted march.

In this day's operations, however, Marmont won. He outmarched and outflanked the British, and when night fell his dusty and exhausted soldiers held the ford of Huerta on the Tormes. He had nothing to do but to keep that position till his reinforcements reached him, then Salamanca and Wellington's line of retreat to Portugal lay under his stroke. The night set in wild and stormy. Rain fell with tropical violence. The hill-slopes were slippery with a thousand rills; a furious thunderstorm broke over the valley, where the tired armies, in great confusion, were trying to take up their positions. The peals of thunder were so deep and echoing, that a whole troop of British cavalry horses, familiar with the roar of artillery, broke loose in terror, and galloped riderless into the French camp. Hundreds of frightened horses, too, dashed through the British lines, and were mistaken for charges of French cavalry. Never was a wilder scene. But, through it all, the soldiers of the immortal light division "were seen by the fiery gleams to step from the river to the bank, and pursue their march, amid this astounding turmoil, in close and beautiful order, defying alike the storm and the enemy."

Wellington recognised that in this strife of tactics Marmont had won; but he clung with iron tenacity to his position, in the hope that the Frenchman, instead of waiting till his reinforcements came up and made a battle hopeless, might attempt a rash stroke on his own account. But he wrote a letter to the Spanish general, Castaños, saying he must retreat. The orderly carrying the letter was captured by the French, and his despatch, falling into Marmont's hands, tempted him to his doom. The French insisted afterwards that this letter was a subtle *ruse de guerre* on Wellington's part. It was written to trick Marmont, not to inform Castaños; and its capture was part of the trick. The letter, it is quite true, tempted Marmont to make the rash stroke which ruined him; but it also exactly expressed Wellington's purpose. Retreat was the only course possible to him if Marmont stood on his defence till his reinforcements came up.

A glance at the map shows that the Tormes forms a great loop north of Salamanca. Marmont, on the night of July 18, had seized the ford at Huerta, at the crown of the loop, and could move down either bank of the river to Salamanca. Wellington entrenched his third division on the right bank of the river, opposite the ford of Santa Marta, to bar Marmont's advance, but with the bulk of his army crossed the river, and took up a position perpendicular to its course, his extreme right touching, but not occupying, one of a pair of rugged and isolated hills, called the Arapiles. He thus covered Salamanca against Marmont's advance from Huerta, on the left bank of the river.

The two wearied armies watched each other for a day and a half; but Wellington had learnt that Marmont's reinforcements from the north would reach him on July 22 or 23, and the British general decided that he must retreat. Still, he hung on, hoping for some chance of a dramatic stroke, and this suddenly offered itself. Marmont had crossed to the left bank of the Tormes, and, on the morning of the 22nd, he suddenly made a leap at the outer of the two hills we have named. The hills were about 500 yards apart, and the British, quick to see the French movement, made a dash at the hill near them. The French, vehement and swift-footed, reached the hill on the side first, seized it, and dashed on to the sister hill, which the slower, but more stubborn, British had half climbed. There was a struggle, fierce, short, and bloody; but at its close the French and the British held their respective hills, and these two savage splinters of rock formed, so to speak, the menacing heads, from which two great armies threatened each other. But the capture of the French Arapiles gave Marmont a great advantage. It made his right unassailable, and he could swing round from the hill as from a pivot, and strike at the Ciudad Rodrigo road, along which Wellington must retreat. Wellington met the situation thus created by using the English Arapiles as a fixed point, and swinging round his army till his right rested on Aldea Tejada. What had been his first line facing Huerta, thus became his rear, and the army now looked eastward to meet the wheel of the French left.

The long summer day crept on, both armies grimly watching each other. Wellington had resolved to fall back as soon as night came. Marmont, on his part, was fretted to fever by the dread that Wellington would slip out of his hands before his reinforcements came up. The English commissariat waggons were already on the road to Ciudad Rodrigo, and the dust, rising high in the sky, made Marmont believe that Wellington was actually in retreat; and, taking fire at that thought, he launched his left, consisting of two divisions under

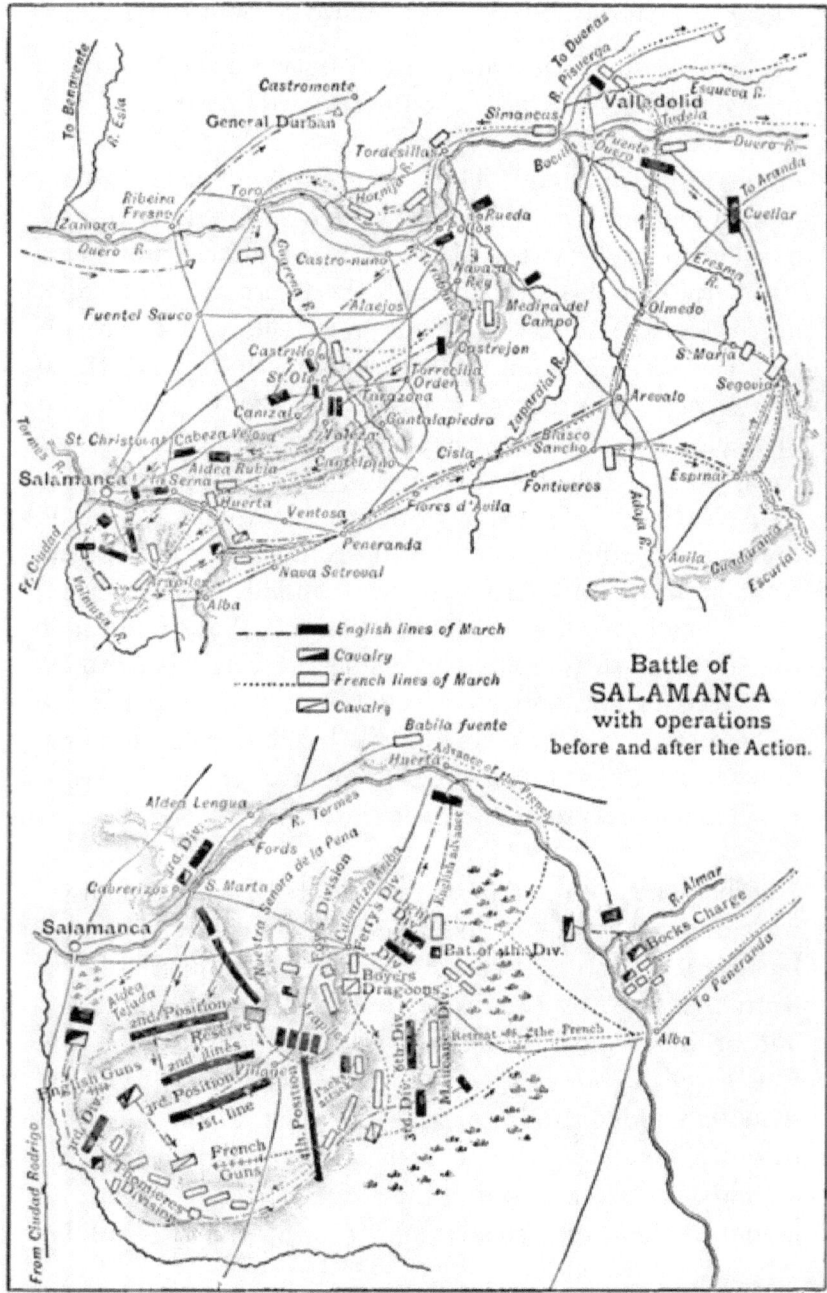

Maucune, with fifty guns and some light cavalry, along a ridge of low hills which ran in a curve past Wellington's right towards Salamanca. The two armies, in fact, occupied the opposing crests of an oval-shaped amphitheatre, whose axis, from east to west, was about two miles long, the transverse axis, from north to south, being about a mile and a half; and to the northern tip of this natural amphitheatre the two Arapiles acted, so to speak, as gate-posts.

Marmont's left was now in movement, and its march quickly created a steadily widening gap in the French line of battle. Wellington's keen and soldierly eye instantly detected the flaw in his enemy's tactics. The French left wing was entirely separated from the centre. The fault was flagrant, and, in Napier's terse phrase, Wellington "fixed it with the stroke of a thunderbolt." Croker, in his journal, relates a conversation at Strathfieldsaye, many years afterwards, in which Alava, while Wellington was present and listened, and smiled at the story, drew a realistic sketch of the manner in which Marmont's unlucky move was detected by the British general:—

"He (Wellington) had been very busy all the morning, and had not thought of breakfast, and the staff had grown very hungry; at last, however, there was a pause (I think he said about two) near a farmyard surrounded by a wall, where a kind of breakfast was spread on the ground, and the staff alighted and fell to. While they were eating, the Duke rode into the enclosure; he refused to alight, and advised them to make haste; he seemed anxious and on the look-out. At last they persuaded him to take a bit of bread and the leg of a cold roast fowl, which he was eating without knife from his fingers, when suddenly they saw him throw the leg of the fowl far away over his shoulder, and gallop out of the yard, calling to them to follow him. The fact is, he had been waiting to have the French sighted at a certain gap in the hills, and that was to be the signal of a long-meditated and long-suspended attack. 'I knew,' said Alava, with grave drollery, 'that something "very serious" was about to happen when an article so precious as the leg of a roast fowl was thus thrown away!'"

Wellington, in brief, waited coolly till Marmont's faulty movement was developed past remedy; then he made his terrible counter-stroke. He fixed Marmont's right to its ground by making a dash at the French Arapiles; he smote the head of Maucune's columns with the third division brought up at the double from Aldea Tejada, and, at the same moment, he launched at their flank the fifth division. How swift and dramatic was the development of Wellington's attack is best told in Napier's vivid sentences:—

"A few orders issued from his lips like the incantations of a wizard, and suddenly the dark mass of troops which covered the English Arapiles, as if possessed by some mighty spirit, rushed violently down the interior slope of the mountain and entered the great basin, amidst a storm of bullets which seemed to shear away the whole surface of the earth over which they moved. The fifth division instantly formed on the right of the fourth, connecting the latter with Bradford's Portuguese, who hastened forward at the same time from the right of the army; and the heavy cavalry, galloping up on the right of Bradford, closed this front of battle."

The first and most decisive blow of the great fight was struck by the third division. These were Picton's men; but that brave soldier was absent through sickness, and the division was under the command of Pakenham, Wellington's brother-in-law, a soldier of excellent fighting quality. Wellington gave his orders in person to Pakenham. "Do you see those fellows on the hill, Pakenham?" he said, pointing to where Maucune's columns were now showing. "Move on with your division, and drive them to the d——!" Pakenham saluted, and there are two versions of his reply. "I will, my lord, by G——," is the reply put in his mouth by Robinson in his "Life of Picton." Napier's version of the reply is, "Yes, if you will give me a grasp of that all-conquering hand." The first version is needlessly profane, the second is tumid and un-British; but about the intelligence and fire with which Pakenham carried out his orders there is no doubt. Wellington himself watched the division as it deployed into column and moved fiercely to attack—an attack which was described by an eye-witness as "not only the most spirited, but the most perfect thing of its kind ever seen." "Did you ever see a man," said Wellington to his staff, "who understood his orders better than Pakenham?"

Pakenham's columns, as they drew near the French, swung into line, the companies bringing forward their right shoulders at a run as they marched, and with bent heads and levelled bayonets, but not yet firing a shot, pressed sternly on the French, who, expecting to look down on the Ciudad Rodrigo road crowded with a retreating enemy, instead suddenly found themselves threatened by swiftly moving lines of steady infantry, glittering from end to end with shining bayonets at the charge. But the French were hardy veterans, and broke instantly into an angry fire of musketry. Their guns, too, swung round and poured a storm of grape on the steady British lines.

These never wavered or halted. The gaps in their front were filled instantly. On they came, their disciplined tread sounding louder and nearer, till they burst into dreadful and fast-following volleys, and the French were swept away as with the blast of a whirlwind. The French officers were gallant men, and did desperate acts to keep their men steady. The colonel of a French regiment, for example, snatched a musket from a grenadier, ran forward a few yards, and shot Major Murphy, in command of the 88th or Connaught Rangers, who was in advance of his men. One of the 88th in return shot the Frenchman dead; but Murphy's horse galloped wildly across the front of the regiment, dragging his dead rider, whose foot was entangled in the stirrup, with him.

The sight kindled the 88th to madness. The line began to sway forward with the eager fury of the men; and Pakenham, who rode near, shouted to Wallace, who commanded the brigade, to "let them loose." The word of command ran down the line, repeated from officer to officer; the bayonets fell as with one impulse to the level; and, "let loose," the men with a sudden shout dashed at the enemy. Amid the smoke of the French line a single officer could be seen lingering to fire the last gun. But, crushed as though smitten with a tempest of aërolites, the French columns broke in hopeless flight. The French cavalry rode at the flanks of the victorious British, and for a few minutes horsemen and footmen were mingled in desperate fight. The French cavalry, however, was quickly driven off; and, steadily moving on its path, the third division struck with its fire the second line of the French, while the fifth division was pouring its volleys at the same moment into the French flank.

Then came one of the most memorable cavalry charges on record. The heavy brigade—the 3rd and 4th Dragoons, and the 5th Dragoon Guards—under Le Marchant, and Anson's light cavalry, found the opportunity of a decisive attack. The squadrons were launched at speed:

"While Pakenham, bearing onward with a conquering violence, was closing on their flank, and the fifth division advancing with a storm of fire on their front, the interval between the two attacks was suddenly filled with a whirling cloud of dust, moving swiftly forward and carrying within its womb the trampling sound of a charging multitude. As it passed the left of the third division, Le Marchant's heavy horsemen, flanked by Anson's light cavalry, broke forth from it at full speed, and the next instant 1200 French infantry, though formed in several lines, were trampled down with a terrible clamour and disturbance. Bewildered and blinded, they cast away their arms and ran through the openings of the British squadrons, stooping and demanding quarter; while the dragoons, big men on big horses, rode onwards, smiting with their long glittering swords in uncontrollable power; and the third division followed at speed, shouting as the

French masses fell in succession before the dreadful charge."

The charging cavalry struck first the 66th Regiment of the French, formed in a sort of column of half battalions, thus presenting six successive lines which broke into a heavy musketry fire as the cavalry dashed on their front. Over these the British horsemen rode at a gallop, simply trampling them out of existence. A second battalion of six hundred was served in the same fashion. Onward swept the eager horsemen. By this time the open trees, under which the British cavalry was galloping, grew closer, and the front of the charging line was greatly broken. A solid French brigade, which stood in the shelter of the trees, poured a stream of fire into the galloping squadrons, and scores of saddles were emptied. Yet the stubborn horsemen kept on, and crushed to fragments this, the third body they had encountered; and Lord Edward Somerset, with a single squadron seeing beyond him a battery of five guns, pushed on his attack and captured them. This memorable charge destroyed Maucune's three divisions, as a military body, and captured five guns and 2000 prisoners. But Le Marchant himself, perhaps the best cavalry leader in the British army, had fallen, and the three regiments of the heavy brigade at nightfall could muster only three squadrons.

One curious incident marked the cavalry charge. Captain Mackie of the 88th, who acted as aide-de-camp to Wallace, the commander of the brigade, was, about this stage of the battle, reported as "missing." No one had seen him fall, but he had disappeared. Some half-hour later he reappeared through the smoke from the enemy's front, covered with dust and blood, his horse stumbling from fatigue, and nothing left of his sword but the hilt. As the English cavalry swept past the 88th, on their great charge, Mackie's Highland blood had kindled to flame; he galloped to the flank of the cavalry, shared in the tumult and rapture of their mad ride, and, when it was over, returned to his regiment in the fashion we have described.

It was five o'clock when Pakenham attacked, and before six o'clock Marmont had been carried disabled off the field; his successor, Bonet, was wounded; the French left had been destroyed as a military body, and had fallen back in tumultuous and disorderly retreat. But two circumstances for a brief space changed the fortunes of the conflict, and seemed to make the final issue doubtful. Clausel, who assumed command of the French when Bonet fell, was a fine soldier, stubborn of courage and fertile in resource. He not only rallied the broken left and shaken centre, but, with the instinct of a valiant soldier, he attempted a daring counterstroke on Wellington's left; and chance for a moment seemed to offer him a golden opportunity. Wellington assailed the French Arapiles with Pack's Portuguese brigade. Pack's men were 2000 strong, and Pack himself was "a fighting general" of fine courage. The hill, too, was held by a single French battalion, and the success of the attack seemed assured. And yet it failed! Pack led his men up within thirty yards of the summit in solid column; then over the crest and round the flank of the hill the French came in a furious charge, pushed home with fiery valour; and the Portuguese broke. "There was a cloud of smoke, a shout, a stream of fire, and the side of the hill was covered with the killed, the wounded, and the flying Portuguese." French valour in this attack was heightened by contempt of the Portuguese, and Portuguese courage, it may be added, was rebuked by a lurking consciousness of inferiority to the French. But it is not easy to excuse 2000 men for permitting themselves to be routed by less than 600.

French valour is always most dangerous when the imagination of victory gleams like a flame in it. The 4th division of the British had at that moment reached the edge of the southern ridge. Pack's defeat exposed their flank, and Clausel, seizing the critical moment, smote hard on their front with two strong unbroken regiments, and the British were driven in tumult and confusion, but fighting desperately, down the hill. Cole, in command of the division, fell badly wounded. Beresford brought up a Portuguese brigade to restore the fight, but the brigade was carried away, and Beresford himself was disabled. The French heavy cavalry was coming on to the attack, and the moment was critical. Wellington, riding quickly to the scene, brought up Clinton's division, which had not yet fired a shot, and the fury and thunder of the fight grew still deeper.

Night was falling. The dry grass on the slope where the hostile lines were exchanging close and deadly volleys, and making furious rushes with the bayonet, took fire, and ran in crackling flames over the bodies of the wounded, and under the trampling feet of the combatants. But the stubborn close-fighting valour of the 6th overbore the fiery daring of the French, and the changing current of battle set finally in favour of the British. The whole volume of the French retreat flowed in wild far-reaching tumult along the Alba de Tormes road. Still its rear-guard, however, clinging to every vantage of ground, covered the retreat with sullen and desperate courage, and Foy in command of it showed fine skill. The fragments of Maucune's division held the last defensible ridge on the edge of the forest through which the French retreat, with loud clamour, was flowing. It was night, black and moonless; and Clinton, scornful of tactics and flank movements, led his division straight up the hill. To those who watched the fight from a little distance, the eddying fortunes of the attack and the defence were written in ever-changing characters of fire on the hill-slopes.

"In the darkness of the night the fire showed from afar how the battle went. On the English side a sheet of flame was seen, sometimes advancing with an even front, sometimes pricking forth in spear-heads, now falling back in waving lines, anon darting upwards in one vast pyramid, the apex of which often approached yet never gained the actual summit of the mountain; but the French musketry, rapid as lightning, sparkled along the brow of the height with unvarying fulness, and with what destructive effects the dark gaps and changing shapes of the adverse fire showed too plainly: meanwhile Pakenham turned the left, Foy glided into the forest, and, Maucune's task being then completed, the effulgent crest of the ridge became black and silent, and the whole French army vanished as it were in the darkness."

The French must cross the Tormes in their flight at Alba de Tormes or at Huerta. Wellington had placed a Spanish garrison at the first, and he pushed on to the second with the light division. If he could seize that, the French army must surrender or be destroyed. The Spanish garrison, however, had abandoned Alba de Tormes without reporting the circumstance to Wellington; and the French army crossed the Tormes at that point in safety, and pushed on their retreat with such speed that, on the day after the fight, Clausel was forty miles from Salamanca. Wellington overtook the French rear-guard with his cavalry a little before noon on the 23rd, and launched the heavy German dragoons and Anson's light horsemen at them. Then ensued a cavalry exploit of singular brilliancy. Anson's troopers broke the French cavalry; but the Germans, riding fast, with narrow front, up the valley, discovered some solid squares of infantry on the slope above them. The left squadron of the regiment instantly swung round and rode at the nearest square. The two front ranks, kneeling, presented a double row of deadly steel; and over their heads, the French infantry, standing four deep, poured a stream of fire into the swiftly moving mass of men and horses before them. The Germans, however, gallantly led, pushed their charge up to the very points of the bayonets. A horse struck by a bullet stumbled forward on to the square, and broke for a moment its solid order, and the Germans—big men on huge horses—swept through the gap, and in an instant the battalion was cut down or trampled out of existence.

Meanwhile the second squadron, taking fire at the exploit of the squadron next to it, also swung round and rode fiercely at the second French square. Its fire was angry and damaging; but its ranks had been shaken by the spectacle of the destruction which had just ridden over the square below it. One or two French infantrymen ran from their places, and in an instant the tempest of galloping horses and furious swordsmen broke over the square. A third square, according to one version, was in like manner destroyed by the triumphant cavalry; but the remaining square stood firm and succeeded in covering the French retreat. The charge was a memorable feat. Three squares were broken and 1400 prisoners captured. Yet a great price was paid for this triumph. "The hill of La Serna offered a frightful spectacle of the power of the musket—that queen of weapons—and the track of the Germans was marked by their huge bodies. . . . In several places man and horse had died simultaneously, and so suddenly that, falling together on their sides, they appeared still alive, the horse's legs stretched out as in movement, the rider's feet in the stirrup, his bridle in hand, the sword raised to strike, and the large hat fastened under the chin, giving to the grim but undistorted countenance a supernatural and terrible expression."

Salamanca is one of the great battles of modern history. The French army was practically destroyed as a military body. "I never saw an army receive such a beating," wrote Wellington, the least exaggerative of men. But the immediate results of Salamanca were its least important consequences. It destroyed the splendid prestige of the French. It delivered Madrid. It raised the siege of Cadiz. It rescued Andalusia and Castile from the French occupation. Napoleon heard the tidings of the defeat the night before Borodino, and it filled him with fury—and with reason. He could henceforth hope for no reinforcements from Spain; he must drain his strength, indeed, when he most needed it, to feed the war there. "The Spanish ulcer," said Napoleon long afterwards, "destroyed me." But it was Salamanca that made the Spanish ulcer incurable.

SIR AUGUSTUS FRAZER, K.C.B.

THE SIEGE OF SAN SEBASTIAN

1813

"The siege of San Sebastian, a third-rate fortress, garrisoned only by 3000 men, hastily got together during the tumult of defeat which succeeded the battle of Vittoria, cost the allied army 3800 men, 2500 of whom, including 1716 British, were struck down in the final assault, and it detained the army sixty-three days, of which thirty were with open trenches and thirty-three blockade. . . . It must be admitted that a stronger proof can hardly be imagined of the vital consequences of fortresses in war, or of the decisive effect which the courageous defence even of an inconsiderable stronghold often has upon the fortunes of a campaign, or the fate of a monarchy."—ALISON.

A RUGGED breach in a long line of parapeted wall, at whose base a river creeps sluggishly to the sea. The breach is black with drifting smoke, and crowded with red-coated soldiers. Many lie dead under the feet of their comrades; many have crept, with streaming wounds, to either flank. The faces of the soldiers yet on the breach are black with powder, fierce with the passion of battle. From the walls above them, from a line of higher parapets that sweeps round at right angles, and commands the breach, a hundred streams of fire converge on the swaying mass of red-coated soldiers. They are dying in hundreds. Suddenly, from beyond the stream, and from the iron lips of fifty great guns, a tempest of shot roars above the heads of the

British soldiers, and sweeps the edge of the wall where the fiercely triumphant Frenchmen have defied for two separate hours the utmost valour of the British. For twenty minutes the British guns maintain that overwhelming fire above the heads of their own troops—the most brilliant bit of artillery practice on record. The French parapets are swept as with a besom of flame, the traverses are wrecked, the lines of steadfast infantry are rent to fragments. Then, with a flame of passion scarcely less fierce than the flame of the bellowing guns, the British stormers swept in one red wave over the blackened parapets, and San Sebastian is won! This is the scene which, through the long afternoon of August 31, 1813, makes the siege of San Sebastian one of the most picturesque in military history.

Three great sieges—those of Ciudad Rodrigo, of Badajos, and of San Sebastian—stand out like flaming beacons in the stern landscape of the Peninsular war. Each siege has its special characteristic. That of Ciudad Rodrigo was a swift and brilliant stroke of arms; it resembles, indeed, nothing so much as the flash of a glittering blade in the hands of a great swordsman. That of Badajos is notable for the masterful and furious daring with which the great breach was carried. The capture of San Sebastian is not marked by the swift brilliancy of Ciudad Rodrigo, nor yet by the tempestuous and half-scornful valour of Badajos. Its characteristic consists of the sullen daring, with a note of wrath running through it, which marked the temper of the soldiers. It is the most bloody and tragical of all the Peninsular sieges. Wellington's sieges in the Peninsula, it may be added, are not shining examples of scientific warfare. In each of them he was short of guns, of warlike material, and, above all, of time. In each he had to make the blood of his soldiers compensate for the blunders of his engineers, and the well-nigh incredible neglect, or equally incredible folly, of the War Office authorities in England. It was, perhaps, the sullen consciousness on the part of the private soldiers, that they had to pay in life and limb for stupidity, or neglect, in the administration of the war, which explains the exasperated temper in the ranks with which the siege of San Sebastian was conducted, and the blast of licence and cruelty with which it was closed.

San Sebastian, while the French held Central Spain, was a neglected third-rate fortress, with foul wells, dismantled batteries, and practically no garrison. But the great defeat of Vittoria made this sandy peninsula, with its steep rocky tip, a place of the first importance to both armies. The French clung to it, as it would be a thorn in Wellington's flank if he advanced through the passes of the Pyrenees. Wellington coveted it, as its harbour would be a new base of supply for him, and he dared not leave unsubdued what might be easily turned into a strong place of arms, as he pushed on the track of the defeated French through the wild mountain defiles which led to France.

San Sebastian resembles a lion's head thrust out from the coast of the Bay of Biscay, just where the spurs of the Pyrenees run down to the sea. The "neck" of the lion is a flat sandy isthmus, some 350 yards wide; the lion's head looks to the north, the bay is under its chin to the west; on the east flows into the sea in a wide shallow tidal channel the river Urumea. The seaward tip of the lion's head is a rocky cone, some 400 feet high, called Monte Orgullo, crowned by the castle of La Mota. Across the sandy isthmus ran a high solid curtain with a huge hornwork, shaped like the point of an arrow, at its centre. Betwixt this wall and the base of Monte Orgullo stretched the town, having a population of something like 10,000 people. A line of ramparts ran along the eastern face of the town, betwixt the curtain across the neck of the isthmus and Monte Orgullo. The Urumea washed the foot of this rampart, and the frowning heights of Monte Orgullo commanded with their batteries the whole town.

Fortune gave to the French, in the person of General Rey, a commander for San Sebastian with a singular genius for defensive war. Rey, indeed, in personal appearance was quite unheroic. Fraser, who was second in command of the British artillery at the siege, met Rey after the surrender, and describes him as "a great fat man," in appearance resembling rather a pacific and heavy-bottomed Dutch burgher, than one of the most brilliant soldiers of the Napoleonic wars. Rey was not present at Vittoria; he left the day before the battle in command of a great convoy. The convoy passed on to France, but Rey, with his escort, entered San Sebastian, and set himself with stern energy, and the genius of a fine soldier, to prepare for the siege which he knew to be inevitable. Part of the wreck of Vittoria a few days afterwards flowed in wild tumult and confusion into the town; but Rey, with great resolution, swept the town of non-combatants, armed all his batteries, cleared out his

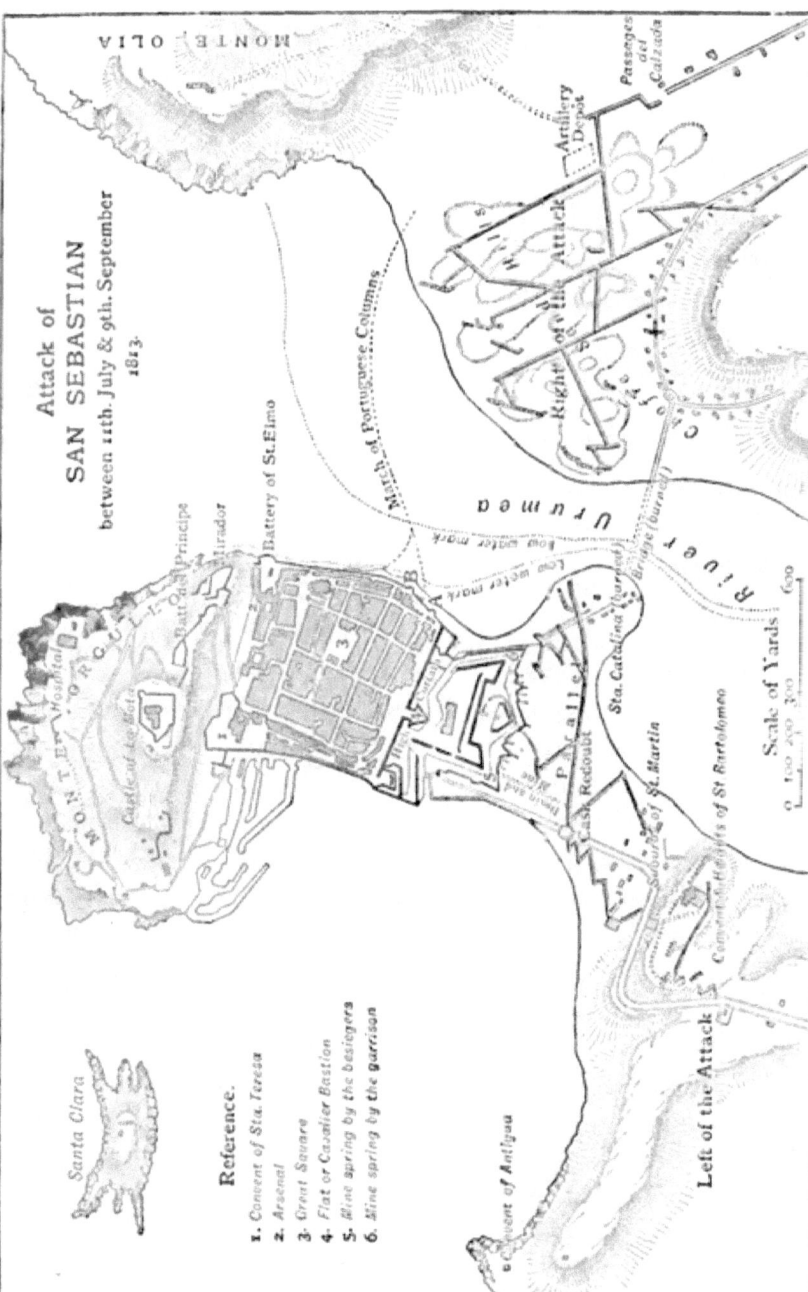

trenches and wells, turned the convent of San Bartolomeo, some 600 yards in advance of the curtain crossing the isthmus, into a strong place of arms; and, with all the art of a veteran soldier, set himself to hold San Sebastian against all comers. He had a garrison of some 3000 men; and 10,000 British and Spanish troops, under Sir Thomas Graham, the "hero of Barossa," one of Wellington's most trusted lieutenants, were moving down the slope of the Pyrenees to besiege him.

The Frenchman, however, had many things in his favour. San Sebastian lent itself easily to a stubborn defence. San Bartolomeo formed a strong outwork to the south; behind this, on the main road which crossed the narrow neck of the isthmus rose a great circular redoubt, formed of casks, and flanked by ruined houses, strongly held. These in turn were covered by the strong rampart which crossed the isthmus, with a powerful hornwork rising high in its centre. Thus, no less than three lines of defence had to be broken through before the town was reached. The town itself must be carried by obstinate street-fighting, while Monte Orgullo, with the stroke of its batteries, covered the whole field of combat, and could be held independently after the town itself had been carried.

The happiest feature for the French was the fact that they had practically an open sea base, and were in daily communication with France. It is an amazing fact that, eight years after Trafalgar, and while Great Britain was absolutely mistress of the sea, Wellington could not secure any adequate naval assistance in the siege of San Sebastian. A single British frigate, the

Surveillante, represented all the naval help the Admiralty could afford. Wellington's transports were captured almost daily by French privateers. The French garrison was perpetually fed by supplies sent directly from France. Vainly Wellington appealed to the Admiralty for ships. "Since Great Britain had been a naval power," he wrote bitterly, "a British army had never before been left in such a situation at a most important moment." Wellington's genius, however, was essentially practical. "If the navy of Great Britain," he wrote to Lord Bathurst, "cannot afford more than one frigate and a few brigs and cutters, fit, and used only, to carry despatches, to co-operate with this army in the siege of a maritime place, the possession of which before the bad season commences is important to the army as well as to the navy, I must be satisfied, and do the best I can without such assistance." "We have been obliged," he says in the same despatch, "to use the harbour boats of Passages, navigated by women, in landing the ordnance and stores, because there was no naval force to supply us with the assistance we require in boats." Wellington, in brief, in this siege of a hostile port, had to leave the aid of British ships out of his calculation.

But the aid the French derived from the open sea was simply past calculation. Boats came nightly to the garrison from Bayonne, bringing engineers, artillerymen, supplies of every kind, with news from the outside world, promises from Soult of immediate relief, and decorations, badges of honour, and crosses of the Legion of Honour in profusion to the soldiers who, from day to day, distinguished themselves in the siege. In this way the imagination of the besieged French was fed, as well as their material wants supplied. And the sense that a way of escape to the rear was open, that France was watching their defence, and that every act of valour brought an immediate reward in the shape of some "decoration," or of promotion, bred such a spirit of daring and enthusiasm in the garrison that, says Maxwell—who was actually a prisoner in San Sebastian—"I believe the garrison, individually or collectively, would not have hesitated attempting any enterprise, however difficult or dangerous."

The principles of war are changeless, and Wellington's engineers adopted the very plan of attack employed by the Duke of Berwick, who besieged San Sebastian in 1719. Strong batteries were erected on the Chofres sandhills, to smite with their fire the comparatively weak eastern wall across the stream of the Urumea. Approaches were simultaneously to be pushed along the isthmus, so as to take in flank the wall which the breaching batteries were smiting in front, and to smash the defences by which the breach, when made, would be guarded. The plan was able, and if it had been carried out the siege would never have attained what Napier calls its "mournful celebrity." Wellington, however, was guarding the passes against Soult, and left the conduct of the siege to Graham; and Graham allowed the eager spirits about him to over-ride what their impatience regarded as the too formal approaches of the engineers. They inverted, in a word, Vauban's well-known maxim, "Never attempt to carry anything at a siege by open force which may be gained by art and labour." The British leaders at San Sebastian scorned to postpone the bayonet to the spade or the linstock! So there became visible in the conduct of the siege that "raw haste" which is something more than "half-sister to delay."

Batteries were marked out on the night of July 10, 1813; by the morning of the 14th the guns were thundering across the front of the isthmus on San Bartolomeo; but not till the 20th did the breaching batteries across the Urumea begin to smite with their fire the eastern wall of the town. Even at this early stage in the siege the British began to feel the strength of the defence. Frazer writes in his diary on July 19: "The enemy has some good head in the fortress; we must feel for it. He fires and takes his measures with judgment."

Nothing could well surpass the energy with which the siege was pushed. The great breaching battery had ten guns in action, and in fifteen and a half hours of daylight the fire from these averaged 350 rounds a gun; "such a rate of firing," says Jones in his "Journal," "was probably never equalled at any siege." The sustained fury of the fire on both sides, indeed, quickly affected the guns in use. The guns fired from the fortress, for example, gave the appearance of two explosions when discharged; the vent of the gun, in a word, being so enlarged that the flash from it was almost as clear as that from the muzzle; while in the English batteries, Jones records, that "some of the vents of the guns were so much enlarged that a moderate-sized finger might be put into them."

The attacks on the two faces of the defence were

of course part of one scheme, and should have been pushed on with a wise balance of energy. But Graham, apparently, found it impossible to keep the too eager spirits of his force in check; and, as a result, the attack on the isthmus was urged on with fiery energy, and without any regard to the operations against the eastern front of the town. By the 17th, San Bartolomeo was almost knocked out of shape; and though the batteries had not yet opened fire against the eastern front it was impossible to cool the impatience of the attack on the southern face. On the 17th the convent was assaulted. From the engineering point of view the attack was premature; but it was a brilliant and picturesque feat of arms.

The convent stood upon a steep ridge, and was open to the fire of both besiegers and besieged. From the batteries on the Chofres sandhills, and from the rocky height of Monte Orgullo, the French and British alike eagerly watched the fierce struggle for the convent. No less than sixty guns indeed concentrated their fire on the building while the attack raged—the French guns smiting the assailants, the British guns trying to crush the defenders. At ten o'clock the storming party in two columns came over the crest of the hill which looked down on the convent. It consisted of Wilson's Portuguese, supported by the light company of the 9th British, and three companies of the Royals. Colin Campbell, afterwards Lord Clyde, led the men of the 9th. The Portuguese came on slowly, and the four companies of the British pushed forward with impatient eagerness, carried the redoubt, jumped over the convent wall, and thrust the French fiercely out. The French clung stubbornly to the houses which stretched beyond the convent towards the town, but the other companies of the 9th coming up with great resolution the French were still thrust back, while the cheers of the British troops watching the struggle from the farther bank of the Urumea, could be heard above the tumult of the fight. The reckless daring of the British carried them too far; they tried to carry the great circular redoubt, which stood betwixt the convent and the town. Musket and bayonet were vain, however, to carry a work so strong, and the too eager soldiers were driven back with sharp loss.

The convent was at once turned into batteries against the southern front of the defence, and the eastern wall of the town began to crumble under the stroke of the guns from the Chofres hills. A parallel was carried by the British across the neck of the isthmus, and in its course laid bare an ancient aqueduct, a great drain four feet high and three feet wide. A young officer, Reid, of the Engineers, crept up this drain; he found it ran for 230 yards towards the curtain across the isthmus, and ended in a door in the very counterscarp itself. A space of eight feet at the end of the aqueduct was stopped with sandbags, and thirty barrels of gunpowder were lodged against it, thus forming a globe of compression. This was to be fired at the moment of the assault, and it was hoped would blow, as through a tube, enough rubbish over the counterscarp as would fill the ditch of the hornwork, and thus make a way for the stormers.

Meanwhile the eastern wall crumbled fast under the fire of the batteries across the river. On July 23, the great breach was declared practicable. A day was spent in making a second breach a little to the north of the first, and the assault was fixed for the next morning. When the troops, in the grey dawn, however, were waiting in the trenches for the signal to attack, the houses behind the great breach broke into flames, and the attack was postponed to the next day—a very unhappy circumstance.

The proposed attack was in violation of the simplest rules of engineering. A breach was to be stormed, in a word, before the defences which covered it with their fire had been mastered. Rey had made these defences exceedingly powerful. The hornwork, or cavalier, at the centre of the southern front, rose fifteen feet above the other defences, and swept the breach with the fire of its guns. A tower on either side of the breach raked it with a flanking fire; the houses immediately behind the breach were strongly defended. The British, too, could only attack by leaping from the eastern extremity of the trench which crossed the isthmus, and advancing at the double for 300 yards along the slippery strand left at low water betwixt the Urumea and the undestroyed wall of the town, till they reached the breach. For those 300 yards they were under a flank fire of musketry from the wall; while Rey had piled the parapet with live shells to be rolled down on the struggling British. The attack was directed by Wellington to take place "in fair daylight," so that the batteries across the Urumea might keep down the fire of the defenders. Unfortunately, the signal for the attack was given whilst the night was still black, and the batteries on the Chofres hills were unable to open fire on the defenders, except at the risk of smiting their own troops.

The attacking force consisted of 2000 men of the 5th division: Frazer led a battalion of the Royal Scots against the great breach; the 38th, under Greville, was to attack the more distant breach; the 9th, under Cameron, supported the Royals, while the forlorn hope consisted of twenty men of the light company of the 9th, and the light company of the Royals, with a ladder party, under Colin Campbell. The opening from the trench was too narrow, and the formation of the troops was broken at the very outset. The 300 yards to be traversed was slippery with weeds and rocks, and broken by deep pools of water, while at every step a fierce fire scourged the flank of the broken soldiers. The assault, in a word, from its very first step became the rush of a mob, instead of a disciplined and orderly attack. The globe of compression in the aqueduct, already described, was indeed fired with a blast that filled the surrounding hills with its echoes, and the surprise of it drove the French for a moment from their defences.

Frazer and the principal engineering officer, Harry Jones, led eagerly on to the great breach, followed by the soldiers immediately about them; but the mass of the attacking party halted in the dark to fire at a gap in the wall which they mistook for the breach. In a few minutes the halt filled the narrow interval betwixt the wall and the river with a struggling crowd of soldiers, aflame with the passion of battle, but without order or leaders. Colin Campbell, with a few men, struggled past the flank of the crowd, and climbed the great breach, and a few disconnected parties followed up the rough slope. These gallant men reached the broken crest of the breach, but the French had meanwhile recovered from their surprise. Those who reached the crest of the breach saw below them a deep black gulf, beyond which, in a curve of fire, was a wall of flaming houses, and from every quarter a tempest of shot swept the rugged edge of broken stone on which they stood. Frazer of the Royal Scots, leaped down the farther side of the breach, reached the flaming houses, and died there. Greville, Cameron, Campbell, and other gallant officers broke through the tumult of the crowd, climbed the breach, and fell on its crest. Twice Campbell ascended, and twice he was wounded. Meanwhile, the mass of British soldiers below, with the black river—now filling again with the returning tide and climbing the rocks fast—on one side, and the hostile wall, with its perpetual hail of bullets on the other side, swayed to and fro with sullen shouts and angry answering fire of musketry. But, with military cohesion destroyed, and scourged on both flank and front by the fire of the French, the mass crumbled into clusters, and surging backwards, slowly regained the trenches. When day broke, Frazer of the Artillery, watching from the batteries beyond the Urumea, thought that nothing more than a false attack had taken place; till, in the clearer daylight he could see the rough slope of the great breach mottled with red spots, the fallen bodies of officers and men.

This bloody and ill-managed assault resulted in a loss to the British, in killed, wounded, or prisoners, of forty-four officers and nearly 500 men. Perhaps the best account of the attack and its failure, is to be found in a private letter written by Colin Campbell at the time, and published in his life :—

"It was dark, as you know, when ordered to advance. All before me went willingly enough forward, but in a very straggling order, arising, in the first instance, from the order of formation previous to attack being extended the whole length of the parallel in a front of fours, which it (the parallel) would admit of by packing when halted, but was not of sufficient width for troops to maintain that front when in movement. We thus debouched from the mouth of the opening made from the parallel, which was not quite so wide as the latter, in twos and threes. The space we had to traverse between this opening and the breach—some 300 yards—was very rough, and broken by large pieces of rocks, which the falling tide had left wet and exceedingly slippery, sufficient in itself to have loosened and disordered an original dense formation; and the heavy and uninterrupted fire to which they were opposed in advance, increased this evil—these different causes combining to make our advance look more like one of individuals than that of a well-organised and disciplined military body.

"On arriving within some thirty or forty yards of the demi-bastion on the left of the main front, I found a check. There appeared to be a crowd of some 200 men immediately before me, opposite the front of this work—those in front of this body returning a fire directed at them from the parapet above, and which was sweeping them down in great numbers, and also from an entrenchment which the enemy had thrown across the main ditch, about a yard or two retired from the opening into it. I observed at the same time a heavy firing at the breach; and as the larger portion of the right wing appeared to be collected, as I have described, opposite the demi-bastion, it was very manifest that those who had gone forward to the breach were not only weak in numbers for the struggle they had to encounter, but it was apparent they were also unsupported. I endeavoured with the head of my detachment to aid some of their own officers in urging and pushing forward this halted body. They had commenced firing, and there was no moving them. Failing in this, I proposed to Lieutenant Clarke, who was in command of the light company of the Royals, to lead past the right of these people, in the hope that, seeing us passing them, they might possibly cease firing and follow. I had scarcely made this proposition when this fine young man was killed; and several of my own (9th) detachment, as also many of the light company Royals, were here killed and wounded. In passing this body with the few of my own people and most of the light company Royals, some might have come away, but the bulk remained. Their halting there (opposite the demi-bastion) thus formed a sort of stopping-place between the trenches and the breach, as the men came forward from the former on their way to the latter. . . . On arriving at the breach, I observed the whole lower parts thickly strewed with killed and wounded. There were a few individual officers and men spread on the face of the breach, but nothing more. These were cheering, and gallantly opposing themselves to the close and destructive fire directed at them from the round tower and other defences on each flank of the breach, and to a profusion of hand-grenades which were constantly rolling down. In going up I passed Jones of the Engineers, who was wounded; and on gaining the top I was shot through the right hip, and tumbled to the bottom. The breach, though quite accessible, was steep, particularly towards the top, so that all those who were struck on the upper part of it rolled down, as in my own case, to the bottom. Finding, on rising up, that I was not disabled from moving, and observing two officers of the Royals, who were exerting themselves to lead some of their men from under the line-wall near to the breach, I went to assist their endeavours, and again went up the breach with them, when I was shot through the inside part of the left thigh.

"About the time of my receiving my second hit, Captain Archimbeau of the Royals arrived near the bottom of the breach, bringing with him some eighty or ninety men, cheering and encouraging them forward in a very brave manner through all the interruptions that were offered to his advance by the explosion of the many hand-grenades that were dropped upon them from the top of the wall, and the wounded men retiring in the line of his advance (the narrow space between the river and the bottom of the wall). Seeing, however, that whatever previous efforts had been made had been unsuccessful—that there was no body of men nor support near to him, while all the defences of and around the breach were fully occupied and alive with fire, and the party with him quite unequal in itself—seeing, also, the many discouraging circumstances under which the attempt would have to be made, of forcing its way through such opposition — he ordered his party to retire, receiving, when speaking to me, a shot which broke his arm. I came back with him and his party, and on my way met the 38th, whose advance became interrupted by the wounded and others of the Royals returning."

The attack had thus failed; and in the British batteries the supply of ammunition was exhausted; Soult was coming fiercely on through the passes of the Pyrenees, and Wellington had no choice but to turn the siege into a blockade till fresh supplies arrived from England. Thirty days had been spent in open trenches, and thirty days of blockade followed; days, as far as Wellington, who was covering the siege, was concerned, of desperate and bloody fighting. But Soult's gallant host, at the close of these operations, was sweeping, a broken mass, in wild tumult back to France, with a loss, in killed, wounded, and prisoners, of not less than 20,000 men. Then Wellington resumed the siege. On August 19, a battering train arrived from England; on the 23rd came a second battering train; but, with a touch of administrative stupidity delightfully characteristic, ammunition for only a single day's consumption was sent out with the guns!

On the morning of the 26th, the batteries opened in thunder on the doomed city. No less than 114 guns were in action at once. For four days that tempest of fire was maintained. By August 30 two wide breaches gaped in the eastern wall, the fire of the place was almost silenced, three mines had been run from the southern attack towards the curtain crossing the isthmus, and everything seemed ready for the final assault. The gallant French commandant, however, had spent the thirty days of the blockade in perfecting his defences; and, with a wise prevision of the difficulties before them, Frazer records in his "Diary" on August 22: "This St. Sebastian is destined to be a thorn in our sides, or a feather in our caps." At this stage the "thorn" was more visible than the "feather"!

Rey, the French commandant, did not hope to maintain an equal duel with the furious British batteries; his plan was to make assault on the breach hopeless. He constructed immediately behind the great breach an interior rampart, 15 feet high, with outstanding bastions. The apparent breach, therefore, was, in effect, a death-trap. On reaching its crest the storming party would find before it a huge pit, from 20 to 35 feet deep, its bottom strewn with every sort of impediment; and beyond it a new and unbroken rampart, loopholed for musket-fire, with traverses at either extremity. A mine charged with 12 cwt. of powder was driven beneath the slope along which the stormers must come; two other mines were designed to blow down part of the sea-wall on the British columns as they passed along it to the attack. Never, in fact, was a more desperate task than that of carrying San Sebastian. And it is to be noted that the engineering blunder which made the first attack a failure was repeated. The defences that covered the breach were left undestroyed.

On the night of August 29, a false attack was made on the breach, in order to tempt the besieged to spring their mines, and show the direction and scale of the fire they had prepared for the assaulting column. Lieutenant Macadam, of the 9th, was ordered, with a handful of men nearest him, to make a pretended attack on the breach. Macadam leaped out of the trench, seventeen men of the Royals at the word of command followed him; and, running forward, reached the foot of the great breach, and in extended order, with loud shouts, and discharging their muskets, proceeded to mount it. They were, of course, flinging their lives away. If the trick had succeeded, these brave men, by their very success, would have been blown into fragments. The French, however, kept their coolness, and shot these brave fellows down, one by one, their leader alone regaining the trenches.

Meanwhile Wellington, dissatisfied with the conduct of his men in the first attack, called for fifty volunteers from each of the fifteen regiments in the 1st, 4th, and light divisions; "men," the appeal ran, "who could show other troops how to mount a breach." That stinging phrase was felt by the gallant men of the 5th division like the stroke of a whip; but the response in the other divisions was eager, and even tumultuous. Here is a picturesque little passage from the "Private Journal" of Larpent:—

"There was nothing but confusion in the two divisions here last night (the light and 4th), from the eagerness of the officers to volunteer, and the difficulty of determining who were to be refused and who allowed to go and run their heads into a hole in the wall, full of fire and danger! Major Napier was here quite in misery, because, though he had volunteered first, Lieutenant-colonel Hunt of the 52nd, his superior officer, insisted on his right to go. The latter said that Napier had been in the breach at Badajoz, and he had a fair claim to go now. So it is among the subalterns; ten have volunteered where two are to be accepted. Hunt, being lieutenant-colonel, has nothing but honour to look to; as to promotion, he is past that. The men say that they don't know what they are to do, but they are ready to go anywhere."

The "Historical Record" of the 52nd says that when Wellington's appeal reached that regiment "entire companies volunteered, and the captains had a difficult task in selecting the men most fit for such an undertaking, without hurting the feelings of the others; in many cases lots were resorted to to settle the claims of those gallant fellows who contended for the honour of upholding the fame of their regiment." When the order was communicated to the 4th division, and volunteers were invited to step to the front, the whole division moved forward!

Leith, however, who commanded the 5th division, was much aggrieved at the slight put upon his men, and he placed the 750 volunteers who were to " show other troops how to mount a breach " in support, and gave the men of the 5th division the post of honour. The men of that division, indeed, were so exasperated with the slight put upon them that there was some risk of them firing on the volunteers themselves, instead of on the French!

The assault was fixed for 11 o'clock on the morning of August 31. Robinson's brigade was formed in two columns. One was to storm the eastern end of the curtain that crossed the isthmus, the other was to assail the great breach; Bradford's Portuguese were to cross the river and assault the smaller and more northerly breach.

The morning broke gloomy and black. A dense mist drifted down from the high valleys of the Pyrenees, and girdled San Sebastian with a shroud of grey vapour, so dense that the besieging batteries could not fire. As the day advanced, however, the fog lifted, and a tempest of shot was poured for more than two hours on the defences of the city. Eleven o'clock struck; the batteries suddenly ceased. Robinson's men leaped from their trench, and a river of scarlet uniforms swept towards the breach. It was known that heavy mines were in the path of the column; but twelve men led by a sergeant ran forward at speed, and leaped upon the covered way to cut the fuse by which the mine was to be exploded. Startled by their rush, the French hurriedly fired the mine. The sergeant and his brave band were instantly destroyed, and the great sea-wall was thrown, with a terrific crash, upon the flank of the advancing column, crushing some forty men beneath it. Had it been fired some five minutes later it would have slain hundreds. As it was it did not arrest the attack for a moment. Macguire, of the 4th, who led the forlorn hope, "conspicuous," says Napier, "from his long white plume, his fine figure, and his swiftness, bounded far ahead of his men in all the pride of youthful strength and courage. But at the foot of the great breach he fell dead, and the stormers went sweeping, like a dark surge, over his body."

On pressed the stormers. Their array was broken by the slippery rocks, over which they stumbled as they charged, and by the fire which scourged them from the summit of the wall on their left. But they reached the breach, swept up it without a pause, and gained its narrow crest. They found themselves on

THE BREACH AT SAN SEBASTIAN.

the edge of a gulf, barred at its further edge by a frowning rampart, from which flashed incessantly the flame of the French muskets; while from every side a storm of bullets swept over them. The flow of the eager soldiers up the breach was constant, but there was no living in the deadly fire that played on the crest. The attack on the half bastion of St. John was equally obstinate and bloody, and equally ineffective. The breach was flanked by a traverse held by French grenadiers; it was scourged by guns from every angle. The British could not force their way; they would not yield, and they fell fast and thick. Still the attack was fed by fresh troops; but both breaches were barred as by a sword of flame.

The volunteers from the other divisions had been held back with difficulty so far, and were now calling out to know "why they had been brought there if they were not to lead the assault." They were at last let loose; and, to quote Napier, "went like a whirlwind to the breaches, and again the crowded masses swarmed up the face of the ruins; but reaching the crest line they came down again like a falling wall. Crowd after crowd were seen to mount, to totter, and to sink. The deadly French fire was unabated. The smoke floated away, and the crest of the breach bore no living man."

This dreadful struggle, with its tumult and bloodshed, the passionate heroism of the attack, the unyielding valour of the defence, lasted for two hours. The lesser breach had been assailed by the Portuguese, under Snodgrass, with no better fortune.

Graham had watched the long struggle from a battery on the farther side of the Urumea. He saw that valour could accomplish no more on the bloodstained breaches, and he resorted to an expedient of singular daring. He turned fifty heavy pieces on the parapet of the high curtain whose fire barred the breach. The British soldiers clung to the slope of the breach only a few feet below the level at which the British guns were firing; but the British gunners, after five days' continuous firing, knew the range precisely, and the practice was perfect. A tempest of shot swept along the edge of the high curtain, broke down its traverses, and slew the exultant French infantry that lined it. For thirty minutes, with this whip of flame, the ramparts of the curtain were scourged; then, suddenly, a series of explosions ran along the crest of the parapet. All the stores of powder-barrels, live shells, hand-grenades, &c., piled there took fire. The curtain was lost for a moment to sight in a cloud of smoke through which ran the shock, and the wavering flame of the explosion. Three hundred French grenadiers were destroyed in a moment; then through the smoke, on the staggering French came the British stormers, mad with the passion of combat, and the rage bred of the long slaughter they had suffered. The French colours on the hornwork were plucked down by Lieutenant Gathin of the 11th. The French clung to their broken defences with amazing valour, but were thrust back fiercely and triumphantly by the British; and, after five hours of dreadful combat at the walls, the whirlwind of battle swept into the town.

Frazer, who watched the assault from a battery across the river, describes the spectacle of the assault as "awful." He took pencil notes of the assault, from moment to moment, part of which is reproduced here. It gives the great struggle, so to speak, as in the present tense.

Minutes taken during the assault of San Sebastian, August 31:—

"It begins (5 minutes before 11)! They reach the top of the breach. A mine springs, but behind them! All seems well. They reach the top and halt—if they are supported it will do.

"Mirador and St. Elmo do not fire. Men run too much to old breach—too little to junction of demi-bastion and curtain. 11.35: Much firing. Troops do not advance. Bugles sound advance. Head of Portuguese column cross to left in detached columns, men pass creek up to knees; advance nobly at double quick; fourteen taken back wounded with grape, about fifty more turn back; main body advance. Lieutenant Gathin, 11th Regiment, acting engineer, runs to the Portuguese to storm with them. The Portuguese get across at 11.45, but with great loss. At the breaches all is stationary. Another reinforcement runs from trenches to breach. 11.50:

O

More reinforcements from trenches to breach. Noon: Much grape in all directions from the enemy's batteries. Breaches are filled. . . . 12.10: Fire slackens on all sides. At a quarter-past eleven a letter was brought across the water by Private O'Neil, of the 4th (Portuguese run from the breach), from Lord Wellington, asking Sir Thomas Graham if he can spare Bradford's brigade, as Soult comes on in force. 12.15: Advancing from breach of retired wall; smoke prevents clear view. Lodgment apparently secure. Two more mines blown up on curtain. 12.25: Ditch toward low communication filled with troops. More reinforcements from trenches to breach. 12.30: Troops again try the end of curtain; our own shots strike close over their heads. The place will be taken! Our men run from the curtain. . . . 12.40: Men going down from the old breach into the town. It will do; they wave their hats from the terre pleine of the curtain. Another reinforcement from trenches. Our men fire from right of right round tower. This bounds our ground to right. 1 P.M.: More reinforcements from trenches. This duty is well performed, whoever may direct it. Men enter the town, principally by the end of old breach next round tower. One man of 1st Guards runs alone to the part of the parapet, twenty yards to the right of the right tower, and a sergeant and a few Portuguese by right breach of all. They gain it by getting on the old foundation of Marshal Berwick's wall. The enemy lines the stockade. The enemy runs from the rampart behind that stockade. All goes well. 1.10: Two of our shots go through the stockade; the enemy abandons it. One brave French officer and two men alone remain; they too are gone.

1.15: Enemy still holds end of the curtain next the cavalier; he should be forced at that point. The gun at St. Elmo fires. 1.20: And again—it must be silenced. Very heavy fire of musketry in the town. Horn-work decidedly ours. 1.25: The gun at St. Elmo more and more troublesome. Firing in the town continues and increases. Few men comparatively on breaches; chiefly in hollow of retired wall between end of curtain and left tower; they are now entering the town. The flag was struck on the castle when the assault began. 1.35: More reinforcements to breach from trenches. No fire or men to be seen on trenches. Wind very high; sand blows and destroys the view. Many prisoners brought into trenches from the town. Tide has begun to flow. 1.45: Heavy musketry in the town. Our bugles sound the advance in all parts of the town. Our men are pulling prisoners out by the breach. The enemy retire. 1.55: Fire in town slackens. 2 P.M.: Marshal Beresford and Sir Thomas Graham come to the battery. Town seems again on fire near the right breach. 2.5: News of Sir Richard Fletcher's death! 2.15: Firing in town continues, but is decreasing. Gabions carrying into town from trenches. 2.48: Great fire and smoke in centre of town near the square. Two mines explode in the town. The enemy still hold a church and the left part of the town. 3 P.M.: Mules with ammunition going from trenches to town. Three fires in the town. Between rain, and smoke, and black sky, it is very dark. 3.30: Great fire in the town; as dark as it is generally at half-past six. Nothing of the town to be seen from excessive smoke."

A thunderstorm which had been gathering round the

crest of the shaggy summits of the nearest mountains now broke upon the city; and perhaps a wilder scene than that which was now presented has seldom been witnessed. The town was in flames. The streets were filled with the crash of musketry volleys, the oaths and shouts of contending men; while overhead rolled the deep voice of thunder, and from the black sky the incessant lightning leaped. The French commandant fell back, fighting with sullen valour, to Monte Orgullo, from which he was only to be driven by a new siege; but the town itself had fallen. Yet at what a price had this victory been won! The slaughter at the breaches was dreadful. Of the 750 volunteers who were "to show other troops how to mount a breach" every second man had fallen. The total loss of the assault, in killed and wounded, amounted to 2000 men. Many officers of rank fell. The troops, it may be added, when they broke into the town, got completely out of hand; and a shadow which blackens the fame of the splendid and obstinate valour by which the breaches were carried is cast by the scenes of cruelty and license which followed the assault. The men who swept the streets of the unhappy city as that night fell were drunk with the long madness of the fight, and Graham had no fresh troops at hand which he could march into the town to enforce order.

Frazer, it may be added, gives a realistic picture of the town as seen after the attack:—

"I have been in the town, and over that part of it which the flames or the enemy will permit to be visited. The scene is dreadful; no words can convey half the horrors which strike the eye at every step. Heaps of dead in every corner; English, French, and Portuguese lying wounded on each other; with such resolution did one side attack and the other defend. The town is not plundered; it is sacked. Rapine has done her work, nothing is left. I had occasion, in going to General Hay, to go into several houses, some had been elegantly furnished. All was ruin; rich hangings, women's apparel, children's clothes, all scattered in utter confusion. The very few inhabitants I saw said nothing. They were fixed in stupid horror, and seemed to gaze with indifference at all around them, hardly moving when the crash of a fallen house made our men run away. The hospitals present a shocking sight: friends and enemies lying together, all equally neglected."

Napier says that "the place was won by accident"—the "accident" being the explosion of the powder-barrels and grenades along the high curtain. But that accident was due to Graham's happy use of the British artillery in the very crisis of the assault. Jones in his "Journal," says that "on inspecting the defences it was found that the tremendous enfilade fire on the high curtain, though it lasted only twenty minutes, had dismounted every gun but two. Many of these pieces had their muzzles shot away, and the artillerymen lay mutilated at their stations. The parapet was thickly strewed with headless bodies." But the terrible effects of that cannonade only suggest how gross was the blunder of not making this use of the batteries earlier. It belongs to the alphabet of the engineer's art that the fire which guards a breach should be mastered before the breach itself is assailed. A great siege, however, like a great battle, is usually a catalogue of blunders. In the story of San Sebastian these blunders are thrown into even blacker relief by the dazzling splendour of the courage shown by both men and officers in that great struggle on the bloodstained breach, and through the blackened streets of the city the French had defended with so much skill and courage.

SIR EDWARD CODRINGTON AT NAVARINO

October 20, 1827

"Navarino was as honest a victory as was ever gained by the arms of any power from the beginning of the world."—LORD JOHN RUSSELL (Speech in the House of Commons).

"Fast as the flaming beacon which conveyed the news of the fall of Troy to Argos, the joyous tidings were transmitted from mountain to mountain, from crag to crag, from isle to isle, and one throb of exultation and thankfulness was felt in every bosom. Never since the defeat of Hasdrubal by the Consul Nero, on the banks of the Metaurus, had such a sensation pervaded the heart of a nation. Every one felt as if he himself were delivered from captivity or death. . . . Christendom had come to the rescue; again, as in the days of the Crusades, the Cross had been triumphant over the Crescent."—ALISON'S "*History of Europe.*"

MEMORY has a very limited office in politics. The typical politician is essentially an opportunist, much exercised about to-day, but with no memory of yesterday, and not much thought of to-morrow. Yet it is curious how completely all the editors who have written, and all the orators who have discoursed about the recent struggle betwixt Greece and Turkey, forgot how exactly, as far as the Eastern question is concerned, 1897 was a reproduction of 1827. The Greek struggle for Crete which we have just watched is, in all its essential features, the drama of the Greek War of Independence acted over again, on the same stage, and by the same performers, and with the same passions and ambitions. There are differences, of course, in the two situations. The Turkey of 1897, considered as a fighting power, was immeasurably stronger than the Turkey of 1827. France, too, that to-day bears to Russia the relation that the tail bore to the dog in Lord Dundreary's famous apologue, was seventy years ago hostile to Russia by the whole trend of its policy. The differences betwixt the two periods, in a word, are almost as significant as their agreements. But the most tragical difference is that to-day we have no Navarino. English, French, and Russian admirals in the present struggle have been firing on the wrong side. We have Canea instead of Navarino!

The Greek revolt against Turkey broke out in 1821, and all righteousness was on its side. The land of Homer and of Plato, of Marathon and of Salamis, was the prey of Turkish pashas. The governing methods of the pashas are described with great plainness in a Greek manifesto of the period. "Any virgin that pleased them they took by force. Any merchant who was making money they beheaded, and seized his goods. Any proprietor of a good estate they slew, and occupied his property. And every drunken vagabond in the streets could murder respectable Greeks and was not punished for it." Armenia makes that statement credible. The Turk of 1897 is the replica of the Turk of 1827. But the national life of Greece was beginning to revive. The trade of the Greek islands brought prosperity; with prosperity came education, and education made slavery intolerable. When the Greeks revolted, their chances seemed as desperate as those of Holland against Spain under Philip II. A population of less than 2,000,000 plunged into battle against one of 30,000,000! The hopes of the Greeks rested at first on the Russian Emperor Alexander. Thrice already Russia had incited the Greeks to revolt; and the immemorial policy of Russia seemed a sufficient pledge of help to a movement which would rob Turkey of one of her provinces. But there was a revolutionary movement throughout Europe; in Spain, and Naples, and Piedmont, there were risings against despotic government. And much as the Czar hated Turkey, he hated popular movements still more. "I discerned in the troubles of the Peloponnesus," he said, "the revolutionary mark. From that moment I kept aloof from them." The Emperor William might have written that sentence to-day. The League of the Three Emperors in 1897, in a word, is but the reproduction, in another form, of the Holy Alliance which governed Europe in 1821.

Left to themselves, the Greeks fought with magnificent courage. Nothing can well be more striking, indeed, than the contrast betwixt the resisting power of Greece to-day, and that of seventy years ago. The struggle was a true Seven Years' War. On the part of the Greeks, it was a guerilla war, a war of sudden surprises, of wild onfalls and ambuscades; while on sea they fought and destroyed Turkish fleets with fire-ships. This style of warfare suited both Greek geography and Greek genius, and army after army, despatched by the exasperated Sultan, perished in the contest.

That the war was marked by terrific savagery goes without saying. The Turk, when his wrath, or his religious fanaticism, is aroused, is the most cruel of human beings; and the Sultan Mahmud, during the early stages of the struggle at least, made stupendous cruelty his deliberate policy. Thus on Easter Sunday in 1821, he hung the Greek patriarch in Constantinople on the lintel of his own gate, with three of his own bishops. A few weeks afterwards, no less than five archbishops and three bishops were hanged in the streets of Constantinople without trial. The tale of massacres in that war almost, if not quite, equals the Turkish performances in Armenia in our own times. Nobody quite knows how many were massacred in Smyrna in 1821; but the victims rose in numbers to tens of thousands. Cyprus was almost entirely depopulated by a similar massacre. In Scio, to quote Professor Ramsay, "30,000 people were massacred within two months; 32,000 were made slaves; 30,000 destitute refugees escaped to other lands." The story of Chios is almost more tragical still. "Every corner of the island was ransacked," says Alison; "every house burned or sacked, every human being that could be found slain or carried off into captivity. Modern Europe has never witnessed such an instance of bloodshed or horror. To find a parallel to it we must go back to the storming of Syracuse or Carthage by the Romans, or to the sack of Bagdad or Aleppo by Timour." It was calculated that 25,000 persons were slain, and 45,000 women and children dragged into slavery. A curious feature of that fierce struggle was the enormous number of Christians—mostly women and children—whom the Turks sold as slaves, usually in the Egyptian market. As a postscript to the Smyrna massacre, 10,000 women and children—all Christian—were publicly sold in the market-place of Salonica. After the capture of

Missolonghi, Ibrahim Pasha boasted that he had "collected 3000 heads, and sold 4000 women and children"!

The Greeks, it may be frankly admitted, sometimes rivalled the Turks themselves in cruelty. They had suffered 1400 years' bondage, Byzantine or Mohammedan, and they had the vices of slaves. Massacre, too, was answered by massacre—deep calling unto deep. At the beginning of 1821 there was a Mussulman population of more than 20,000 persons scattered through agricultural Greece, and, says Finlay, "before two months had elapsed the greater part was slain; men, women, and children were murdered without mercy or remorse"—and all by Greeks!

Europe could not watch a struggle at once so heroic, so tragic, and so prolonged, without being profoundly stirred. The pulse of generous sympathy beat strongest, perhaps, in British blood, and—again as in 1897—not a few English volunteers lent both their swords and their purses to the cause of Greek freedom. A curious degree of ill fortune, however, attended all attempts of private persons to assist Greece. Hastings, a gallant sailor, fit to have led fleets, lost his life in an inglorious sea-skirmish. Gordon was driven from the Greek service by sheer disgust. The Greeks hired the services of that immortal free-lance of the sea, Lord Cochrane, at a generous rate, paying him £50,000 to take command of their fleet; but even the genius and daring of Cochrane could achieve nothing in such a warfare. Sir Richard Church, too, was engaged to command the Greek land forces; but both Church and the Greeks misunderstood each other. The Greeks, to quote Finlay, expected

Church to prove a Wellington, with a military chest well supplied from the British treasury; Church expected the irregulars of Greece to execute his strategy like regiments of the Guards! The truth is, Greek politics were a chaos, and Greek patriots, though they could fight, could not obey. The National Assembly appointed Church "arch-general," and Cochrane "arch-admiral," giving these unfortunate officers extraordinary titles as a substitute for ordinary power.

Byron was the most famous ally the Greek cause won. After carrying "the pageant of his bleeding heart" across Europe, this "pilgrim of eternity"—to quote Matthew Arnold—took it to the assistance of Greece. Byron, in a sense, rendered the Greek cause no practical service. He was neither a politician nor a soldier. He hated war, while he regarded politics, according to one of his critics, as the art of cheating the people by concealing one-half of the truth and misrepresenting the other! Byron landed at Missolonghi on January 5, 1824, and died on April 19, thus giving only the last three months of his life to the cause of Greek independence. But his fame, and the pathos of his death, helped to quicken the generous sympathy of Europe on behalf of Greece. Byron, perhaps, served Greece better by dying so promptly than if he had lived longer and actually fought for her. The financiers of Europe rendered as little real help to Greece as its soldiers and sailors and poets. Thus, in 1824, the first Greek loan was floated. It was for £800,000 at 5 per cent., and each £100 stock brought £59. The Greeks, that is, received £280,000, and contracted a debt for £800,000! A loan of £2,000,000 was floated next year at only

£55, 10s. The money-lenders of Europe were greedy, and it is with not unmixed regret one remembers that they never received either principal or interest! The Greeks had no financial conscience. "They appear to have considered the loan," says one historian, "as a small payment for the debt due by civilised society to the country that produced Homer and Plato"!

Meanwhile, though the Greeks still continued to win victories, their cause grew desperate. One-third of the adult population had perished when the war had lasted only two years; at the end of six campaigns the complete extermination of the Greek people was an end visibly near. The country was in a state of anarchy. The fields were untilled. The regular troops had practically disbanded. The sailors of the islands were lapsing into piracy as a vocation. At the end of 1826 the Greek Treasury contained only sixteen piastres—about five shillings! Turkey, too, had found a formidable ally in Egypt, where Ibrahim Pasha had, like Lord Kitchener to-day, trained and hardened the fellaheen into soldiers of high quality. Pity for Greece grew acute throughout Europe, and the siege of Missolonghi crystallised it into action. The Greeks held that swamp-girdled village against Ibrahim Pasha as the British held the shallow ditches at Cawnpore against Nana Sahib. When food was exhausted, and their last charge of powder had been fired, the inhabitants—men, and women, and children—joined in one reckless, heroic, night assault on the Turkish line, and, for the most part, perished fighting. "The siege," says Finlay, a somewhat grudging critic, "rivals that of Platæa in the energy and constancy of the besieged; it wants only a historian like Thucydides to secure for it a like immortality of fame."

Europe at last intervened. The Emperor Alexander was dead, and his successor Nicholas hated Turkey even more than he hated "the revolution." Canning has the merit of shaping the policy which delivered Greece. He opened communication with the Greek leaders, and sent the Duke of Wellington to St. Petersburg, nominally to congratulate the Czar on his accession, really to consult on the affairs of Greece. On July 6, 1827, what is known as the Treaty of London was signed betwixt England, France, and Russia. The object of the treaty was declared to be "the reconciliation of the Greeks and Turks." An armistice was to be proposed, and, if necessary, enforced. Greece was to be self-governed under the suzerainty of the Sultan, to whom an annual tribute was to be paid. The Sultan, with a paroxysm of wrath, rejected the treaty, but for once the "Concert of Europe" meant business, and was prepared to deliver itself from the iron lips of cannon and the glittering points of bayonets.

A combined fleet under Sir Edward Codrington made its appearance in Greek waters. It consisted of three English line-of-battle ships and four frigates, four French line-of-battle ships and one frigate, and four Russian line-of-battle ships and four frigates. The combined Turkish and Egyptian fleets lay in the bay of Navarino —a great armament of sixty-five sail, with a weight of fire nearly double that of the allied fleet; and Codrington's business was to prevent that great fleet carrying on operations against Greece. In an interview with Ibrahim Pasha, Codrington warned him that any attempt to act in defiance of the treaty would bring on instant attack by the allied fleet. Ibrahim replied that he was a soldier, and must obey orders, and his orders were to carry on the war, and this he would do at all costs. Finally, however, he pledged his word of honour to observe the armistice till he received fresh instructions from Constantinople. He broke his word. The smoke of burning villages told of the ravages of his troops. His fleet twice attempted to leave the harbour, and only retired before the grim menace of Codrington's open portholes. To maintain a winter blockade outside Navarino, however, was impossible, and on October 19, Codrington determined to run in to the harbour and anchor his fleet, ship by ship, alongside the Turkish and Egyptian ships.

Never had a sailor a more difficult task than Codrington. He commanded a mixed fleet—he is the only British admiral, indeed, in history who had a French squadron and a Russian squadron in his line-of-battle. Only eleven years before, it must be remembered, Russian troops had occupied Paris; the retreat from Moscow was still a recent memory. And one of Codrington's anxieties was lest his French and Russian allies should turn their guns against each other! Scandal, indeed, has it that, in the battle which followed, the French ships actually fired into the Russian squadrons to "avenge Moscow"! It is certain that Codrington, in his plan of battle, anxiously interposed the English ships betwixt the Russians and the French, so as to lessen the risk of his allies turning their guns on each other. Navarino, too, was a battle fought without war being declared. Codrington, in a word, had to enforce peace by the argument of cannon-shot. He sailed into Navarino as into an ostensibly friendly port. He was cleared for action it is true, but his lower-deck ports were not hauled flat against the ship's sides, but kept square, as at sea in fine weather, as a visible symbol that he did not mean battle. And as the great column of line-of-battle ships—the *Asia*, Codrington's flag-ship, leading—glided into the harbour before a gentle breeze, nobody knew whether the batteries on either side would open on them or not.

Never, however, was a sailor better fitted for this difficult task than Codrington. He was not merely a gallant sailor of Nelson's school, a seaman of the utmost skill, familiar with ships and battles since he began his career as a middy of thirteen, more than forty years before Navarino. He was a gentleman to his fingertips, of crystalline simplicity, and integrity of character; and, to a degree rare even amongst British soldiers or sailors, he combined the faculty for swift decision with the quality of unshakable composure.

Codrington underwent his "baptism of fire" in Howe's great victory of June 1. He was lieutenant on the *Queen Charlotte*, Howe's flag-ship, and had charge of seven guns on the lower deck. The *Queen Charlotte*, it will be remembered, broke the French line by suddenly tacking and passing betwixt the stern of the French flag-ship and the next ship following. He commanded the *Orion*, the fourth ship in Collingwood's column at Trafalgar, and was, perhaps, the coolest and hardest fighter of all Nelson's captains. In that battle of giants he strictly ordered his men to reserve their fire till he could put the ship in the position he desired.

The ships not merely before him, but behind him, were girdled with the thunder of broadsides; but the *Orion* kept grimly silent. Codrington, indeed, had to hail a British ship near him not to fire into the *Orion!* "Passing down as the *Orion* did," he wrote afterwards, "through the whole group of those ships whose fortune it was to be placed foremost in the attack, and who then were all engaged with their various opponents, without firing a single gun to impede my view, although the ship next astern, as well as all those ahead of us, were firing broadside after broadside, I had an opportunity of seeing more of what was doing than perhaps any other captain in the whole fleet. I suppose no man ever before saw such a sight as I did, or, rather, as we did; for I called all my lieutenants up to see it. So grand, so awful, so tremendous was the scene before me that the impression will ever be fresh in my mind." The coolness which made Codrington reserve his fire so long in such a scene, was linked to a skill which made his fire, when he did deliver it, effective in the highest degree. He chose as his antagonist the *Swiftsure*, a ship bigger than his own, rounded under her stern, and poured in one blast of darting flame and tempest of flying shot, a broadside so overwhelming that it carried away the three masts of the Frenchman, and made the unfortunate ship strike without waiting for a second discharge! A sailor of this quality was, plainly, admirably qualified for leading the allied fleet into the bay of Navarino.

The Turkish and Egyptian fleets had spent some three days, under the direction of a French naval officer of great skill in the Turkish service, in preparing for Codrington's approach. The fleet formed, in brief, a huge crescent, the lighter ships filling up the gaps in the first line occupied by the heavier ships. A cluster of fire-ships formed either tip of the crescent. Navarino is only a tiny bay, about three miles long by two broad, and as the tips of the crescent almost touched the batteries on either headland of the entrance, the allied

BATTLE OF NAVARINO.

fleet, entering the harbour in a long and straggling column, would be met by the converging fire of the 2000 and odd guns of the Turkish and Egyptian fleets, to say nothing of the headland batteries. Ibrahim Pasha, however, allowed Codrington to enter without firing a shot. He calculated that the allied fleet would anchor betwixt the horns, so to speak, of the crescent;

then, when night fell, the fire-ships from either tip of the crescent would be launched on the allied fleet, the whole crescent would break into a tremendous converging fire, and the allied fleet, he did not doubt, would be destroyed.

This ingenious plan was spoiled by Codrington's adroitness. With a quick, sure glance he read Ibrahim's purpose directly he saw the crescent-shaped formation of his fleet. The *Asia* was a noble example of the wooden three-decker now extinct, a stately ship of about 3500 tons burden, quick and weatherly, and making, with her triple pyramids of sails, a singularly noble and stately spectacle, as about three o'clock on the afternoon of October 20, 1827, she came through the headlands of the bay of Navarino; and, ship after ship following in perfect order, moved across the crescent we have described, straight for a huge 84-gun ship flying the flag of the Turkish admiral. Next to it was the Egyptian flag-ship under Moharrem Bey. Nothing could be more impressive than the silent, menacing fashion in which the British flag-ship came on, passed close to the ship of Moharrem Bey, where the men were all at quarters, clewed up her topsails, rounded to, and dropped anchor with the most beautiful accuracy alongside the Turkish flagship. Ship after ship of the allied fleet came up in succession and anchored alongside an enemy's vessel, the French squadron taking the south-east curve of the crescent, the Russian the opposite curve. The corvettes and brigs of the fleet under Captain Fellows, of the *Dartmouth*, were detailed to "attend" to the enemy's fire-ships. Codrington had given the strictest orders that not a gun was to be fired without his orders; but if any ship fired on the allied fleet she was to be instantly destroyed.

It may easily be imagined that the Turkish captains watched the cool, steady, silent approach of Codrington's ships with very mingled feelings. Their men were at quarters; the guns were run out, loaded to the muzzles with shot, broken bars, rusty iron, &c. But whether a battle was to take place, or when, or at what signal, nobody exactly knew. But the signal for battle quickly came. The *Dartmouth* sent a boat—or boats—to the fire-ships requesting they would "move a little farther off." One of the fire-ships discharged a musketry volley into one of the *Dartmouth's* boats, killing the lieutenant in charge with part of the crew; the *Dartmouth* instantly fired on the fire-ship; the *Sirène*, the French flag-ship near by, also fired, but used only muskets. Then one of the Egyptian ships discharged a round shot at the *Sirène*; and, with a deep, intermittent, broken roar that ran—sometimes pausing but then leaping forward again—round the whole crescent of the Turkish and Egyptian fleet, the battle began.

For four hours the tumult of it never ceased. High above the eddying thunder of the combat broke, in quick-following blasts of sound, deep, distinct, and lion-like, the roar of the *Asia's* broadsides. For three-quarters of an hour Codrington poured a tempest of fire on the Turkish flagship; at the same time no less than five ships were pouring their fire into the *Asia*, two of them delivering a raking fire across her stern. In three-quarters of an hour, however, the Turkish flagship was a wreck, had cut its cables, and was drifting mastless out of the line of battle, having lost 650 men out of a crew of 850! The Egyptian flagship at first did not fire; Moharrem Bey, indeed, sent a boat to say he did not intend to fire. But on Codrington's sending a boat in return with the assurance that he would not, in that case, fire on Moharrem Bey, the boat was fired into, the officer in charge killed, and the Egyptian flag-ship opened its guns on the *Asia*. Codrington instantly broke into fire, by way of reply, and so swift and destructive were his broadsides that in ten minutes Moharrem Bey's ship was a wreck! The coolness and deadly precision of the *Asia's* fire satisfied even Codrington's fastidious taste. His son, who was a middy on board, wrote to his brother, "How astonished I was at the coolness and intrepidity shown by all the men during the action! For my part, I was hopping about here and there and everywhere, hurrying them on, for I had not that cool way at all; but devil a bit would they hurry, and they went on in a way that actually made me stare. My father says that he never saw any ship's fire equal to ours from our main and lower decks in precision and steadiness."

Evening fell on the sea. The crescent of Turkish and Egyptian ships was a jagged curve of blackened or flaming wrecks. The Turks, too, as each ship in turn was overcome, abandoned it, first setting it on fire. Ship after ship in this way broke into flames, and ended its existence with the blast of an explosion. "We have had," wrote Codrington himself the next day, "some thirty-seven beautiful explosions! All through the night the hills round Navarino shone with the light of burning ships, or shook to the blast of their explosions. The white fires of the stars in the Eastern night-sky above grew faint in the red glow of so many conflagrations. When morning dawned the Turkish fleet had vanished, or floated as mere blackened fragments on the surface of the bay. A tiny cluster of transports, a few brigs and schooners, alone survived. More than sixty ships had been destroyed, with a loss to the vanquished of more than 7000 lives.

Nothing could surpass the skill and courage shown by the allied fleet. English and French and Russian vied with each other in daring and energy. A great fight has always its humours, and the amusing element in the great drama of Navarino is supplied by the *Hind*, a little cutter of 150 tons, which served as tender to the *Asia*. She had been despatched on some errand a day or two before, and came in sight of the allied fleet just as the leading ship had disappeared within the headland of Navarino. Its commander, a quite youthful lieutenant, felt bound to "support" his admiral, and he did so by running down to the battle-line, and placing his tiny craft on the inshore side—the exposed side, that is—of the flagship! In this position the tiny Hind was struck with no less than twenty-three round shot, half its crew were killed, its two midshipmen each lost a leg, and on one occasion the very surgeon had to leave his patients and join in the business of repelling boarders. The *Hind* afterwards was known through the fleet as "His Majesty's line-of-battle cutter"!

Of Codrington's own cool courage it is almost unnecessary to speak. Almost every one about him was shot down, and at one time he stood the only uninjured man on his own quarter-deck. His hat was shot through, his watch was crushed by a bullet, his coat was pierced. Tahir Pasha, the Turkish vice-admiral, told afterwards how, as he watched Codrington—"tall as a mast," to use his own words—on the quarter-deck of the *Asia*, he drew up a company of riflemen and told them the only hope of victory lay in shooting that tall Englishman, and the riflemen fired repeated volleys at him, but somehow failed to hit him. It will give some idea of the tumult and distraction of a great fight to read Codrington's description of the noise, of the smoke which was so thick that the men could not see the ships at which they were firing, &c.; and how, at last, when the Turkish flagship had vanished, "in my anxiety to ascertain that we were not firing into each other, I tried to make the general signal to cease firing; but as fast as the flags could be attempted to be shown, either the men hoisting them were killed, or the means by which the signals were to be displayed were shot away. I then tried to despatch a boat with this object, when it was found that we had no boat that would swim; an attempt by hailing to get one from the *Genoa* was equally unsuccessful, and I was obliged to give up the attempt, and leave things to take their course."

Navarino was the first and last battle in which the *Asia* took part. For forty years she has been lying in Portsmouth Harbour as a reserve guardship. Imagination is not a strong feature of the British character, or a ship which has played a part in history so great and noble would not be dismissed to forgetfulness, or allowed to go to decay with such amazing indifference. England might easily place in the chief port of each of her colonies some ship like the *Asia*, or the *Victory*, which might be a perpetual object-lesson in national pride.

Certainly the *Asia* made a great contribution to the world's history. The fight in Navarino Bay on 20th October 1827, won freedom for Greece, and added a new Christian State to Europe. The exploding Turkish wrecks in that Syrian bay all through that wild night were the symbols of a perishing despotism. On the night of Navarino, to quote Alison, " Hellas rose from the grave of nations, scorched by fire, riddled by shot, baptized in blood." Yet was it a true resurrection? All this surely is a tale to be remembered to-day, when Greece and Turkey have met in battle once more, with ill-fortune to Greece, and no Navarino, alas! to save her.

THE HON. SIR GEORGE CATHCART, G.C.B.

From an authentic portrait, painted in 1852, by CAPTAIN GOODRICH, *of the Cape Mounted Rifles*

INKERMANN

November 5, 1854

> "Scarce could they hear or see their foes,
>   Until at weapon point they close—
> They close in clouds of smoke and dust,
> With sword-sway and with lance's thrust;
>   And such a yell was there
> Of sudden and portentous birth,
> As if men fought upon the earth
>   And fiends in upper air."
>
> —Scott.

INKERMANN is emphatically "a soldier's battle." The bayonet of the private counted for everything in it, the brains of the general for almost nothing. It is simply one of the most distracted, planless, muddle-headed, yet magnificent battles in British history; and as an illustration of the chivalrous daring of the British officer, and the dogged, unconquerable fighting quality of the British private, Inkermann has scarcely a rival in the long roll of famous battles. There are some scenes in the military history of our race the recollection of which always stirs the blood—the steadfast, long-enduring patience of the infantry squares at Waterloo; the stern valour of the Fusiliers at Albuera; the wild daring of the stormers of Badajoz. But none of these surpasses, as an example of the fighting quality of the British soldier, the strife that, for nine hours on that November Sunday in 1854, raged amidst fog and rain on the rugged slopes of Inkermann. It was on the British side, at least, in the truest sense of the word, an Homeric fight—a long succession of single combats; of desperate charges undertaken by tiny clusters of men, with leaders evolved by mere supremacy of fighting power at the moment. Generalship was non-existent; tactics were forgotten; regiments were broken up into unrelated fragments, and fought like Hal o' the Wynd for their own hand.

The general physiognomy of the battle may be described in a dozen sentences. The scene of the fight was a long and narrow spine, rising from steep and wooded ravines. Some 40,000 grey-coated Russians, with more than 100 guns, were being thrust into the flank of the British camp. They formed a river of dingy-grey overcoats, closely-cropped bullet heads, broad, high-boned, pasty-looking faces. Across the ridge was drawn a knotted, irregular line of British soldiery—for the first three hours of the fight not exceeding 3000 in number—men of all regiments, mixed together, many of them pickets who had been on duty for twenty-four hours, and without food for twelve. The ground was heavy with rain, thick with scrub, broken with rocks, a mist lay heavy on it, and the red flash of the guns had the strangest effect as it flamed and vanished through the eddying masses of vapour. The steadfast red wall, edged with fire, and fretted with the gleaming bayonets, which we expect in a British line of battle, had no existence here. But that knotted, irregular, and swaying line of British soldiery which kept back the huge Russian masses was

unpierceable. To quote Hamley, it was made up of
"scanty numbers, but impenetrable ranks." "Colonels
of regiments," he adds, "led on small parties and fought
like subalterns, captains like privates. Every man was
his own general." Nobody could see many yards from
the point where he stood and fought or died. When
at any given point the huge grey mass of the Russians
swayed upwards, a cluster of British — sometimes a
single officer leading, sometimes a sergeant, a corporal,
or a private soldier of exceptional daring — would run
forward fiercely with bayonets at the charge; and
always the few thrust back the many. About the
combatants eddied the thick, white fog. Above them
rolled incessantly the sullen thunder of the Russian
guns, and over the crest to which the swaying line of
the British clung so stubbornly rushed incessantly the
tempest of Russian shot.

No one can adequately tell the story of Inkermann.
If translated into the language of tactics, it is the
coldest and shortest of tales. If written as a pure
chapter of adventure, it overwhelms both writer and
reader by its wealth of detail. Kinglake devotes an
entire volume to Inkermann; and, in patches, his story
is of amazing brilliancy. It is, in fact, a sort of dithy-
rambic hymn of praise in honour of the British private.
But no one will form any clear mental picture of the
great fight from Kinglake. His landscape is too wide
and crowded. You cannot see the forest for the trees!

Inkermann represents on the part of the Russians
an effort of daring generalship. The allied forces, numbering 65,000 men — not including Turkish auxiliaries
— were besieging a great stronghold, fortified by the

genius of Todleben, and defended by forces numbering 120,000 men. The allies, moreover, were spread along an exterior line of twenty miles; the Russians held interior lines only four miles long. The Russians had already attacked Balaclava at one extremity of the allied position; Inkermann was a daring, well-planned, and powerful effort to pierce the other extremity of that position.

The scene of the fight, surveyed from the British camp, is a tiny and steep plateau, shaped like the butt-end of a musket or the letter L turned the wrong way. The post-road from Sebastopol bisects the cross-ridge, which runs east and west, and at its rear was the camp of the Second Division. The crest lent itself perfectly to defensive uses. On the east it fell by a steep ravine to the Tchernaya; on the north, the "fore ridge," as the upright part of the letter L was called, sank into the Quarry Ravine; to the west the gloomy depths of the Careenage Ravine protected the crest. A few entrenchments and a dozen guns in position would have made the hill impregnable. But not a battery had been erected, not a trench dug, not a square yard of scrub cleared! Such was British generalship! On the tip of the Fore Ridge, or half-way down its slope, stood what was called the Sandbag Battery. It was without guns, and so badly constructed that the soldiers who undertook to hold it against the enemy found themselves in a death-trap. The parapet from the inside was so high that they could not see over it or shoot over it. Sandbag Battery had no relation to the defence of the ridge, and it is an illustration of the distracted quality of the battle that round this useless

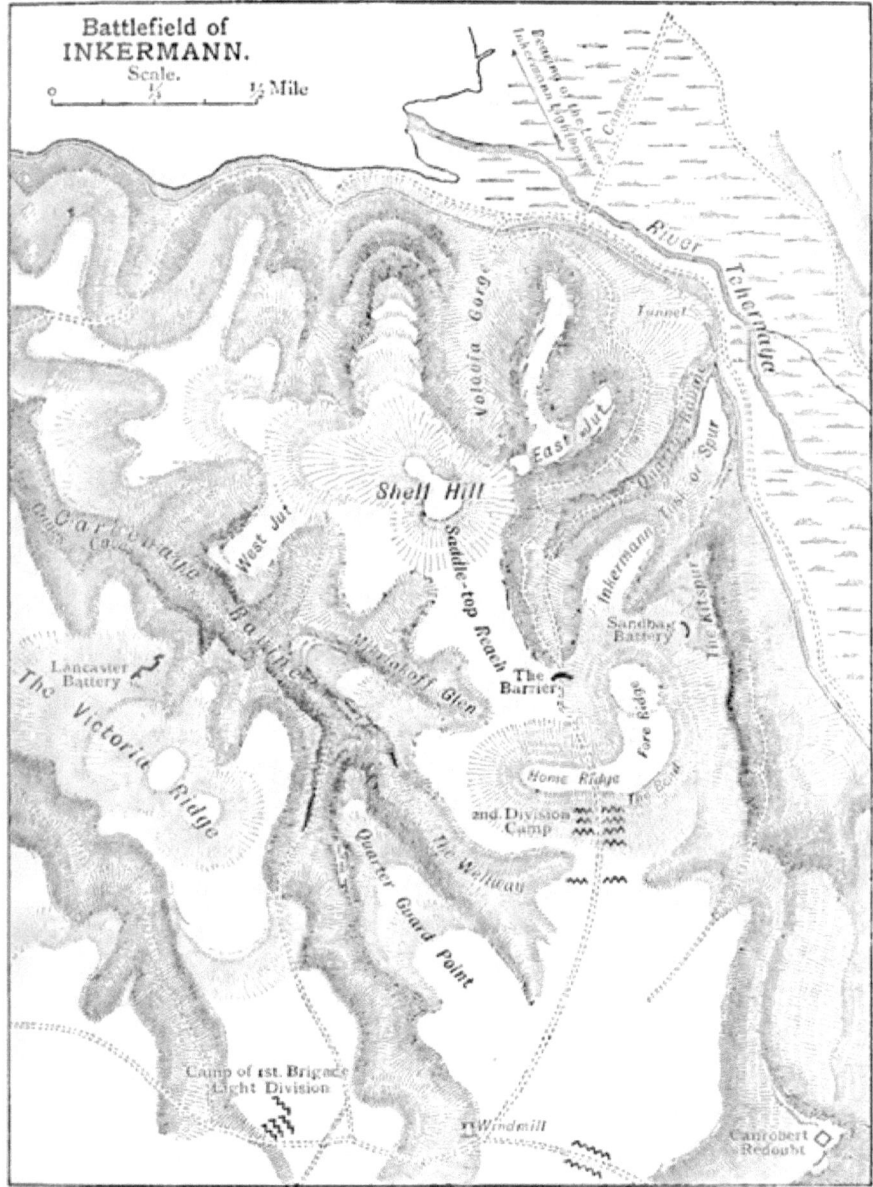

point the most desperate fighting of the day took place. Guards and Russians fought round it muzzle to muzzle and breast to breast till the dead lay on the blood-wet ground literally in strata. More than 1100 dead bodies were counted after the fight round the Sandbag Battery. It was as though two football teams in a great match forgot football, umpire, and goals, and fought to the point of exhaustion over a bit of orange-peel!

The Russian plan was that a column of 19,000 men and 38 guns, under General Soimonoff, should advance before daybreak, seize Shell Hill—a summit to north of the crest of Inkermann, and commanding it—plant its guns there, and crush the scanty British regiments holding the crest with its fire. Another force of 19,000 men and 96 guns, under General Pauloff, was to cross the harbour head, climb up the Quarry Ravine, join hands with Soimonoff, and together break through the British defence. Prince Gortschakoff, with another force of 20,000 men and 88 guns moving from Balaclava, was to add himself to the attack, or, at all events, detain the French by feints from moving to the British help. As a further distraction a powerful sally was to be made on the French siege-works from Sebastopol itself. The British force holding Inkermann was only 3000 strong; the Russians calculated that they would brush this force aside, roll up the British lines to the south, and 60,000 victorious Russian soldiers would compel the allied forces to abandon the siege, or even themselves surrender. It was able strategy; and, in its earlier stages, ably carried out.

Soimonoff moved from the city in the blackness of

the winter morning, while the stars yet shone keenly in the sky. His gun-wheels were muffled, the sternest silence was enforced in the ranks, and, without alarming a British outpost, he climbed the West Sappers' Road, as it was called, and moved on towards Shell Hill. It was a great feat to move 20,000 infantry with guns and tumbrils through the darkness to within 1300 yards of the British position undetected. But the silent grey line of Russian battle stole on, and no murmur of human voices, no sharp clang of steel, no rumble of tumbril or gun, broke through the fog and the darkness to the listening—or, perhaps, the dozing—British sentries. At last a sentry of the 41st, on the northern slope of Shell Hill, saw the dim outlines of a huge gliding column mounting from the ravine. He called his officer, who, satisfied as to the character of the approaching body, opened fire upon it with his tiny picket, and clung to his position with almost ludicrous obstinacy—a handful opposing an army. The sound of their muskets rang loudly across the ravines, and the British sprang everywhere to arms. But Soimonoff's men pushed forward, his guns swung round from the crest of Shell Hill, and opened their tempest of shot on the very tents of the Second Division, and many men and officers, running out at the sound, were slain before they knew that the enemy was within striking distance.

The Russian generals had thus carried out part of their scheme. Almost without discovery, and with no other resistance than a few shots from an obstinate picket, they had made themselves masters of three-fourths of Inkermann, and were pouring an overwhelming fire into the very tents of the British camp. Pauloff's men, too, were by this time moving up the Quarry Ravine from the east. It was possible now to throw some 40,000 men, with over 100 guns, upon the 3000 British soldiers who formed the Second Division. The Guards, 1300 strong, were half a mile to the south; a brigade of the Light Division, 1400 strong, was a mile and a half distant to the west!

Now the character of the resistance offered by the British was determined partly by accident, and partly by, not so much the military skill as the fighting temper of the British general, Pennefather, who temporarily commanded the Second Division. De Lacy Evans, its general, a war-wise and experienced soldier, had his own plan for the defence of the crest. He would have allowed his pickets to fall back, and the Russian columns to climb the ridge and come along the narrow front of 800 yards, covered by the fire of his field batteries. Thus he would concentrate his own forces, cover them with the fire of his field batteries, and with a minimum of loss he calculated he could crush the Russian attack. But De Lacy Evans was lying ill on board a ship in Balaclava Harbour, and Pennefather was left to take counsel of nothing but the effervescing and warlike blood in his own veins. He was a type of soldier familiar enough, and valued enough, in the British army: an Irishman, who borrowed his tactics from Donnybrook; of obstinate and combative temper, loud of speech, cheerful of face, an ideal leader for a forlorn hope. Pennefather's expletives were the jest of the camp. Years afterwards he was appointed to the command at Aldershot, and the Queen on chancing to ask, "Has the new general taken up his command yet?" was told, with a touch of sly humour, which mocked the royal ear, "Yes, your Majesty, he swore himself in yesterday"!

Now Pennefather's senses were stirred, and his fighting temper delighted, by the obstinacy with which his pickets on the lower slopes of the ravines held their ground against the Russian advance. Kinglake says he was "enchanted" with the tenacity of their resistance. The sound of the exploding muskets coming up through the fog drew him on as with a magic spell. He would "feed" his pickets—he would make the Russian fight for every foot of ground he gained; so he commenced to push forward in succession, company after company, wing after wing. The mist, the brushwood, the huge rocks which pierced the sloping hillside, broke these up into yet tinier fragments under independent leaders.

The men and officers, it must be admitted, enjoyed this method of fighting. It gave play to personal courage and to individual qualities of leadership. The starch of discipline melted in the heat of such a struggle; the natural fighting man emerged. But in this piecemeal fashion nearly Pennefather's whole command was by-and-by fighting in fragments at the outposts, and beyond the control of any single commanding brain or will. And the fortunes of these clusters of unrelated fighting men, all in the highest mood of battle, were sometimes very extraordinary.

Soimonoff was so tormented by the fire of the obstinate British pickets that he determined to move without waiting for the arrival of Pauloff's forces, and a mass of 9000 men moved down the slope of Shell Hill and across the valley towards the centre and left flank of the British position. The extreme left was held by a wing of the 49th, under Major Grant, and through the mist the British could hear the multitudinous hum of thousands of voices, the massive and regulated tread of thousands of feet, as the enemy came on. The moving acres of flat-capped Russian heads now became visible, and Grant's four companies—245 men facing 9000—fell slowly back, firing as they went fiercely. At the same moment 6000 men of Pauloff's command came into action on the English right. Some of their battalions, spreading out to their own right, stumbled across the Sandbag Battery, held at that moment by six men under a sergeant, and with a rush seized it. Here were 15,000 men attacking the British front at either extremity, while the great batteries from Shell Hill thundered on its centre.

Some five companies of the Connaught Rangers, with Townsend's battery of six guns, had by this time found their way up from the Light Division, and stumbled full upon the advancing Russian battalions on the left. The British gunners delivered one hasty shot when the Russians were within ten yards of the guns, and were then submerged. Miller, in command of the battery, bade his gunners draw swords and charge, and himself rode straight into the Russian ranks, while the artillerymen, in a tempest of rage, fought with swords and rammers, and even with naked fists, for their guns. It was an heroic, but vain struggle. Three of the guns were captured, and the Russian column moved steadily on.

They were next struck by four companies of the 77th, under Colonel Egerton. This particular Russian column, indeed, winding like some gigantic and many-jointed reptile up the Careenage ravine, had passed the point occupied by the 77th; its head was debouching on the plateau. A lieutenant named Clifford stood at the extreme left of the 77th: he shouted to the men nearest him, "Come on, boys, and charge with me!" and flung himself upon the flank of the great Russian column. Scarcely more than fifty men heard his cry or grasped his meaning, but these instantly followed, and this gallant rush actually broke through, and, so to speak, fractured the spine of the long Russian column. The files at its head, actually within sight of the tents of the Second Division, hearing the tumult of the fight behind them, believed themselves cut off, and came tumbling back in panic. A picket of Grenadier Guards, on a post on the shoulder of the hill overlooking the Careenage Ravine, had by this time discovered the huge gliding column of the enemy beneath, and opened fire upon it, with the effect that the column halted, seemed to sway to and fro, and then fell back. The fire of a picket, and the sudden dash upon its flank of less than fifty men, that is, actually thrust back Soimonoff's whole right column at the very moment when it seemed at the point of success!

Soimonoff himself, however, was personally leading his second, or left, column—nearly 8000 strong—up the slopes of Saddletop Ridge on the British front, Grant's four companies doggedly trying to bridle its advance. Colonel Egerton, with his four companies of the 77th still advancing, found himself on the flank of the great mass, and, without pause, he fired a volley and charged. The great Russian mass, as Kinglake describes the scene, heard the British words of command, saw the long line of British muskets fall suddenly to the level and break into flame, then the bristling edge of bayonets moved swiftly towards them. They saw here and there, moving in dimness, the shadowy form of a rider, the naked gleam of a sword, and to the Russian imagination the two or three company officers who happened to be mounted, became the leaders of a cavalry charge, terrible as that which, only ten days before, had ridden up the Valley of Death! The long stretch of grey-coated battalions seemed to quiver and shrink, and before the line of moving steel points smote it, it broke, and the men of the 77th tumbled through the disordered mass, and pushed it, with shouts, and oaths, and shocks of angry steel, down the hillside. Many Russians flung themselves down on the ground till the slender British line swept over them, then they rose and followed their retreating comrades, and these grew so numerous that the 77th, an irregular line not 300 strong, had a mass of "resurrection boys"—as, with grim humour, they were called—behind them treble themselves in number. The British, however, treated them with grim good-humour, as beaten men, and allowed them to run past their flank without harm and join the main body. General Soimonoff himself perished in that fierce charge of the 77th.

Farther east, part of General Pauloff's force, 6000 strong, was advancing, and two Borodino battalions, in particular, were moving along the post-road, crossed, half-way down the ravine, by a rough stone wall called "The Barrier." This point of the British line was held by 200 men of the 30th, under Colonel Mauleverer. The 30th tried to open fire on the Russian advance, but their pieces were damp, and the exasperated men found themselves practically without the power to fire a shot. Mauleverer, a cool and daring soldier, took his men forward at the double to "The Barrier," and made them lie down behind it. He waited till the multitudinous tread of the Russians showed they were within a yard or two of the other side of the Barrier, then, with a shout, he himself and a couple of officers sprang upon the summit of the wall, and leaped down almost upon the Russian bayonets. How the 30th followed their officers may be imagined! The astonished Russians beheld a sudden swarm of British tumbling over the wall and running upon them with levelled bayonets. The officers who leaped over the wall first were shot or stabbed, but the men of the 30th were by this time tearing their way through the yielding mass of the Russians, and here was seen the amazing spectacle of the slender line of the 30th, not 200 strong, driving a broken mass of Russians ten times their own number across the Quarry Ravine and up the slopes of Shell Hill! The 41st, under General Adams, by a like brilliant charge, drove off the section of Russians holding the Sandbag Battery.

It was not yet half-past seven o'clock, and yet the first assault of the Russians had been defeated, and defeated too, with much slaughter. The Russians had attacked with 25,000 men and 38 guns, and of this number 15,000 had been thrust forward into actual and desperate conflict with the British, who, up to this stage, had less than 4,000 men in their fighting line.

But the individual courage displayed on the part of the British, the close and deadly quality of their fire, and the resolute daring with which clusters of men numbering a few score threw themselves, again and again, on massed battalions to be counted by the thousand, had given a tiny few the victory over the many.

Soimonoff's attack was delivered simultaneously on the British front and left; General Dannenberg, who now took the command, attacked almost at the same moment the British right, at the Sandbag Battery, and its centre, and the story of each attack makes a marvellous tale. The Russian general had 19,000 troops supported by 90 guns; Pennefather, to resist this force, had in hand scarcely 1400 men, with some 18 guns; but 1200 men of the Guards, and 2000 under Cathcart, from the Fourth Division, were rapidly coming up to the line of battle.

The Guards moved to the extreme British right; where Adams at the Sandbag Battery, with 700 men, principally of the 41st and 49th, was trying to bar the march of 10,000 fresh troops. The fighting at this point was desperate, and often hand to hand. In the tangle of the brushwood, and the bewilderment of the fog, it was impossible to keep regular formation, and the British line really consisted of irregular and swaying clusters of desperately fighting men. One instance tells the mood into which men were kindled. Four officers of the 41st—all of them young, one of them desperately wounded—challenged each other by name, ran in on their own account upon the Russian mass, and all died desperately fighting. Adams himself, who commanded at this part of the line, fell mortally wounded, and just at this stage the Grenadier Guards and the Scots Fusiliers, 700 strong, came into the fight, marching straight upon the huge Russian mass over 7000 strong in front of them.

When within a few yards of the enemy the Grenadiers flung forward their muskets and tried to fire, but only a snapping of caps followed. The rifles were damp, and from the long line of bearskins rolled up a curious growl of wrath. The bayonet remained, however, and the men went forward at a run, smashed in upon the Russian front, and flung it, broken and disordered, over the crest of the ravine, the Scots Fusiliers on the left of the Grenadiers performing a similar feat on the masses opposed to them. Again and again the Russian battalions, rallied by their officers, re-formed under the shelter of the ridge, and came over its crest, always to be hurled back again by the Guards, who, however, steadily dwindled in numbers, and whose cartridges had begun to fail. Some of the men, in default of better missiles, actually picked up the loose stones lying underneath their feet, and hurled them at the Russians. At this critical moment, through the smoke, another line of bearskins could be seen advancing—it was the Coldstreams, whose fire soon swelled the thunder and tumult of the fight.

The Russians ignite slowly, but by this time they were kindled to a flame of valour. They came on, repeatedly, with the utmost resolution, a cluster of officers with swords gleaming high in air leading them. One Russian officer, little more than a lad, clambered, with a single private at his side, to the summit of the

Sandbag Battery, and actually leaped down upon the British Guardsmen who held it!

But fierce as was the oft-repeated advance of the Russian battalions, the tough and knotted line of British soldiers never broke. The trouble was to keep the men, after they had flung the broken Russians over the crest, from following them down the ravine. The ardour of the attack and the pursuit threatened to carry them completely away. At last, indeed, the restraining power of the officers failed, and after one particularly stubborn assault, and specially fiery repulse, of a Russian column, a cluster of the Coldstreams, in one hot rush, went with the broken enemy down the slope. At that moment, Cathcart, with some 400 men of the 68th and 46th, came up. It was intended that he should fill the gap on the edge of the plateau betwixt the Sandbag Battery and the Barrier on the post-road; but Cathcart thought he saw the opportunity of following the pursuing Coldstreams down the slope, and striking the yet unbroken Russian battalions on the flank.

This was a fatal movement! It was a movement, for one thing, which carried with it nearly the whole line of Guardsmen. Cathcart's lads, as they ran out at the double, sent a pulse of flame along the whole British front. The men holding the Sandbag Battery poured out; at various points of the line officers and privates charged forward, and a score of desperate duels betwixt slowly retiring Russians and fiercely pursuing Englishmen were fought. Kinglake tells at length the story of thirteen Grenadiers, headed by Captain Burnaby, who ran upon the Russian mass, pierced it deep with desperate fighting, and sent it staggering backwards. One private named Pullen stopped coolly, almost within touch of the Russian line, swore he would "shoot nothing less than a general," adjusted the sight of his rifle, while men panted and stabbed and wrestled on all sides of him, and brought down the only mounted officer within sight! Another private named Bancroft was assailed first by two Russians, then by three simultaneously, and with bayonet, and fist, and boot, slew all five!

Bancroft's feat is described at length by Sir Evelyn Wood. As, following his officer, he leaped out of the Sandbag battery, a cluster of Russians charged at him. He killed one by a bayonet thrust in the chest, but at the same moment had a Russian bayonet thrust through his open jaw. He staggered back, and was again wounded by a second assailant. Bancroft kept his eye fixed on the man who had stabbed him in the face, and shot him dead; his third assailant he thrust through the body with his bayonet. Two Russians then charged him with levelled bayonets, and he fell wounded once more, but leaped up, drove his bayonet through one of the two attacking him, who fell, and, only slightly wounded, clutched the Englishman by the legs. Bancroft himself, bleeding from half-a-dozen wounds, and with a fallen Russian pulling at his legs, had to meet in an upstanding fight the one assailant remaining. Him he stabbed, and at the same time freed his feet from the fallen Russian by violently kicking him; a performance which, being observed by his sergeant, brought on Bancroft a loud rebuke for "kicking a man when he was down"!

The sight of these little fighting groups and their performances carried the Guardsmen out of all control; the Duke of Cambridge shouted himself voiceless trying to hold his line back. He kept in hand, perhaps, a hundred men immediately in his own neighbourhood, but the rest, in one furious, overmastering charge, sent the Russian battalions immediately before them tumbling down the ravine, and followed them with triumphant shouts, slaying as they ran. It was a magnificent but fatal charge! Another huge grey column of Russian infantry, separated from the torrent of pursuers and pursued by a shoulder of the hill, moved up, thrust itself through the gap which Cathcart should have filled, and formed on the crest the Guards had just abandoned.

The Duke of Cambridge, with the flags of the Guards, and 100 men formed a group on one side of this new body of the enemy; Cathcart's men, with the disordered Fusiliers and Grenadiers, were in broken fragments on the other. The panting Guardsmen below looked up, and through the eddying mist and smoke-charged air, saw the crest they had left barred by the solid and threatening masses of the enemy. Some of the broken Guardsmen worked round the flank both of the hill and of the enemy, and regained the British position, but the gallant line that went in a tumult of victory down the slope but a few minutes before had ceased to exist as a military force.

Cathcart's men were overtaken with fatal disaster. Scourged by the fire of the column above them they yet plunged into the column on their flank, a few of the 20th actually piercing their way across it. Cathcart himself, standing on the slope of the hill, within a few yards of the Russian column, gathered some fifty men of the 20th, and sent them back under Maitland to attack the force on the crest. It was fifty men climbing uphill to attack 700; but some, at least, of those gallant fifty actually tore their way through the Russian mass. Others died in its midst; yet others were flung back wounded and breathless down the slope. Cathcart then sent Maitland down the slope to try and bring up any scattered men he might find, but before Maitland could return Cathcart himself fell, shot dead.

Meanwhile, the Duke of Cambridge, with 100 Guardsmen and the colours, found himself with one powerful Russian battalion in his rear and two in his front, 2000 in all. He turned, and charged uphill on the force in his rear, and succeeded in forcing his way past its flank. The last regimental colour in the tumult was at one time surrounded by not more than a dozen Guardsmen; but some one shouted "Carry the colours high!" and, borne still more proudly aloft through the battle-smoke and the hail of bullets, the gallant group brought their colours safely through.

Some score of the broken 20th drew together on the slope, the regimental surgeon being one. Nature meant the doctor for a soldier; he was carrying, at the moment, not a lancet, but a firelock. "Fix bayonets," he shouted to the men, "and keep up the hill." And the daring group actually ran upon the massed battalion of their foes, and rent their way through it! The Russian battalions, however, pressed hard upon the broken Guardsmen. The men were mad, partly with battle fury, and partly with fanatical religious passion, and as the mass came on, Kinglake says, there could be heard above the tumult of the fight the multitudinous strains of a hymn roaring up from its depths! Burnaby thought if the colours were to be saved this formidable mass must be checked. He gathered round him some score of men—Guardsmen and men of the line—and asked them "if they would follow him." "I thought it perfectly useless," said one of the brave little group afterwards, "a few of us trying to resist such a tremendous lot. But for all that I did so." The twenty men, in fact, ran in upon the advancing mass of Russians, and kindled a fight in its ranks which actually drew the whole battalion to a pause, though only seven of the twenty survived. The sight of a French battalion, visible through the smoke, yet further served to stay the Russian movement. After a sort of bewildered pause, the battalion, with the stormy chorus of its hymn suddenly fallen dumb, fell back; but round the colours of the Guards stood only 150 men, gathered from all quarters, and from various regiments, smoke-begrimed, breathless, many of them wounded.

The last to join was a little cluster of the No. 1 Company of the Fusilier Guards, under Ensign Lindsay, afterwards known as Lord Wantage, V.C. This company had been on picket all night, and was relieved at 5.30 A.M. When the firing broke out on the outpost line, Lindsay led his men at the double towards the sound of the firing, took part in the confused fighting at the outposts, held his place in the knotted line by the Sandbag Battery, and shared in the fatal rush on the broken Russians down the hill. When they found themselves cut off by the Russians on the crest, Lindsay consulted for a moment with his colour-sergeant, then led his men at the run, with levelled bayonets, on to the Russian line. Lindsay himself ran at the Russian officer, who stood in front of his own men, ran him through the throat, plunged into the mass behind, and broke through, living to report, as an interesting detail, that the close-packed Russian ranks exuded a peculiar odour, pungent, leather-like, and overpowering! His colour-sergeant following Lindsay bravely, was killed, but most of his men broke through.

A strong Russian column had meanwhile climbed from the Quarry Ravine, and attacked the British centre. Colonel Mauleverer, with 200 men of the 30th, held the post here, and this resolute handful of men, by steady firing till their ammunition was expended, and incessant bayonet charges till the men were worn out, kept back the ever-repeated waves of Russian infantry climbing the narrow ridge. When at last the men fell back to the crest, and had a short breathing-space, they dropped, with smoke-blackened faces, and muskets hot from firing, on the ground, and, while their officers watched, and the clamour of the battlefield thundered above them, the men actually slept! Presently the stern call, "Up, 30th," told them the enemy was coming on again, when the men instantly started up, fell swiftly into line, and resolutely charged the advancing Russians.

Pennefather himself held the centre, and Kinglake's picture of the temper in which he carried on the fight is unconsciously amusing. He rode to and fro, noisy, wrathful, exultant, enraptured with the tumult and passion of the fight. The soldiers would see, moving through the fog and smoke, a horseman with vehement gestures, and, as some favourite and well-known oath roared cheerily through the smoke, they knew it was "old Pennefather," and with a grim laugh gave themselves anew to the fight. Of leadership, in any other sense than an example of cool, quenchless, and dogged courage, there was none. Steevens, in his "Crimean Campaign," says that the four companies of the Connaught Rangers, who played a gallant part in the fight, caught a glimpse of General Pennefather once when going into the fray, but no other general officer or staff-officer came near them till long after the battle was over.

Steevens adds that Colonel Shirley, who, from the British trenches, was watching the fight, and could see the Russian reserves, apparently some 10,000 strong, on a hill about two miles distant, was approached about this time by some forty sailors, armed with ships' cutlasses only, who requested that he would lead them to attack that huge mass of Russians! These forty tars belonged to the Naval Brigade, and, as the fight was going on, they wanted to join in, and were ready to take in hand as their share the entire Russian reserves!

Just at this time yet another Russian column climbed from the gloomy depth of Quarry Ravine, swung slightly to the left, so as to avoid the stubborn resistance offered by the 30th, and moved up betwixt the post-road and the Sandbag battery. It was met by a wing of the 20th, counting 180 men, under Colonel Horn. The 20th instantly advanced, firing. The Russian line immediately in front of them seemed to crumble under their fierce volleys, but the flanks were obstinate, and the mass seemed to thrust out huge lateral claws, so to speak, along the flanks of the 20th, so that they found themselves in a concave of fire. At that moment their own ammunition gave out! Nothing throughout this Homeric fight, however, is more wonderful than the eager promptitude with which the British—no matter with what inferiority of numbers—would fling them in a bayonet charge on the foe. The 20th cherish a particularly hideous yell, known as the "Minden yell" —it having been, apparently, evolved originally in that bloody fight. Somebody in the ranks of the 20th raised the "Minden yell"; it ran a wave of ear-splitting sound down the front of the regiment, and the men instantly leaped forward with the bayonet, cleft the mass before them in twain, and drove it, confused and broken, down the hillside!

The right battalion of the Russian column, however, still stood, massive and undestroyed, higher up on the shoulder of the ridge, and against this moved a wing of the 57th, 200 strong, who had just come into the fight, led by their captain, Stanley. The 57th was one of the famous "fighting regiments" of the Peninsular War; it won the name of "the Die-hards" at Albuera; and Stanley turned the warlike traditions of the regiment to useful purpose. Just as the bayonets fell to the charging level, he shouted, "Men! remember Albuera!" Stanley himself fell mortally wounded, but the impulse of his shout sent the line of the 57th forward in a charge which finally cleared the whole of what was called the Home Ridge. Where else in the history of battles can we find such amazing examples of the overthrow of the many by the few?

The truth is, however, that the extraordinary state of the atmosphere in which Inkermann was fought— the clinging, smoke-thickened fog which hung about the combatants—told, on the whole, in favour of the British. The Russians could not see how slender was the line of gleaming bayonets charging on them, and they resisted less stubbornly on that account. On the other hand, the British could not see the real scale and depth of the mighty battalions upon which they flung themselves, and so they charged with a degree of confident daring which otherwise would have been impossible.

It was now half-past eight, the fight had raged for nearly three hours, and during that period a force of British infantry, numbering a little over 4000, had resisted the assaults of 40,000 Russians, aided by the fire of nearly 100 guns! It was a marvellous feat! But the battle was not yet over. The Russian general had still 17,000 untouched troops, sustained by the fire of 100 guns, which he could throw into the fight, and he had only to show himself in possession of the English crest to bring Prince Gortchakoff's 20,000 men into the fight. The resisting power of the British, too, was steadily shrinking. Many of the men were utterly exhausted; they had been on duty for the previous twenty-four hours. The number of killed and wounded, too, was dreadful. "All the field," says Hamley, "was strewn with the dead and wounded. But the space in front of the two-gun battery, where the Guards fought, bore terrible pre-eminence in slaughter. The sides of the hill up to and around the battery were literally heaped with bodies. It was painful to see the noble Guardsmen with their large forms and fine faces lying amidst the dogged, low-browed Russians." It is true that on an average four Russians had fallen for every

Englishman who was killed, a result due largely to the superior penetrating power of the Minié rifle, with which the British were armed. But how could this fight against overpowering odds be longer maintained?

The scene of the fight, let it be remembered, is a ridge, thrust out like the horn of a rhinoceros to the north; the ground sinking in deep and gloomy ravines on three sides. A dense fog brooded over the whole ridge, reddened incessantly with the flash of the guns and the sparkle of musketry. The cannonade was like the deep-voiced roar of the surf on a rocky coast; and through fog and smoke the figures of the charging lines and the wrestling groups flitted ghostlike. A knotted irregular fringe of British infantry clung to the edge of the slopes of the ridge on its three sides. Every few minutes up from the blackness of one of the ravines— east, west, or north—a huge, flat-capped, grey-coated mass of Russians thrust itself, and the nearest cluster of British soldiers—an officer, a sergeant, sometimes a private leading—flung itself at the mass, and never failed to thrust it back into the ravine. The slaughter was dreadful, the valour sublime, the battle a chain of swaying, desperate Homeric combats of the few against the many, the few always winning, but growing swiftly and tragically ever fewer. As has been already explained, the daring of the British was greatly sustained by the fact that the whirling mist forbade their seeing the real weight and power of the masses by whom they were attacked. Thus, when battalions of Russian infantry, 6000 strong, were thrusting themselves against the Sandbag Battery, a soldier of the Grenadier Guards was heard to shout in delighted accents, "I am d——d if there ain't scores of 'em!" As a matter of fact, there were thousands; but that particular British soldier could see only scores, and he exulted in the number of possible victims he saw before him. "That man, multiplied by the number of English bayonets in action," as Kinglake argues, is the central explanation of the amazing failure of the Russians at Inkermann.

By half-past eight, however—the close of what Evelyn Wood calls the Fourth Attack, or Kinglake's "Second Period"—nearly one half of Pennefather's unconquerable infantry—only 4700 in all, counting all the reinforcements that had come up—were struck down; ammunition had begun to fail; the men who were still fighting were exhausted with fatigue and want of food. And the awful strain of the unequal combat was affecting the imagination of many of the British officers. They fought with cool and sustained fury, but with none of that careless delight in fighting which so often marks the British soldier. The men who were carried back wounded were often like men broken-hearted by mere grief, the grief of brave men who felt that bravery was vain. "Bentinck," says Russell, "as he went from the Sandbag Battery towards the camp with a shot through his arm, was like a dying man—and a man dying in despair and grief. Sir George Brown, with head uncovered, was carried past me on a litter, so white and wan that I thought he was dead, till he waved his uninjured arm in recognition of my salute, for I took off my cap as the soldiers bore him by. In answer to my inquiry if he was badly wounded, he said, 'I don't know—nor care. Our men are overpowered—that's all! You'll have a bad story to tell if you live to tell it.' The towering figure of Adams, blood streaming from his boot, was propped on his horse, on the shoulder of which he leant, bowed with pain. His countenance was anxious. 'Unless we are helped,' he said, 'and that very soon, my brigade will be destroyed. Your old friends of the 41st and 47th are suffering terribly. Good-bye.'"

At this moment, it must be remembered, Dannenberg was scourging the narrow British front with the fire of many guns, and was preparing to launch upon it 17,000 infantry, 9000 of which were fresh troops. He was opposed, in all, by 3300 British infantry, and 1600 French troops, who had just come up, and thirty-eight guns. The air, too, at this time grew clearer, and the fire of the Russian guns more deadly. The Russian attacks, moreover, were sent home with greater daring and confidence than at any other period of the fight.

The grey-coated columns broke over the crest of the ridge at half-a-dozen points, the first and most daring rush being made on the western edge of the Home Ridge. The massive whirling column swept over a half-battery of British guns. Two British gunners, named Henry and Taylor, drawing their short artillery swords, fought with desperate valour against the mass for their gun. They received, in an instant, a dozen bayonet thrusts; Henry, in particular, received in his chest the upthrust of a bayonet delivered with such strength as to lift him from the ground. Taylor was killed, Henry, with twelve bayonet wounds in his body, survived; but the guns were lost for a brief space. They were recaptured a few minutes afterwards by a charge of some men of the 63rd and 21st, aided by a little body of sixty French Zouaves, who, of their own accord, and drawn by the mere lust of battle, had wandered down to the fighting line. A little farther along the ridge, however, the endless Russian battalions were forcing their eager way upward, and, as it happened, no tiniest thread of British infantry covered the gap through which they came. The fighting elsewhere was too fierce to allow of this particular irruption of the enemy to be, for a moment, so much as seen.

As it happened, a French battalion, the 7th Léger, had just moved into the gap, along which the Russians were coming. The Russian advance, as the red caps of the French gleamed through the grey mist, paused, and the French moved forward a few paces. Then a curious tremor ran along their front, and a murmur rose in the ranks. The men, apparently, were protesting against an advance in line—one quite opposed to French traditions. A British staff officer galloped to the front of the line, and, with loud shouts, urged the mass forward. Slowly the onward movement was resumed, but the British officer, struck by a bullet, fell, and the French once more paused; the formation began to crumble, the line swayed backward. Lord Raglan and his staff were watching the scene, and it is said that at this moment alone, during the whole fight, Lord Raglan's face lost for an instant its cheerful calm. He had sent an aide-de-camp to Pennefather to ask how the fight was going on in the part of the line he commanded. That officer, in all the rapture of a desperate fight, sent back the cheerful message that everything was going on well, the enemy's infantry showed symptoms of retiring, and if a few more troops could be sent to him he would follow the enemy up and lick them to the d——!" The blast of that courageous message stirred the blood of the somewhat despondent staff like the note of a bugle; Canrobert in particular breaking out into exclamations, "Ah! quel brave garçon, quel brave homme; quel bon général!"

At this moment some 200 men of the 77th, led by Colonel Egerton, came up by fours, and at the double. The men brushed roughly against the flank of the retiring French battalion. One of Egerton's captains remonstrated with a French officer, whom he found retreating, and aided his remonstrance by taking the French officer by the collar. "Mais, monsieur," said the unhappy Frenchman, pointing to the formidable Russian front, "there are the Russians!" The French still continued to fall back, but Egerton's men falling swiftly into line, opened a steady fire on the Russian front.

The decisive check to the Russian column, however, was given by a small body of the 55th, 100 strong, who took the column on its flank, poured a close fire into it at a distance so close that the flame of the muskets seemed to scorch the grey mass, and then tore their way into its entrails at the point of the bayonet. The 7th Léger, too, had been rallied, thrown into the formation of column familiar to it, and came forward with great resolution, and the Russian attack on the western crest fell back shattered.

But meanwhile the great trunk column of the Russian attack, 2000 strong, with a dense fringe of skirmishers running before it, was moving up from the Quarry Ravine, and to oppose it were some 250 men, the wrecks of several regiments—the 55th, 57th, and 77th—and less than 1000 Frenchmen—the 7th Léger. The French troops were young, and of uncertain quality.

In one mood they deployed across the front of the advancing Russians with a swift coolness altogether admirable, and maintained a fire so close and sure that the slaughter in the Russian ranks was dreadful. But in the interval between the volleys, when busy reloading, the young French soldiers were apparently seized by the thought that the Russian line, already so close, might deliver a bayonet charge, and the mass began to change its structure, to shrink back, and then to fall back! Their officers made gallant attempts to rally them. Pennefather, with his staff, galloped down to them, and in energetic British-French, punctuated, it is to be feared, by many oaths, exhorted them to stand. A French officer, his sword high in air, a mere youth, ran out several paces in the front, a British officer ran to his side, a third and a fourth joined the group. Some voice called out in French, "Drums to the front," and drummers and buglers ran out, and sounded and screamed the pas de charge; and still the great battalion swayed to and fro, undecided between an heroic rush on the enemy or mere ignoble flight.

Here, again, as so often throughout the battle, the audacious and almost absurd daring of a cluster of British infantry changed the fortunes of the day. Colonel Daubeny found himself with thirty men of the 55th, on the flank of the Russian column. The second Russian battalion was at quarter-distance in the rear of the leading battalion; it was in the act of deploying to its right, when Daubeny, with his thirty men, charged into the gap between the two battalions! The jam was fierce—so close, indeed, that shot or bayonet-thrust for a few seconds became impossible, and Daubeny was cool enough to exchange a half-laughing nod with a Russian officer close to him, and pinioned, like him, with the weight of the mass. But the British infantry, by sheer strength—sometimes with stroke of fist, sometimes with a murderous clutch at an enemy's throat—made space for themselves, and the heroic thirty actually fought their way through this body of 600 men, from flank to flank, half of them dying in the effort. And it was that heroic dash of thirty British soldiers through what may be called the spine of the great Russian column, which broke its strength, and froze into powerlessness the attack at its head. The 7th Léger by this time coming bravely on again, the great trunk column swung back, broken and demoralised.

Another Russian attack on the north-east shoulder of the ridge had, in the meanwhile, been gallantly met and defeated by the 21st Fusiliers and some companies of the 63rd. Both regiments were Irish—the Fusiliers a regiment of veterans; the companies of the 63rd in the main raw recruits from Dublin. Drawn up in line, these troops maintained a fire so fierce and cruel that the Russian masses halted, and fell in huge and bloody heaps. Then a line of Celtic fire swept through Fusiliers and 63rd alike! With a fierce shout they ran forward. The scrub and rocks broke their ranks; many a gallant soldier fell; but the rush was irresistible. On swept the charge, down the slope, across the post-road, far in advance of the British front, down into the jaws of the Quarry Ravine, into which a stream of broken Russian battalions was by this time flowing. Thus, if the enduring valour of the general British line defeated the innumerable attacks of the Russians, it was the *élan* and daring of these two Irish regiments which carried the decisive counter-attack deep into the heart of the Russian army.

All through the day the Russians had an overpowering superiority in artillery fire, and the roar of their 100 guns never ceased. To this the British replied with the fire of 38 guns, mostly of lighter calibre than the Russian guns; but at this stage Lord Raglan drew two 18-pounder guns into the fight. The huge pieces, each weighing 42 cwt., were dragged with ropes into position, 150 men toiling at the task, while man after man fell under the enemy's fire. The guns were dragged into a commanding position, and opened fire on the Russian batteries. The answering fire was fierce and cruel, and, of the men working the guns, one in ten was struck down within the first few minutes. But the two great guns, laid with cool and deadly accuracy, and worked with almost incredible speed, wrought great mischief, and in less than half an hour obtained a complete ascendancy over the Russian batteries on Shell Hill. Some French guns of heavy calibre, too, came up, and it was plain that the dominion of the Russian guns was ended. It was equally plain, moreover, that the strength of the Russian attack was broken; and from this time the Russians, as a matter of fact, commenced to fall back in slow and sullen retreat.

At most points of the battle-line, the exhausted British could only stand where they had fought; but at some points there was still energy enough to assume the offensive. Thus Lieutenant Acton, in command of some sixty men of the 77th, was ordered to gather under his command two other tiny British companies close at hand, and attack the most western Russian battery on Shell Hill. Both Sir Evelyn Wood and Kinglake tell the story in detail, and a very remarkable story it is.

Acton drew the three companies into line fronting the battery, some 800 yards distant. He explained to the officers his orders, and said he would lead his detachment on the battery front, if the other two companies would attack on either flank. The other officers refused to join in the attack, saying the force was too hopelessly small. "If you won't come," said Acton, "I will attack with my own men;" and, turning to them, said, "Forward, lads." But the men had heard the dispute between the officers, and refused to move. To undertake with one company what was pronounced a task too desperate for the three companies seemed mere madness. "Then," said Acton, "I'll go by myself!" Turning his face towards the battery he marched off, single-handed, to attack it! But it is not the way of British soldiers to forsake their officers. Acton had advanced some fifty yards, when a private of the 77th, named Tyrrel, ran out of the ranks after him, reached his side, and said, "Sir, I'll stand by you!" From one of the other companies a second man ran up, and the three brave men clambered up the slope to attack the battery thundering round-shot over their heads. Great, however, is the magic of a brave example. The 77th could not see their lieutenant with only two followers moving up unsupported to attack a battery; and, with a shout, they ran out, an eager crowd, caught up to him, and fell into rank behind him.

He divided his sixty men into three groups, sent twenty under the command of a sergeant against either flank, and himself led another twenty on the battery front. The other two companies, in the meanwhile, were coming up fast, and the Russian gunners, after a few hasty discharges, wheeled round their guns and made off!

By one o'clock the fight was practically over, and the victory won; and there is no more astonishing victory in the history of war. Todleben afterwards explained the Russian defeat to Russell by saying, "You were hidden by the fog, and you had a thin front; but your fire into our dense masses was deadly. Then, again, our men fancied that they had all the siege guns playing on them. Every little obstacle appeared to be a fort or a battery," &c. The mist and the uncertainty of the fight, in a word, only hardened the courage of the British: they stirred with a ferment of alarmed uneasiness the imagination of the Russians.

The slaughter was great. On the three-quarters of a mile front, along which the battle raged, lay nearly 14,000 dead or wounded men. The British loss amounted to 3258 killed or wounded; the French lost less than 1000; the Russian killed and wounded, according to their own published figures, reached nearly 11,000. It is suspected to have been much greater. This huge slaughter amongst the Russians is explained by the fact that they were crowded together on a narrow neck of ground, they attacked in solid masses, the firing was close, and the hard-hitting Minié bullets often would pass through half-a-dozen men. The British losses, however, in proportion to their numbers, were of startling severity. Thus, at the close of the day, no fewer than eight British generals were lying on the field, while of the Guards 594 men were killed and wounded out of 1098 in the space of a single hour!

It was a great and memorable victory: but what arithmetic can measure the price at which it was bought! Here is a pen picture of the scene the day after the fight:—" Parties of men busy at work. Groups along the hillside, forty or fifty yards apart. You find them around a yawning trench, 30 feet in length by 20 feet in breadth and 6 feet in depth. At the bottom lie, packed with exceeding art, some forty or fifty corpses. The gravediggers stand chatting, waiting for arrivals to complete the number. They speculate on the appearance of the body which is being borne towards them. 'It's Corporal ——, of the —th, I think,' says one. 'No; it's my rear-rank man. I can see his red hair plain enough,' and so on. They discuss the merits or demerits of dead sergeants or comrades. 'Well, he was a hard man. Many's the time I was belted through him!' or 'Poor Mick! he had fifteen years' service—a better fellow never stepped.' At last the number in the trench is completed. The bodies are packed as closely as possible. Some have still upraised arms, in the attitude of taking aim; their legs stick up through the mould; others are bent and twisted like fantoccini. Inch after inch the earth rises upon them, and they are left 'alone in their glory.' No, not alone; for the hope and affections of hundreds of human hearts lie buried with them."

FAMOUS CAVALRY CHARGES

> "Then down went helm and lance,
> Down were the eagle-banners sent,
>   Down reeling steeds and riders went,
> Corslets were pierced, and pennons rent;
>   And to augment the fray;
> Wheel'd full against their staggering flanks,
> The English horsemen's foaming ranks
>   Forced their resistless way."
> —Scott.

NO rational man to-day cares to reflect much on that historical tragedy known as the Crimean War. In that war Great Britain expended the lives of 24,000 brave men, and added £41,000,000 to her national debt, with no other result than that of securing to "the unspeakable Turk" a new opportunity of misgoverning some of the fairest lands in the world—an opportunity which made possible the Armenian horrors. As a matter of fact, the Crimean War only secured a truce of some twenty-two years in the secular quarrel between Russia and Turkey, and it was scarcely worth while spending so much for so little.

But this war, begun for an inadequate end, was also one of the worst-managed wars known to history. It deserves to stand beside the famous Walcheren expedition as an example of colossal blundering. Lord Wolseley has described one particular incident in the war—the assault on the Redan—as "crazy, ignorant, and childish," and those adjectives might be extended to the strategy and tactics of the whole campaign. The generalship was contemptible; the transport broke down; the commissariat fell into mere helpless bankruptcy; the state of the hospitals, at one stage, would have made a Turk blush. Great Britain was mistress of the seas, yet through the bitter winter of 1854 her brave soldiers, on the frozen upland above Sebastopol, died of mere hunger and cold, with a port crowded with British ships within eight miles. The camp was wasted with scurvy while an illimitable supply of fruits and vegetables lay within a day's sail. The feats of non-intelligence performed by the British commissariat would sound incredible even in a burlesque. Steevens in his "Crimean Campaign" relates how, while the camp hospitals had neither medicine nor candles, yet wooden legs at the rate of four per man were laboriously sent out from England! This may be a mere flight of camp humour, but it is historic that a large consignment of boots, on being opened, was found to consist exclusively of boots for the left foot! The troops were thoughtfully provided with coffee, but it was with green coffee-beans; and the fireless soldier who had to extract coffee from a combination of cold water and green coffee-beans naturally expended much theological language on the authorities who were amusing themselves at his expense. In January 1855, the sick cases in the British camp reached the appalling number of 23,076. For every man killed by bullet or sword in the Crimean campaign, eight died from sickness, cold, or hunger.

In the black sky of that mismanaged war there gleams only one star. History can show nothing to exceed, and not much to equal, the quenchless fortitude, the steadfast loyalty to the flag, the heroic daring of the men and officers who kept watch in the trenches round Sebastopol. The Crimean War created only one military reputation—that of Todleben, the great Russian engineer who defended Sebastopol—but it has enriched British military history with some deeds, the memory of which will endure as long as the race itself. Two of these are the great cavalry charges, which took place on the same day on the open plains just above Balaclava, and the story of "Scarlett's Three Hundred," and of the yet better known charge of the Light Brigade, are well worth telling afresh to a new generation.

SIR JAMES YORKE SCARLETT

From a lithograph, after the portrait by E. HAVELL

I. "SCARLETT'S THREE HUNDRED."

" The charge of the gallant three hundred—the Heavy Brigade!
Down the hill, down the hill, thousands of Russians,
Thousands of horsemen, drew to the valley—and stayed;
For Scarlett and Scarlett's three hundred were riding by
When the points of the Russian lances arose in the sky;
And he called, "Left wheel into line!" and they wheeled and
    obeyed.
. . . . . .

And we turned to each other, whispering, all dismayed,
"Lost are the gallant three hundred of Scarlett's Brigade!"
"Lost one and all" were the words
Muttered in our dismay;
But they rode like Victors and Lords
Through the forest of lances and swords
In the heart of the Russian hordes."
—TENNYSON.

In the cold grey dawn of October 25, 1854, a British cavalry general and three of his staff were riding towards Canrobert's Hill, the extreme eastern outpost held by the allied armies. A quick-eyed aide-de-camp saw that above the redoubt two flags were flying instead of one. "What does that mean?" asked one. "Why," was the answer, "that is the arranged signal that the enemy is advancing"; and, as he spoke, there broke from the redoubt the sullen roar of a gun fired at some unseen object to the east. The Russians were, indeed, advancing. Balaclava, the base of supplies for the British army, lay temptingly open to a Russian assault, and the open valley that led to it was guarded by nothing better than six redoubts held by Turks, over which a donkey might have scrambled, one battery of horse artillery, part of the 93rd Highlanders, and the Light and Heavy Cavalry Brigades, numbering about 1500 swords.

And on these scanty forces in the chilly dawn of that October day were marching 25,000 Russian infantry, 34 squadrons of Russian cavalry, and 78 pieces of field artillery. Lord Raglan had been warned by spies the previous day of the coming attack, but took no steps to meet it. News that the attack had actually begun was carried to the tent of the sleeping English general at 7.30 A.M., but he did not turn out till past eight o'clock, nor did he get a single British regiment on to the threatened ground before ten o'clock. Lord Raglan certainly could not be accused of the sin of "raw haste"! Meanwhile the Russians were coming on with more than usual decision.

Balaclava is a plain about three miles long and two broad, girdled with hills from 300 feet to 1000 feet high, while a sort of spine of low hills called the "Causeway Heights," runs from east to west across it. The valley is thus divided into two parts, the North Valley, the scene of the famous Light Cavalry charge, and the South Valley, where the charge of the Heavy Brigade took place. Canrobert's Hill, or No. 1 Redoubt, stood in the eastern throat of the South Valley, and five other redoubts known as Nos. 2, 3, 4, 5, and 6—all held by Turks—were scattered along the Causeway Heights. The unfortunate Turks in No. 1 Redoubt—only 500 strong—on the dawn of that historic day, saw an entire Russian army marching upon them! The 93rd Highlanders were two miles to their rear, guarding the immediate approach to Balaclava; at a distance as great, at the western root of the Causeway Heights, whence they project like an extended lance across the valley, stood two brigades of British horse. Turks behind an earthwork can fight stubbornly, but when the tiny cluster of Turks in No. 1 Redoubt saw 11,000 Russian infantry and 38 guns marching straight upon them, with no support in sight, they might be forgiven if their nerve failed. As a matter of fact they returned with their five guns the fire of thirty-eight guns, and held their ground until one-fourth of their number were killed. Then, as the grey-coated Russian battalions came tumbling clumsily, but in resistless masses, over their earthwork, the Turks fled. The solid column of Russian cavalry opened like a fan, long sprays of galloping skirmishers shot out, and soon Cossacks and lancers were busy slaying amongst the flying red fezes.

At that spectacle, and at the steady advance of the masses of Russians, the Turks in each of the other redoubts in succession fled, and Lord Raglan and his staff, who just then rode on to the crest of the hills—which overlooked the green floor of the valley, as the upper seats of an amphitheatre overlook its arena—beheld this disconcerting spectacle. A Russian army—horse, foot, and artillery—was moving swiftly to attack the most vital point in the British lines, its arsenal and base of supplies. The early sun, to quote Russell, shone on "acres of bayonets, forests of sword-blades and lance-points, gloomy-looking blocks of man and horse." The Turks were in full retreat; their guns were in the enemy's hands—nothing stood between the British ships in Balaclava and the Russian guns but some 1100 marines, the immediate garrison of the port, 400 men of the 93rd Highlanders, with 100 invalids on their way to hospital, a battery of light field-pieces, and the British cavalry, apparently withdrawn from the fight altogether.

Liprandi had, up to this, shown a high degree of resolution, and it cannot be doubted that if he had thrust resolutely forward with his full force, he must have reached Balaclava. Just at this point, however, some spasm of doubt seems to have crossed his mind, and his huge grey battalions halted in their march. Perhaps the cluster of generals—British and French— with their staffs and escorts showing against the sky-line on the crest of the western hills, gave him pause. But the Russian cavalry continued its advance, a dense mass, squadron after squadron deploying on a front that widened till it threatened to fill the whole space of the valley, and all flowing steadily forward. The advance guard of the Russian cavalry, 1000 strong, swung over the Causeway Ridge into the South Valley. Nothing seemed to be between them and Balaclava but the famous "thin red line" of the 93rd—by this time increased to 550 men, with a battalion of Turks on either flank—who, at the sight of the Russian lancers, dissolved into mere fugitives. To the spectators—and that a British general and his staff could be mere spectators in such a scene is very wonderful—it seemed as if that great mass of ordered cavalry could brush aside the red fence of men that barred its path. The Highlanders, as it happened, were at that particular moment in a mood of Homeric laughter. As the flying Turks swept through the tents of the Highland camp an angry Scotch wife appeared on the scene, stick in hand, and commenced to belabour the fugitives, while her voice, in strident

Glasgow tones, rang clear in the morning air. One gigantic Turk in particular she captured, and thumped with masculine energy, and loud laughter rose in the Highland ranks at this spectacle.

But the horsemen were coming on fast, and a grim silence fell on the Highlanders. Then, as the beat of the hostile troops sounded deeper and louder, a curious quiver ran down the long two-deep line of the 93rd. The men were eager to run forward and charge. "93rd, 93rd," rang out the fierce voice of Sir Colin Campbell, "d—— all that eagerness!" He had previously ridden down the line and told his soldiers, 'Remember, there is no retreat from here, men. You must die where you stand." And from the kilted privates came the cheerful answer, "Ay, ay, Sir Colin; we'll do that." The Russians were now within range, and the fire of the Highlanders rang out sudden and sharp. A few horses and men came tumbling down, and the Russian cavalry wheeled instantly to the left, threatening the right flank of the Highlanders. Campbell, a cool and keen soldier, saw the skill of this movement. "Shadwell," he said, turning to his aide-de-camp, "that man understands his business." So, too, did Campbell; who instantly deflected his line so as to protect his right, and met the advance with a destructive volley, before which the Russian horsemen at once fell back.

At that moment an officer rode at a breakneck pace down the hill from Lord Raglan to where the British cavalry were drawn up on the base of the hills below, surveying the whole field as mere benevolent spectators. It had occurred to Lord Raglan that his cavalry might be used to assist his infantry, and eight squadrons of the Heavy Brigade were ordered to move off to support the Highlanders. The squadrons moved off promptly under General Scarlett, having the Causeway Heights on the left. The men were picking their way across the encumbrances of their own camp when Scarlett's aide-de-camp, Elliot, happened to cast his eyes to the ridge 600 yards distant to his left, and saw its top fretted with lances, and the whole sky-line broken by moving squadrons. These 600 British troopers, in a word, were moving across the front of a body of Russian cavalry 3000 strong, and had not the least idea of the circumstance until the enemy's squadrons looked down on their flank within striking distance! Kinglake, who was an actual spectator of the fight, says that the huge mass of hostile cavalry, as, at the sound of trumpet, with all the weight of its thousands, it began to descend the hillside, "showed acreage rather than numbers." The Russians were clothed, as a rule, in long grey overcoats, and grey, by its mere mass—as is seen in sky or sea—has almost the effect of blackness. And across this black, threatening, steadily-moving mass was drawn, in the valley below, at a distance of some 600 yards, the vivid crimson line of the English cavalry—the Greys, with their white horses and bearskin caps, the Inniskillings with gleaming helmets. Scarlett was a white-whiskered, red-faced soldier, fifty-five years old, a delightfully simple-minded warrior, who had never heard a shot fired in anger. But as he looked up and saw that huge, threatening mass on his flank, with the instinct of a brave man he took the one possible course. "Left wheel into line," he shouted. The men swung round instantly, faced the Russian front, and quietly moved forward, two squadrons of Greys and one of Inniskillings forming the front line.

The ground was rough with the *débris* of a camp; part of the British cavalry, too, had to cross the site of an old vineyard, bristling with vine-stumps, and girdled by a ditch. By the time they cleared all this, the ranks were somewhat disordered, and the company officers commenced to "dress" their line. This was a dainty process for 300 cavalry, with a huge mass nearly ten times their strength, 600 yards off, and hanging like a threatening cloud on the hill above them, ready to burst in overwhelming tempest. The Russians moved steadily down to within 400 yards of Scarlett's line, and then a spasm of doubt seemed to run through the mass. It halted. The beat of trampling hoofs died away. The officers of the Greys were still, with their backs turned coolly to the enemy, daintily "dressing" the lines of their men, and under that treatment the men's tempers were growing slightly volcanic. The Inniskillings had a clear stretch of grass before them, and the passion to charge thrilled in the men so fiercely that Scarlett could only restrain the line by waving it back with his sword. The troop resembled a high-bred horse, chafing at the curb for a start.

Scarlett saw the huge mass above him, and outflanking him so enormously, draw to a halt, just as the dressing of his own lines was completed. His trumpeter rang out stern and clear the signal to "charge," and Scarlett himself, mounted on a horse of great speed and size, led against the enemy at a trot, which after a few yards quickened to a gallop. His troops, still hindered by broken ground, could not come on so swiftly, and there was the amazing spectacle presented of a red-faced British general galloping headlong and alone into a gigantic mass of Russian cavalry, his aide-de-camp, trumpeter, and orderly following hard on his rear, and more than fifty yards behind some 300 Greys and Inniskillings just getting into their stride. A horse sixteen hands high going at full speed with a white-whiskered British general on its back, is a somewhat discomposing object as it approaches, and as Scarlett smashed in on the Russian front he saw the nearest of the hostile cavalry drop promptly off their horses for safety. Scarlett himself, flourishing his sword, drove deep into the Russian mass; Elliot, his aide-de-camp, a splendid swordsman, came next, and a Russian officer, sitting on his horse a few paces in the front of the line, struck furiously at him as he swept up. Elliot parried the cut, dropped his sword point to the thrust, drove it through the body of his antagonist, and, as the rush of his horse carried him onward, the Russian was literally turned round in his saddle by the leverage of the sword thrust clean through him. Then, as his sword was released, with a flash of the crimson blade, Elliot, too, broke through the Russian line.

How eagerly the three squadrons following were, by this time, riding, may be imagined. The Inniskillings on the right, as the Russian line came within sword-stroke, broke into a shout, sudden, loud, and menacing. The Greys, according to Kinglake, broke out into what he somewhat absurdly calls "a fierce moan of rapture." Grey and Inniskilling had not ridden side by side since the great charge at Waterloo, and the men of 1854 were as gallant as the men of 1815. When before, indeed, was ever seen a spectacle of 300 men galloping up hill to charge 3000! As the squadrons loosened in the gallop the men in the second line seized the opportunity afforded by every interval to add themselves to the first line, and, largely, it was in a single line that Scarlett's 300 flung themselves on a mass of cavalry of almost unknown depth. Colonel Dalrymple White, who led the Inniskillings, was the next man after Scarlett and his little group to pierce the enemy's line; Major Clarke, who led the Greys on the enemy's flank, was the next man in. He rode a horse with a satanic temper, who, driven temporarily mad by the rapture of galloping, plunged so fiercely as to displace his rider's bearskin, and, bare-headed, Clarke rode under that gleaming roof of Russian swords. Then with one sustained and swelling roar of sounds the lines clashed together, the Russians "accepting the files," as it is called—shrinking aside, that is—to yield a passage to their enemies, so that, in a few seconds, the 300 Greys and Inniskillings were simply buried in the black mass of the Russians, and became, to the excited onlookers who hung over the combat from the heights, mere eddying specks of grey and red, of black bearskin and gleaming and plumed helmet, in the gloomy mass of the Russian squadrons.

The British, it must be remembered, were heavy cavalry—big men on big horses; they broke into the Russians in the full rapture of a galloping charge; fiercer blood beat in their veins than in the more stolid Russians. And from the very instant of actual contact the British established a curious mastery over their enemies. The fight was fought on a sloping floor of elastic turf; there was no explosion of fire-arms, nothing but the ring of steel on steel, and the shouts of the combatants. The Russians everywhere were on the defensive, with crouching heads, the gleam of white teeth, and one long-sustained and hissing "zizz," which, to quote Kingslake, resembled the buzz of a thousand factory-wheels. In the tumult and squeeze of this *mêlée* the tall British horsemen bore themselves with an air of assured mastery. The thick greatcoats of the Russians served almost the purposes of a coat of armour; the sword-stroke sometimes rebounded from it as though the stroke had been that of a cudgel, and in more than one instance the sword thrust fiercely at the body of a Russian was bent, as though it had been lead, against the thick fold of the wearer's coat. In the passion of the fight a British soldier, while he cut down a Russian with his right hand, would often clutch another Russian by the throat, and drag him from the saddle. Clarke was cut cruelly across his bare head with the stroke of a Russian sabre, and the rush of crimson blood turned face and neck to the colour of his red coat; yet Clarke himself, in the exaltation of the fight, knew nothing of his wound! Elliot, familiar with war in India, and a fine swordsman, played a great part in the fight; but, overreaching himself for a moment in a thrust, four Russian swords simultaneously struck him on head and face. He received the point of one enemy in the forehead, the blade of a second divided his face transversely by a furious slash, a third smote him behind the ear, a fourth cut clean through his cocked hat. Elliot received in all fourteen sword wounds, yet kept his seat and his sword through them all!

The Russian cavalry formed a huge and solid oblong, but the two front lines were extended considerably beyond the true width of the oblong, so as to greatly prolong the front; and the prolongations on either extremity served as a kind of antennae. They could be swung back so as to protect the flanks of the mass, or swung forward so as to enclose, as within the claws of a crab, a body attacking in front. At this stage of the fight these two "horns," so to speak, wheeled forward, and shut round on the Russian front so as to completely swallow up the tiny squadrons that had followed Scarlett.

What, meanwhile, was Scarlett's second line doing? It was a soldierly impulse on the part of Scarlett which made him instantly swing round, and charge with the three squadrons he had in hand, the huge bulk of Russian cavalry which suddenly appeared on the hill above him. But it was a slur on his generalship that he had not discovered the presence of so formidable a force within striking distance earlier; it was a still further blunder that, instead of striking the enemy with his whole force, his men were left to expend themselves in no fewer than five separate and unrelated attacks.

The 4th Dragoon Guards were moving in the rear of Scarlett's first line when they saw at almost the same moment the dusky mass of the Russians, Scarlett himself, his white whiskers visible beneath his glittering helmet, in their midst flourishing his sword, and the first line at full gallop just crashing on the Russian front. The 4th Dragoons were advancing in leisurely fashion, but, at that spectacle, the men without orders instinctively drew their swords, and their colonel, Hodge, said to his second in command, "Foster, I am going on with the left squadron; as soon as your squadron gets clear of the vineyard, front form, and charge." Hodge was a good soldier; he went at the gallop past the Russian front on its right flank, brought up his left shoulder—still at the gallop—crashed in upon the unprotected Russian flank, and hewed his way at the sword's edge clean from flank to flank of the mass. The Royals had received no orders at all, but the shouts of the combat had set them moving. They came over a ridge of the hill in time to see the right arm of the Russian front fold round on the Greys. That spectacle set the Royals on flame. Some voice cried out, "By G——, the Greys are cut off! Gallop! Gallop!" The men broke into a cheer, the blast of a trumpet pealed out, and, trying to form line as they moved, the Royals galloped up, and smote the wheeling Russian line on its rear, and broke it to fragments.

Still farther to the right were the 5th Dragoon Guards, who also sprang forward, like hounds unleashed, at the sight of the *mêlée*. Some stray troopers off duty joined them—a man or two from the Light Brigade drawn by pure love of fighting, the two regimental butchers in their shirt sleeves. The 5th Dragoons came up at a gallop, and also caught the wheeling Russian line in the rear. A second squadron of the Inniskillings, still farther to the right, was the only one which Scarlett, before he started on his charge, had summoned to follow him. It had a clear field for the gallop; the men came on at full charging pace, shot clear through the Russian left wing—which it also caught trying to wheel in on Scarlett and his men—and drove it with their fiery onset in ruins upon the main body.

Meanwhile, the Greys in the centre of the swaying mass had been rallying round their adjutant, a big man, on a gigantic steed, with a voice famous for its range, who, holding up erect in the air a sword that from point to hilt dripped with blood, shouted, "The Greys! Rally! Rally!" Tormented at its centre by Greys and Inniskillings, rent from flank to flank by the 4th Dragoons, smitten with shock after shock by the charge of the Royals and the first squadron of Inniskillings, what could the Russians do? They swayed to and fro! the clamour of shouting, the stamp of hoofs, the clash of sword on sword grew ever fiercer, till at last the many yielded to the few! The huge bulk broke asunder, and a mere tumbled wreck of squadrons swept in flight over the crest of the hill, down which not many minutes before, in such a threatening shape, it had moved in order so majestic.

The 93rd had watched the sight, and as the Russians broke they cheered madly, while Sir Colin Campbell, with head bare, galloped up to the Greys, his war-battered face shining. "Greys, gallant Greys!" he said, "I am sixty-one years old, but if I were a lad again I would be proud to join your ranks." "That," said one of the French generals who watched the scene, "is the most glorious thing I ever saw."

II. THE SIX HUNDRED.

> "I see you stand like greyhounds in the slips
> Straining upon the start. The game's afoot:
> Follow your spirit, and upon this charge;
> Cry—'God for Harry! England, and Saint George!'"
> —HENRY V.

> "Flash'd all their sabres bare,
> Flash'd as they turned in air,
> Sabring the gunners there,
> Charging an army, while
> All the world wonder'd."
> —TENNYSON.

As the Russians swept back in confusion, they passed right across the front of the Light Cavalry Brigade, seven splendid squadrons brought to white-heat by the gallant fight of the Heavy Brigade, which they had watched as mere spectators. Lord Cardigan, their commander, had received two orders—(1) To "defend the position" he occupied; and (2) "To strike at anything that came within distance" of him. He forgot the second clause of his orders, and remembered only the first. Lord Cardigan was a brave man, but a bad soldier. Nature, in fact, intended him for a lawyer of the old hair-splitting type, and an unkind fate had made him a cavalry officer, and put him in command of seven squadrons of the finest horsemen in the world. All through the fight of Scarlett's men the officers nearest him heard Cardigan explode at short intervals into the sentence, "D—— those Heavies! They have the laugh of us this day." But when the disordered Russians swept past him Lord

THE EARL OF CARDIGAN

From an engraving, after a photograph by JOHN WATKINS

Cardigan's opportunity came. He had amongst his officers one at least—Morris of the 17th Lancers—who had taken part in great battles in India, and he implored Cardigan to strike with the full force of his brigade the flanks of the flying Russians, or, at least, to allow him to charge them with his own two squadrons. But Cardigan had a brain as narrow and as impenetrable as his own sword. He was a precisian, capable of quarrelling desperately about trifles. He had fought two deadly duels when a young man—one about the colour of a bottle, another about the size of a tea-cup. He could easily become the prisoner of a phrase. His orders, too, were to "defend" his position, and Cardigan so little understood his business as a soldier that he thought an order to "defend" meant a prohibition to attack. And to the derision of military mankind, and the wrath of every man in his own brigade, Cardigan flung away his chance.

But the testing hour of the Light Brigade came quickly. About eleven o'clock, as the British yet remained absolutely passive, Liprandi began to remove the guns from the redoubts he had captured. Now, to see British guns carried off under the eyes of a British army was a spectacle that pricked even Lord Raglan's lethargic spirit into anger, and he sent an order to Lord Lucan, who commanded the British cavalry, to advance and recover the Causeway Heights, and added that he would be "supported by infantry." Lucan, however, made no sign of movement. It turned out he was waiting for the infantry which Lord Raglan had somehow failed to provide. After a pause of nearly three-quarters of an hour, Lord Raglan sent a second order, peremptory in tone but vague in expression, directing the cavalry to "advance rapidly to the front" and try to "prevent the enemy carrying away the guns." The order was carried by the ill-fated Nolan, a splendid horseman and sabreur, but a man of vehement temper. Lucan, like Cardigan, was an obstinate and contentious man, who must first criticise an order before he obeyed it. "Attack, sir!" said Lucan to Nolan, "Attack what? What guns, sir?" Nolan, with a gesture, pointed up the valley, and said, "There, my lord, is your enemy; there are your guns!" Lucan had from the first fatally misunderstood Lord Raglan's order, and by this time he was in a white heat of passion, and not in a mood to understand anything.

Kinglake, very happily, likens the position of the Russians to the four outspread fingers of the human hand. The little finger represents the Causeway Heights, the fore-finger the parallel range called the Fedioukine Hills. Betwixt these ran the North Valley, up which the Russian cavalry and guns—representing the second and third fingers—had advanced. But the charge of the Heavy Brigade had flung this force back; the valley was empty, the two central fingers, so to speak, being doubled back. But there remained the parallel heights crowned by Russian batteries, corresponding to the outer fingers of the hand, while the position of the "knuckles" of the reverted fingers was occupied by a battery of eighteen guns, with at least 400 cavalry drawn up in their rear as a support. Raglan meant the cavalry to attack the tip of the little finger. Lucan understood him to mean that the cavalry was to be launched down a mile and a quarter of level turf, under the cross-fire of the hills the whole way, on the eighteen guns at the eastern end of the parallelogram. This was a simply lunatic performance, but Lucan considered he had no choice but to undertake it.

He rode to Cardigan, told him what was to be done, and that the Light Cavalry must lead. Cardigan brought down his sword in salute, said, "Certainly, sir; but the Russians have a battery in our front, and riflemen and batteries on both flanks." Lucan shrugged his shoulders, and said, "We have no choice but to obey"; whereupon Cardigan turned quietly to his men and said, "The brigade will advance," and set off on the ride which has become immortal, saying to himself, as he moved off, "Here goes the last of the Brudenells."

The brigade numbered a little over 600 men, seven dainty glittering squadrons, the perfection of military splendour. When the brigade was in full movement the 17th Lancers and the 13th Light Dragoons formed the first line, the 8th and 11th Hussars and 4th Light Dragoons the second line, under the command of Lord George Paget. Lord Cardigan, quite alone, led. Nolan joined in the charge, but before the brigade had moved a hundred paces he galloped across its head from left to right, shouting and waving his sword. To Cardigan's martinet soul this was an indecorous performance, which kindled in him a flame of anger that lasted at white-heat through the whole fatal charge; but Nolan had, as a matter of fact, discovered the tragical mistake that was being made, and tried to divert the brigade to the true point of attack, the Causeway Heights. That moment a Russian shell—the first fired—exploded in front of Nolan, and instantly killed him. His horse, freed from the rider's hand, wheeled and galloped back on the front of the brigade, Nolan, though dead, sitting erect in the saddle, with sword uplifted, his death-cry still ringing in the air.

Meanwhile from the heights above, the spectators, to their horror, saw the double lines of English horsemen turn their heads straight up the fatal valley, and begin their famous ride "into the mouth of hell." The heights on either side broke into a blast of flame, the white smoke swept across the valley, and within that wall of drifting smoke the gallant lines vanished, their trail already marked by fallen men and horses. Cardigan led magnificently. He chose the flash of the central gun in the battery across the head of the valley, and rode steadily, and without looking back, upon it. The galloping lines behind him quickened as the scourging of the cross-fire became more deadly, but Cardigan put his sword across the breast of the officer who led the Lancers, and bade him not to ride before the leader of his brigade. Fast rode the lines, and fast fell the men, and the iron bands of discipline began to relax. The eager troopers could not be restrained from darting forward in front of their officers, the racing spirit broke out, the thunder of hoofs behind Cardigan pressed ever closer. He could not keep down the pace, but he would not let it outrun him, and his own stride grew swifter, until the thoroughbred he rode was at full speed. When within eighty yards of the great battery, it fired its final blast. Half of the British line went down; not more than sixty horsemen were left untouched, and, with Cardigan still leading, they drove thundering through the smoke upon guns and gunners. They saw the brass cannon gleam before them, their mouths hot with the flame of the last discharge.

Cardigan dashed betwixt two of the pieces, his men broke over them, and fiercely hewed down the artillerymen. Morris, who led the Lancers, took the survivors of his squadron—some twenty horsemen—forward with a rush past the battery, full upon the cavalry behind. Morris himself drove his sword to the very hilt through the officer who stood in front of the Russian squadrons, and the Russian tumbled from his horse. Morris could not disengage his sword, and was dragged with his slain antagonist to the ground, where the lances of a dozen Cossacks were fiercely thrust into him. He was cruelly wounded, but not killed, and had to surrender, though afterwards he broke away and escaped. His twenty Lancers meanwhile smote the Russian squadrons before them with such fury that they fairly broke them. Cardigan himself raced past the guns to within twenty yards of the Russian cavalry, close enough, indeed, to recognise in one of its officers an acquaintance he had met in London drawing-rooms.

But Cardigan was alone; he turned his horse's head round, and rode back to the captured battery. Up the valley he saw some remnants of the 13th and 17th in retreat, but through the whirls of eddying smoke there were no other men wearing the British uniform in sight. Cardigan concluded that the little cluster of troopers in retreat were the sole survivors of his brigade, and he rode off, and joined them, actually leaving his second line and the survivors of the 17th Lancers still in full conflict. The astonished spectators at the other end of the valley presently saw the leader of the Light Cavalry

T

Brigade emerge alone from the smoke, returning without his brigade.

Meanwhile the second line, led by Lord George Paget, rode as gallantly as the first, but with even worse fortune. They had to ride over the bodies of their comrades who had fallen from the squadrons before them. The riderless horses from those squadrons, too, were a source of confusion. A horse in the horror of a great charge, suddenly finding itself riderless, goes half-mad with terror, and dashes, for mere company's sake, into the moving ranks of the squadrons. Paget, who rode in advance of his line, had at one time no fewer than five riderless horses galloping beside him and squeezing up against him. The officers strove steadily to keep down the pace, and hold the squadrons steady, but they were riding in a perfect hail of fire. Still the gallant lines swept onward in good formation, till, suddenly, through the grey smoke, gleamed the brazen mouths of the Russian guns. Then some officer put his hand to his mouth, and delivered a shrill "Tally-ho!" The lines instantly broke into a tumult of galloping horsemen, and over the guns broke the British!

The 11th Hussars swept past the flank of the battery, and dashed at the cavalry drawn up in the rear. The 11th, from their cherry-coloured overalls, are familiarly known as the "Cherubims," and here, says Lord George Paget, "was witnessed the astonishing spectacle of forty Cherubims assaulting the entire Russian cavalry—indeed, the Russian army!" There were now some 230 British horsemen—all military order gone, but each man in the highest mood of warlike fury—hewing fiercely at the Russian gunners or the Russian cavalry, and it is an amazing fact that before that fiery onset the great body of cavalry fell back and back until the mass was practically rent asunder; and then were visible behind them battalions of infantry, falling hastily into square, as though they expected these terrible British horsemen to sweep over them in turn!

The British officers, however, knew that their bolt was shot. They rallied their men, held brief consultation with each other, tried to discover the whereabouts of their first line, and asked one another, "Where's Lord Cardigan?" That surprising officer was at that moment safely back in the British lines. The survivors of the heroic brigade turned their heads back, up the fatal valley, and found a line of Russian cavalry drawn betwixt them and safety! The guns, too, were re-manned behind them, and they were caught betwixt the flame of a Russian battery and the lances of Russian cavalry. They never hesitated, however. The cavalry that barred their path was broken through like a hedge of bulrushes, and "back from the gates of death" and from the "jaws of hell" they rode—but "not the Six Hundred!"

There is no time to tell how the French had, meanwhile, by a gallant attack of Chasseurs d'Afrique, doubled up the batteries on one flank; and, in units, or in scattered clusters, bloody with wounds, and spent with riding, the wreck of the brigade came out of the smoke, and regained the British lines. As each survivor, or cluster of survivors, appeared, a cheer broke from the slope of the hills, and eager faces and friendly hands welcomed them. Lord George Paget was almost the last man to appear, and amongst the officers who welcomed him was Lord Cardigan, composed and formal as ever. "Hullo! Lord Cardigan," said Paget, "weren't you there?" When the broken fragments of the squadrons were re-forming, Cardigan looked at them, and broke out, "Men, it's a mad-brained trick, but it's no fault of mine." And it tells the temper of the men that they answered him, "Never mind, my lord, we're ready to go again!"

Of that mad but heroic charge a hundred incidents are preserved—thrilling, humorous, shocking. A man of the 17th Lancers, for example, was heard to shout, just as they raced in upon the guns, a quotation from Shakespeare—"Who is there here would ask more men from England?" The regimental butcher of the 17th Lancers was engaged in killing a sheep when he heard the trumpets sound for the charge. He leaped on a horse; in shirt-sleeves, with bare arms and pipe in mouth, rode through the whole charge, slew, it is said, six men with his own hand, and came back again, pipe still in mouth! A private of the 11th was under arrest for drunkenness when the charge began; but he broke out, followed his troop on a spare horse, picked up a sword as he rode, and shared in the rapture and perils of the charge. The charge lasted twenty minutes; and was ever before such daring or such suffering packed into a space so brief! The squadrons rode into the fight, numbering 673 horsemen; their mounted strength, when the fight was over, was exactly 195.

It was all a blunder; but it evoked a heroism which made the blunder itself magnificent. And long as brave deeds can thrill the imagination of men the story will be remembered of how—

> "Stormed at with shot and shell,
> Boldly they rode and well,
> Into the jaws of death,
> Into the mouth of hell;
> Noble Six Hundred."

Fate and the poets have been somewhat unkind to Scarlett's Three Hundred. Tennyson's lines on them have not the lilt which makes them live in the ear of a people, though there is an echo of trampling hoofs in some of the stanzas—

> "The trumpet, the gallop, the charge, and the might of the fight,
> . . . . .
> Four amid thousands! And up the hill, up the hill,
> Galloped the gallant Three Hundred, the Heavy Brigade."

But the stanzas which tell the story of Cardigan's men are as immortal as the deed itself:—

> "Half a league, half a league,
> Half a league onward,
> All in the valley of death
> Rode the Six Hundred.
> 'Forward the Light Brigade!
> Charge for the guns!' he said.
> Into the valley of death
> Rode the Six Hundred.
> . .
> When can their glory fade?
> Oh the wild charge they made,
> All the world wondered.
> Honour the charge they made,
> Honour the Light Brigade,
> Noble Six Hundred!"

THE MEN IN THE RANKS

THE story of a great fight, on one side at least, and as far as the commanders are concerned, is a contest, not of bullets, but of brains. Strategy is pitted against strategy, and the general wins who, in Wellington's phrase, guesses most successfully "what is happening on the other side of the hill." The fate of a campaign, indeed, may be decided before a shot is fired, and by purely intellectual forces; by a blunder in calculations on one side, or a failure of imagination, or an infinitesimal waste of time on the other. It is settled, that is, by the relative energy of brain-waves in two heads, adorned with cocked hats, perhaps a score of miles distant from each other! And literature reserves all its honours for what may be called the intellectual side of battle—the wrestle of rival strategies. Even when the actual incidents of a battle have to be described, it is all lost in a vapour of generalities. The unit is nothing, the mass is everything. We are bidden to watch the march of the many-coloured, steel-edged columns, urged by the impulse of some solitary and planning brain; but history is too dignified to take notice of the men in the ranks, of the dusty faces, the stumbling feet, the gasping breath—of the stragglers who limp, sore-footed, in the rear—of the men who drop, as though shot, killed with mere fatigue. A battle translated into literary terms is a haze of impersonal generalities. The batteries thunder along a front of miles; the attacking bodies are made up of "divisions"; the victory consists in driving back this or that "wing" of the opposing army, or in severing, as with the flourish of some unseen sword, its "communications." A fight treated in this fashion is a game of chess, with regiments for pawns, cavalry brigades for knights, and "corps d'armée" for castles. The personal element vanishes. The play of human passions in the long lines of fighting men — of terror and of valour, of despair or of triumph — is overlooked. The men in the ranks are treated as bloodless abstractions, mere symbols in a passionless arithmetic. The story of Waterloo itself, thus treated, becomes as colourless, as completely exhausted of human incident as, say, the demonstration of a theorem in Euclid.

But a battle has, as far as the men in the ranks are concerned, quite another side. It is a tussle of bayonets, a wager of life against life; a wrestle of hot-blooded human beings in an atmosphere of passion, fought under the shadow of death, and with all human emotions at their highest pitch. And this, the human side of a battle, which historic literature usually treats as non-existent, is really that over which the average man is tempted to linger with wide-eyed and awe-smitten curiosity. He hungers to know how the men in the battle-line feel; how they bear themselves; what aspect the faces of their opponents wear. What are the emotions and thoughts that race through the brain-cells of the ordinary private, as he stands a panting — perhaps a swearing — unit in the swaying human line, transfigured by discipline into a chain of steel? What expression does his face wear as he loads and fires amid the drifting battle smoke? What thrill of passion kindles in him as, through the smoke-filled air, he sees the bent heads and sparkling bayonet-points of the hostile line coming on in fiercest charge? This is what every one wants to know, but which no one is able to tell. Literature contains no adequate picture of a great battle as seen through the eyes of the private in the ranks. The men who make history, unfortunately, cannot write it. Yet what human document would be more thrilling than one which gave us the landscape of a battle-field as De Foe painted the incidents of the Great Plague of London; or which did for the fighting line of the regiments at Albuera what Dana did for the forecastle-life of a merchant ship?

But no such "document" exists; probably none ever will exist. The average soldier belongs to the inarticulate class. It is not that, like the "needy knife-grinder" of Canning's squib, he has "no story to tell"; he cannot tell it.

It is worth while, however, to try and give some account of the personal side of a battle, and one of the best examples of what may be called the literature of the private soldier is found in a book, long since gone out of print, entitled "Recollections of Rifleman Harris, of the old 95th." Harris was a soldier of the Peninsula days, a fair sample of the men who stormed Badajoz, who kept the hill of Busaco against Massena, and out-marched and out-fought Marmont at Salamanca. His experiences range from Vimieiro to the tragical Walcheren expedition. His book is quite structureless. It is innocent of chronology. Clear method or orderly description is quite unknown to it. It is a mere tangle of confused incidents and blurred recollections. But Harris had a gleam of untaught literary genius. Every now and again there peeps out from his page a tiny battle vignette of curiously vivid colouring. Odd paragraphs in his book tingle as with the actual clash of bayonets. His story, say, of the horrors of the retreat to Corunna—or rather to Vigo—is, in patches, as vividly realistic as a page of Defoe. Whatever the British soldier of that day suffered or dared, Harris knew by personal experience. And as a picture of a private in the Peninsula, with his hardihood, his drunkenness, his oaths, his splendid fighting gifts, his hatred of retreats, his scorn of all Frenchmen, his childlike trust in his officers, "Rifleman Harris' Recollections" are of much greater value than whole volumes of starched and erudite histories.

Harris was born on the downs of Blandford, in Dorsetshire, and his earliest occupation was to help his father, who was a shepherd. In 1802 he was drawn as a soldier of the Reserve, and afterwards drafted into the 66th, leaving his father, an old man, " with hair growing as white as the sleet of our downs, and his face becoming as furrowed as the ploughed fields around." The 66th was stationed in Ireland, and there Harris, attracted by the smart, dashing look of a detachment of the 95th Rifles, volunteered into that regiment. Six months afterwards the regiment sailed with the expedition to Denmark. The troops, some 30,000 strong, were landed at Scarlet Island, near Copenhagen, and as the men leaped from the boats ashore, their warlike temper broke out. "The whole force," says Harris, "set up one simultaneous and tremendous cheer, a sound I cannot describe, it seemed so overwhelming." Harris heard afterwards on many battlefields that deep, stern, menacing wave of sound—the shout of the British soldier in the presence of the enemy.

In his first engagement Harris met with his first and only example of cowardice in a British regiment. His front-rank man, a tall fellow named Johnson, was visibly shaken by the rolling volleys of the enemy. He hung back, and twice turned clean round, with his back to the hostile lines, as though disposed to bolt. "I was a rear-rank man," says Harris, "and porting my piece in the excitement of the moment, I swore that if he did not keep his ground I would shoot him dead on the spot." Harris had an amusing dislike to tall men—a circumstance perhaps explained by the fact that Harris himself was only a "little fellow of five feet seven inches." All his villains were over six feet high, and he records that in the horrors of the retreat to Vigo, the tall men were the greatest grumblers, the greatest eaters, and the worst fighters in the regiment. "The tall men," he says, "bore fatigue much worse than the short ones." With a regiment of undersized men it is plain Harris would have cheerfully charged at least two regiments of Friedrich Wilhelm's Potsdam giants!

The soldier of that day was cruelly over-weighted. He hated his knapsack almost as much as he hated the halberds, and with excellent reason. "I marched," says Harris, "under a weight sufficient to impede the free motion of a donkey." He carried in addition to his rations and a well-filled kit, a greatcoat rolled into the shape of a sausage, a blanket and camp kettle, a canteen filled with water, a hatchet, rifle, and eighty rounds of ball cartridge. As Harris was the cobbler of his company he bore in addition "a haversack stuffed full of leather, a set of tools, and a lapstone"! It is no wonder that sometimes under this load men on a long march would drop dead in the ranks from sheer fatigue. "Our knapsacks," says Harris, in his account of the retreat to Vigo, "were a bitter enemy on this prolonged march. Many a man died, I am convinced, who would have borne up well to the end of the retreat, but for the infernal load we carried on our backs. My own knapsack was my bitterest enemy; I felt it press me to the earth almost at times, and more than once felt as if I should die under its deadly embrace."

At Rolica the Rifles first came into conflict with the French, and fared badly. The numbers opposed to them were overwhelming, but the skirmishers of the Rifles, scattered an irregular line in the grass, kept up a diligent fire. "The barrel of my piece," says Harris, "was so hot from continual firing that I could hardly bear to touch it, and was obliged to grasp the stock beneath the iron as I continued to blaze away." His right-hand comrade kept pushing in advance, in his eagerness to get near the enemy, and was repeatedly ordered to "keep back" by his officer. Presently a French bullet slew the too daring soldier, and Harris, creeping up to his dead body, made it a rest for his rifle, picking off one Frenchman after another with great coolness and enjoyment. The French galled the Rifles cruelly from a couple of houses on a small rise of ground, until the exasperated men, in Harris's phrase, "would not stand it any longer." "One of the skirmishers, jumping up, rushed forward, crying, 'Over, boys!—over! over!' when instantly the whole line responded to the cry, 'Over! over! over!' They ran along the grass like wildfire, and dashed at the rise, fixing their sword-bayonets as they ran. The French light bobs could not stand the sight, but turned about and fled; and, getting possession of their ground, we were soon inside the buildings."

Harris tells the tale of a comrade's fate in this fight. "Joseph Cochan was by my side loading and firing very industriously about this period of the day. Thirsting with heat and action, he lifted his canteen to his mouth; 'Here's to you, old boy,' he said, as he took a pull at its contents. As he did so a bullet went through the canteen, and perforating his brain, killed him in a moment." After the fight Harris led the dead soldier's wife to the scene of her husband's death. The body lay contorted and rigid. "After contemplating his disfigured face for some minutes, with hands clasped, and tears streaming down her cheeks, she took a prayer-book from her pocket, and kneeling down, repeated the service for the dead over the body."

Harris, it is to be noted, tried to comfort the bereaved woman by offering to make her his wife; but she declined, with emphasis, "ever to think of another soldier"!

Harris' next fight was at Vimieiro. The French came on in solid mass, the British guns playing on them; and, says Harris, "I saw regular lanes torn through their ranks as they advanced, which were immediately filled up again as they marched steadily on. Whenever we saw a round shot thus go through the mass," he adds, with a visible chuckle, "we raised a shout of delight." From the enemy Harris looked round upon his comrades. He says:—

"As I looked about me, whilst standing enranked, and just before the commencement of the battle, I thought it the most imposing sight the world could produce. Our lines glittering with bright arms; the stern features of the men, as they stood with their eyes fixed unalterably upon the enemy, the proud colours of England floating over the heads of the different battalions, and the dark cannon on the rising ground, and all in readiness to commence the awful work of death, with a noise that would deafen the whole multitude. Altogether, the sight had a singular and terrible effect upon the feelings of a youth, who, a few short months before, had been a solitary shepherd upon the downs of Dorsetshire, and had never contemplated any other sort of life than the peaceful occupation of watching the innocent sheep as they fed upon the grassy turf."

The first British cannon shot fired was a bad miss, whereupon a brother gunner—"a red-haired man," as Harris records with De Foe-like gravity—rushed at the fellow who had fired, and knocked him head over heels with his fist. "You fool," he said, "what sort of a shot do you call that! let me take the gun;" which he did, and plied it with deadly effect.

Harris himself was soon busy in the skirmishing line. "I was," he says, "so enveloped in the smoke I created, and the cloud which hung about me from the continued fire of my comrades, that I could see nothing for a few minutes but the red flash of my own piece amongst the white vapour clinging to my very clothes." A gust of wind blew the smoke for a moment off, and he saw the enemy advancing, the sun gleaming on their arms, and tipping them as with gold. Again the smoke blotted out the landscape; it grew yet more dense. "Often," says Harris, "I was obliged to stop firing and dash it aside from my face, and try in vain to get a sight of what was going on, whilst groans and shouts, and a noise of cannon and musketry appeared almost to shake the very ground." He records a droll dialogue under these conditions with his next comrade. "Harris, you humbug," said this cheerful veteran, "I think this will be your last field-day, old boy," &c. When the wind blew the field for a moment clear of smoke, Harris was able to see the charge of the 50th, of which Napier was Major:—

"They dashed upon the enemy like a torrent breaking bounds, and the French, unable even to bear the sight of them, turned and fled. Methinks at this moment I can hear the cheer of the British soldiers in the charge, and the clatter of the Frenchmen's accoutrements, as they turned in an instant and went off, hard as they could run for it. I remember, too, our feeling towards the enemy on that occasion was the north side of friendly; for they had been firing upon us Rifles very sharply, greatly outnumbering our skirmishers, and appearing inclined to drive us off the face of the earth. Their lights, and grenadiers, I, for the first time, particularly remarked on that day. The grenadiers (the 70th, I think) our men seemed to know well. They were all fine-looking men, wearing red shoulder-knots and tremendous-looking moustaches.

As they came swarming upon us they rained a perfect shower of balls, which we returned quite as sharply. Whenever one of them was knocked over, our men called out, "There goes another of Boney's Invincibles.'"

The Rifles, thrown out in skirmishing order, suffered greatly from the immense superiority of the French in numbers, and at last they fell back, firing and retiring. The regiments standing in line near had watched the unequal duel with steadily rising wrath, and when the Rifles began to fall back Harris reports that they cried out as with one voice to charge. "'—— them,' they roared, 'charge! charge!'" General Fane, who was in command, checked his too eager troops. "'Don't be too eager, men,' he said, as coolly as if he were on a drill-parade in old England; 'I don't want you to advance just yet. Well done, 95th!' he called out, as he galloped up and down the line; 'well done 43rd, 52nd, and well done all. I'll not forget, if I live, to report your conduct to-day. They shall hear of it in England, my lads!'" Harris adds :—

"A man named Brotherwood, of the 95th, at this moment rushed up to the general, and presented him with a green feather, which he had torn out of the cap of a French light-infantry soldier he had killed. 'God bless you, general!' he said; 'wear this for the sake of the 95th.' I saw the general take the feather and stick it in his cocked hat. The next minute he gave the word to charge, and down came the whole line, through a tremendous fire of cannon and musketry,—and dreadful was the slaughter as they rushed onwards. As they came up with us, we sprang to our feet, gave one hearty cheer, and charged along with them, treading over our own dead and wounded, who lay in the front. The 50th were next us as we went, and I recollect the firmness of that regiment in the charge. They appeared like a wall of iron. The enemy turned and fled, the cavalry dashing upon them as they went off."

One Rifleman, as the French turned and went off, found himself without a bullet in his pouch; whereupon he "grabbed a razor from his haversack, rammed it down, and fired it after them"!

The British soldier of that day, it is somewhat disquieting to find, was not above plundering his enemy after he had slain him. Harris himself was an expert and diligent investigator of the knapsacks of dead Frenchmen, and it was to that circumstance, mainly, he owed the surprising fact that he emerged from his campaigns with no less a sum than £200 in his pockets! Here is one of his adventures while engaged in plundering the fallen bodies on the field of battle:—

"After the battle, I strolled about the field, in order to see if there was anything to be found worth picking up amongst the dead. The first thing I saw was a three-pronged silver fork, which, as it lay by itself, had most likely been dropped by some person who had been on the look-out before me. A little farther on I saw a French soldier sitting against a small rise in the ground or bank. He was wounded in the throat, and appeared very faint, the bosom of his coat being saturated with the blood which had flowed down. By his side lay his cap, and close to that was a bundle containing a quantity of gold and silver crosses, which I concluded he had plundered from some convent or church. He looked the picture of a sacrilegious thief, dying hopelessly, and overtaken by Divine wrath. I kicked over his cap, which was also full of plunder, but I declined taking anything from him. I felt fearful of incurring the wrath of Heaven for the like offence, so I left him, and passed on. A little farther off lay an officer of the 50th Regiment. I knew him by sight, and recognised him as he lay. He was quite dead, and lying on his back. He had been plundered, and his clothes were torn open. Three bullet-holes were close together in the pit of his stomach; beside him lay an empty pocket-book, and his epaulette had been pulled from his shoulder.

"I had moved on but a few paces, when I recollected that perhaps the officer's shoes might serve me, my own being considerably the worse for wear, so I returned again, went back, pulled one of his shoes off, and knelt down on one knee to try it on. It was not much better than my own; however, I determined on the exchange, and proceeded to take off its fellow. As I did so I was startled by the sharp report of a firelock, and, at the same moment, a bullet whistled close by my head. Instantly starting up, I turned, and looked in the direction whence the shot had come. There was no person near me in this part of the field. The dead and the dying lay thickly all around; but nothing else could I see. I looked to the priming of my rifle, and again turned to the dead officer of the 50th. It was evident that some plundering scoundrel had taken a shot at me, and the fact of his doing so proclaimed him one of the enemy. To distinguish him amongst the bodies strewn about was impossible; perhaps he might himself be one of the wounded. Hardly had I effected the exchange, put on the dead officer's shoes, and resumed

U

my rifle, when another shot took place, and the second ball whistled past me. This time I was ready, and turning quickly, I saw my man; he was just about to squat down behind a small mound, about twenty paces from me. I took a haphazard shot at him, and instantly knocked him over. I immediately ran up to him; he had fallen on his face, and I heaved him over on his back, bestrode his body, and drew my sword-bayonet. There was, however, no occasion for the precaution, as he was even then in the agonies of death.

"It was a relief to me to find that I had not been mistaken. He was a French light-infantry man, and I therefore took it quite in the way of business—he had attempted my life, and lost his own. It was the fortune of war, so, stooping down, with my sword I cut the green string that sustained his calabash, and took a hearty pull to quench my thirst."

One of the dreadful incidental vignettes of a battle scene flashed across Harris's vision at this stage: "I had rambled some distance," he says, "when I saw a French officer running towards me with all his might, pursued by at least half-a-dozen horsemen. The Frenchman was a tall, handsome-looking man, dressed in a blue uniform; he ran as swiftly as a wild Indian, turning and doubling like a hare. I held up my hand and called to his pursuers not to hurt him. One of the horsemen, however, cut him down with a desperate blow, when close beside me, and the next wheeling round, as he leaned from his saddle, passed his sword through the body." The actors in this shameful scene, it may be added, were Portuguese, not British.

Harris took part in the tremendous marches which

preceded the battle of Salamanca. The army, as the campaign began, was in the most splendid order. "I love to remember the appearance of that army," says Harris, "as we moved along at this time. It was a glorious sight to see our colours spread on these fields, the men seemed invincible; nothing, I thought, could have beaten them." The dreadful marches against the light-footed French, urged by Marmont's vehement strategy, which followed, sorely tried the endurance of the British regiments. "The load we carried," says Harris, "was too great, and we staggered on, looking neither to the right nor to the left." Harris himself fell as the exhausted Rifles reached the streets of Zamora; "the sight left my eyes, my brain reeled, and I came down like a dead man."

The sternest experience of war, however, which Harris had, occurred when the 95th were caught in the backward rush of Sir John Moore's retreat on Corunna. The detachment joined Moore's forces at Sahagun. The 95th had seen much service in the south, and when they marched into the camp of Moore's fresh-faced regiments, they were gaunt, ragged, sunburnt; many of them were shoeless; there was not an ounce of superfluous flesh in the whole detachment. The grim, war-hardened veterans, it may be added, were welcomed with a tempest of cheers by their comrades. Two days afterwards these four companies joined the headquarters of their regiment, which had come with Moore from England, and were made pets and heroes of at once.

Moore, it will be remembered, had pushed forward on Napoleon's flank, pricking his communications to the quick, until the French Emperor, arresting his southward march, swung round in tempestuous energy upon the tiny force threatening his flank. Moore instantly fell back, and then commenced the terrible retreat which ended at Corunna. Harris marks, with his usual minuteness, the exact moment when the retreat began. "General Craufurd was in command of the brigade, and riding in front, when I observed a dragoon come spurring furiously along the road to meet us. He delivered a letter to the General, who turned round in his saddle the moment he had read a few lines, and thundered out the word 'Halt!' A few minutes more, and we were all turned to the right about, and retracing our steps of the night before;—the contents of that epistle serving to furnish our men with many a surmise during the retrograde movement."

There was no pause nor rest in that march. Napoleon, with an overwhelming host, was thundering on their rear: great mountain-ranges, snow-capped, wind-swept, desolate, and seamed with a hundred angry mountain torrents, lay betwixt the British and their ships, and the retreat was urged with iron resolution. The close of the first day's march brought the British again into Sahagun, but there was no rest possible.

"We remained enranked in the convent's apartments and passages, no man being allowed to quit his arms or lie down. We stood leaning upon the muzzles of our rifles, and dozed as we stood. After remaining thus for about an hour, we were then ordered out of the convent, and the word was again given to march. There was a sort of thaw on this day, and the rain fell fast. As we passed the walls of the convent, I observed our General (Craufurd), as he sat upon his horse, looking at us on the march, and remarked the peculiar sternness of his features; he did not like to see us going rearwards at all; and many of us judged there must be something wrong, by his severe look and scowling eye.

"'Keep your ranks there, men!' he said, spurring his horse towards some Riflemen who were avoiding a small rivulet. 'Keep your ranks and move on,—no straggling from the main body.'"

All that day the tiny army pushed on. The commissariat waggons were abandoned. "A sergeant of the 92nd Highlanders, just about this time, fell dead with fatigue, and no one stopped, as we passed, to offer him any assistance. Night came down upon us, without our having tasted food, or halted—I speak for myself, and those around me—and all night long we continued this dreadful march. Men began to look into each other's faces, and ask the question, 'Are we ever to be halted again?' and many of the weaker sort were now seen to stagger, make a few desperate efforts, and then fall, perhaps to rise no more. Most of us had devoured all we carried in our haversacks, and endeavoured to catch up anything we could snatch from hut or cottage in our route. Many, even at this period, would have straggled from the ranks, and perished, had not Craufurd held them together with a firm rein."

For four days the force marched at this terrific rate, the men being in total ignorance of their goal. "Where are you taking us to?" a Rifleman asked his officer.

"To England," was the answer, "if we can get there." The soldiers then learned for the first time the real reason of their terrific marches, and, says Harris, "the men began to murmur at not being permitted to turn and stand at bay,—cursing the French, and swearing they would rather die ten thousand deaths, with their rifles in their hands in opposition, than endure the present toil."

But the march was pushed relentlessly on. Sometimes the tumult of the pursuing French would sound so near that it seemed as if a fight was inevitable; "then, indeed," says Harris, "every poor fellow clutched his rifle more firmly, and wished for a sight of the enemy." Craufurd, who commanded the rearguard, and maintained an iron discipline over it, shared to the full the fighting eagerness of his men. When the distant clamour became more distinct, says Harris, "his face would turn towards the sound, and seem to become less stern;" a gleam of delight swept over his rugged features. But the business of the English was not to fight, but to march; and march they did, as perhaps no soldiers ever marched before or since. Sometimes the hard-riding French cavalry overtook the dogged British rearguard, and then there was a fiery wrestle of horsemen and footmen. Here is a sample of one of these rearguard fights:—

"The enemy's cavalry were on our skirts that night; and as we rushed out of a small village, the name of which I cannot now recollect, we turned to bay. Behind broken-down carts and tumbrils, huge trunks of trees, and everything we could scrape together, the Rifles lay and blazed away at the advancing cavalry.

"We passed the night thus engaged, holding our own as well as we could. Towards morning we moved down towards a small bridge, still followed by the enemy, whom, however, we had sharply galled, and obliged to be more wary in their efforts. The rain was pouring down in torrents on this morning, I recollect, and we remained many hours with our arms ported, standing, in this manner, and staring the French cavalry in the face, the water actually running out of the muzzles of our rifles. I do not recollect seeing a single regiment of infantry amongst the French force on this day; it seemed to me a tremendous body of cavalry—some said nine or ten thousand strong—commanded, as I heard, by General Lefebvre.

"Whilst we stood thus, face to face, I remember the horsemen of the enemy sat watching us very intently, as if waiting for a favourable moment to dash upon us like beasts of prey; and every now and then their trumpets would ring out a lively strain of music, as if to encourage them."

Once a party of British cavalry—some squadrons of the 15th Dragoons, the 10th Hussars, and the German Legion — charged the French cavalry with furious valour.

"The shock of that encounter was tremendous to look upon, and we stood for some time enranked, watching the combatants. The horsemen had it all to themselves; our Dragoons fought like tigers, and, although greatly overmatched, drove the enemy back like a torrent, and forced them again into the rear. A private of the 10th Hussars—his name, I think, was Franklin—dashed into the stream after their general

(Lefebvre), assailed him, sword in hand in the water, captured, and brought him a prisoner on shore again. If I remember rightly, Franklin, or whatever else was his name, was made a sergeant on the spot. The French general was delivered into our custody on that occasion, and we cheered the 10th men heartily as we received him."

Harris marched next day close to the unfortunate French cavalry general, and enjoyed his chapfallen and dejected look, as he rode along in the midst of the green jackets. How wild was the mountainous country across which the British were now pushing their march can hardly be described.

"We came to the edge of a deep ravine, the descent so steep and precipitous that it was impossible to keep our feet in getting down, and we were sometimes obliged to sit, and slide along on our backs; whilst before us rose a ridge of mountains quite as steep and difficult of ascent. There was, however, no pause in our exertions, but, slinging our rifles round our necks, down the hill we went; whilst mules, with the baggage on their backs, wearied, and urged beyond their strength, were seen rolling from top to bottom; many of them breaking their necks with the fall, and the baggage crushed, smashed, and abandoned.

"I remember, as I descended this hill, remarking the extraordinary sight afforded by the thousands of our red-coats, who were creeping like snails, and toiling up the ascent before us, their muskets slung round their necks, and clambering with both hands as they hauled themselves up. As soon as we ourselves had gained the ascent we were halted for a few minutes, in order to give us breath for another effort, and then onwards we moved again."

Through difficulties of this sort the exhausted British regiments, now almost foodless and shoeless, toiled. "The long day," says Harris, "found us still pushing on, and the night caused us no halt." Snow now fell heavily; tempests edged with hail scuffled and shrieked in the mountain passes, and through the pauses of the tempest the British could sometimes hear, coming down the wind as they marched, the sound of the trumpets of their enemies. There were women and children with the British troops, adding a new and terrible pathos to the sufferings of the wild days and starless nights. "Towards the evening of this day," writes Harris, "I remember passing a man and woman lying clasped in each other's arms, and dying in the snow. I knew them both, but it was impossible to help them. They belonged to the Rifles, and were man and wife." These soldiers' wives, however, were of amazing hardihood and endurance. A woman, for example, one wild day towards evening stepped aside from the march and sank down in the snow, and her husband remained with her. The enemy were near; night was falling. "To remain behind the column of march in such weather," says Harris, "was to perish, and we accordingly soon forgot all about them. To my surprise, however, I, some little time afterwards (being myself then in the rear of our party), again saw the woman. She was hurrying, with her husband after us, and in her arms she carried the babe she had just given birth to. Her husband and herself, between them, managed to carry that infant to the end of the retreat, where we embarked. God tempers the wind, it is said, to the shorn lamb; and many years after I saw that boy, a strong, healthy lad."

The force with which the Rifles marched was no longer under Sir John Moore; its retreat was directed to Vigo, and Craufurd was in command. His stern nature and fiery will held the suffering and almost exhausted troops in steadfast control. Craufurd, indeed, is the hero of Harris's story, and he never wearies of singing his praises. "He was," he says, "apparently created for command during such dreadful scenes as we were familiar with in this retreat. He seemed an iron man. Nothing daunted him, nothing turned him from his purpose. He was stern and pale," adds Harris, "and the very picture of a warrior. I shall never forget Craufurd if I live to a hundred years." Men in that retreat caught courage from his stern eye and gallant bearing. "I do not think the world ever saw a more perfect soldier than General Craufurd," is Harris's summary.

Craufurd knew that everything in this retreat depended on the maintenance of discipline, and he enforced this with a will of iron. The Rifles adored him, but dreaded him. He, on his side, cherished a sort of angry and shrewish affection for the Rifles, and showed it by punishing them more sternly than any other regiments! "You think because you are Riflemen you may do everything you think proper," said he one day to the miserable and savage-looking crew around him; "but I will teach you the difference before I have done with you."

One evening, as night was falling, Craufurd detected

two men straying from the main body. He knew that if straggling were permitted the rearguard would quickly dissolve. He halted the brigade with a voice of thunder, ordered a drum-head court-martial on the instant, and they were sentenced to a hundred apiece. Whilst this hasty trial was taking place, Craufurd dismounted from his horse, stood in the midst, looking stern and angry as a worried bulldog.

The whole brigade was sore and exasperated, and some one in the ranks near muttered that "the general had much better try to get us something to eat and drink than harass us in this way." Craufurd heard the whisper, turned round, seized the rifle from a soldier's hands, and felled him to the earth with the butt-end. But he had knocked down the wrong man! The real culprit, a man named Howans, said, "I am the man who spoke." "Very well," returned Craufurd, "then I will try you, sir." But the march could not be interrupted even for a court-martial.

"Craufurd gave the word for the brigade to move on. He marched all that night on foot; and when the morning dawned, I remember that, like the rest of us, his hair, beard, and eyebrows were covered with frost, as if he had grown white with age. We were, indeed, all of us in the same condition. Scarcely had I time to notice the appearance of the morning before the general once more called a halt—we were then on the hills. Ordering a square to be formed, he spoke to the brigade, after having ordered the three before-named men of the 95th to be brought into the square:—

"'Although,' said he, 'I should obtain the good-will

neither of the officers nor the men of the brigade here by so doing, I am resolved to punish these three men according to the sentence awarded, even though the French are at our heels. Begin with Daniel Howans.'"

This was, indeed, no time to be lax in discipline, and the general knew it. The men, as I said, were, some of them, becoming careless and ruffianly in their demeanour; whilst others, again, I saw with tears falling down their cheeks from the agony of their bleeding feet, and many were ill with dysentery from the effects of the bad food they had got hold of and devoured on the road."

Halting at intervals Craufurd carried through his court-martials and flogged, sometimes in spite of the remonstrances of the officers, every man who straggled. Harris declares that from the point of view of the private soldier this was wise conduct. "No man but one formed of stuff like General Craufurd could have saved the brigade from perishing altogether; and, if he flogged two, he saved hundreds from death by his management."

But if Craufurd was severe with the men, he was also considerate. When the soldiers were fording a deep and icy stream Craufurd was "as busy as a shepherd with his flock, riding in and out of the water to keep his wearied band from being drowned as they crossed over." At this moment he discovered an officer who was riding across the stream on the back of a soldier. The indignant general came plunging and splashing down upon the pair, and ordered the soldier to drop his officer into the stream. "Return back, sir," said Craufurd to the unhappy captain, "and go through the water like the others. I will not allow the officers to ride upon the men's backs through the rivers."

Craufurd established an almost wizardlike authority over the Rifles. Says Harris:—

"The Rifles being always at his heels, he seemed to think them his familiars. If he stopped his horse, and halted to deliver one of his stern reprimands, you would see half-a-dozen lean, unshaven, shoeless, and savage Riflemen, standing for the moment leaning upon their weapons, and scowling up in his face as he scolded; and when he dashed the spurs into his reeking horse they would throw up their rifles upon their shoulders, and hobble after him again."

The severities of the march grew yet more terrible. At last Harris himself fell exhausted on the snow. "Let him die quietly," said his captain to the sergeant, "I know him well; he is not the man to lie here if he could get on," and the ranks moved on, leaving Harris to his fate. After a while Harris staggered to his feet. "On the road behind me," he says, "I saw men, women, mules, and horses dead or dying, whilst far away in front I could just discern the enfeebled army crawling out of sight." He found shelter in a Spanish hut, and the next morning crept on the tracks of the army, passing clusters of exhausted soldiers and women sitting huddled together in the road, their heads drooping forward, apparently patiently waiting their end. A party of the 42nd was sweeping up all stragglers who could walk, much as a drover would keep together a flock of tired sheep. "Many of them had thrown away their weapons and were linked together, arm-in-arm, in order to support each other, like a party of drunkards. These were, I saw, composed of various regiments; many were bare-headed, and without shoes; and some with their heads tied up in old rags and fragments of handkerchiefs."

At last from the head of the long straggling column came a faint shout. From the top of the hill the sea was visible, and the tall masts of many transports. "Harris," said a rifleman notorious for his foulness of language, "if it pleases God to let me reach those ships, I swear never to utter a bad or discontented word again," and the tears ran down his haggard cheeks as he spoke. Harris was the very last man who embarked at Vigo. He crawled on to the beach just as the last boat was pushing off, almost totally blind with mere fatigue. The boat put back for him, and he lived to reach Spithead; where, he says, "our poor bare feet once more touched English ground." Never was such a gaunt, ragged, hunger-bitten, war-wasted, shoeless collection of scarecrows as those that landed at Spithead. The Rifles at the beginning of the retreat numbered 900 men in the highest state of efficiency; when they landed at Spithead they paraded some 300 ragged invalids. Harris's company consisted of exactly three men.

Harris took part afterwards in the unhappy Walcheren expedition, one of the worst-managed and most tragical enterprises in the whole Napoleonic war. The forces employed numbered 30,000; in fighting quality they were equal to the men of the Peninsula. "It was as fine an expedition," says Harris, "as ever I looked at, and the army seemed to stretch the whole distance from Hythe to Deal." The expedition was ruined by bad generalship and the ague, and it may be doubted whether the generalship was not the more deadly of these two mischiefs. The Walcheren sickness, it may be added, was of a very dreadful and mysterious character. The victims seized by it were shaken as with an exaggerated palsy; their bodies were swollen up like barrels; they died like flies in a frost. Harris himself, in spite of his constitution tempered to the hardness of steel by three campaigns, was seized, and lying in a ward of the hospital which held eleven beds, he saw these emptied and filled ten times in succession, each batch of patients in turn being carried out to the grave. Harris survived, but his fighting days were ended.

It will be seen that the experiences of this particular soldier were of a very distressing character. He shared the twin horrors of Sir John Moore's retreat and of the Walcheren expedition. And yet there is not a whining note in Harris's "Recollections." He is proud of his flag, of his comrades, of his officers, of his country. Naturally Harris thinks his particular regiment is the finest in the world. "There never were such a set of devil-may-care fellows, and so completely up to their business," he says, "as the 95th. It would be invidious to make a distinction, or talk of any one regiment being better, or more serviceable, than another; but the Rifles were generally in the mess before the others began, and also the last to leave off."

The tales he tells of the daring of his comrades are sometimes quaint, sometimes thrilling, sometimes absurd. At Vimieiro his lieutenant had to check, with angry energy, not unflavoured with oaths, the eagerness of his men :—

"'D—n you!' he said to them, 'keep back, and get under cover. Do you think you are fighting here with your fists, that you are running into the teeth of the French?'"

As another example of the daring of the individual soldier, Harris says :—

"I remember a fellow, named Jackman, getting close up to the walls at Flushing, and working a hole in the earth with his sword, into which he laid himself, and remained there alone, spite of all the efforts of the enemy and their various missiles to dislodge him. He was known, thus earthed, to have killed, with the utmost coolness and deliberation, eleven of the French artillerymen, as they worked at their guns. As fast as they relieved each fallen comrade did Jackman pick them off; after which he took to his heels, and got safe back to his comrades."

But Harris's soldierly pride is not confined to his own regiment. He held that the French officers, man for man, were far behind the British officers. "The French army had nothing to show in the shape of officers who could at all compare with ours. There was a noble bearing in our leaders, which they on the French side (as far as I was capable of observing) had not."

Of British soldiers, as a whole, Harris says :—

"The field of death and slaughter, the march, the bivouac, and the retreat, are no bad places in which to judge of men. I have had some opportunities of judging them in all these situations, and I should say that the

British are amongst the most splendid soldiers in the world. Give them fair-play, and they are unconquerable."

There is, happily, no reason to think that the quality of the British soldier has fallen off since those words were written.

"THE LADY WITH THE LAMP"

> "Thus thought I, as by night I read
> Of the great army of the dead,
>   The trenches cold and damp,
>   The starved and frozen camp,—
>
> The wounded from the battle plain,
> In dreary hospitals of pain,
>   The cheerless corridors,
>   The cold and stony floors.
>
> Lo! in that house of misery
> A lady with a lamp I see
>   Pass through the glimmering gloom,
>   And flit from room to room.
>
> And slow, as in a dream of bliss,
> The speechless sufferer turns to kiss
>   Her shadow, as it falls
>   Upon the darkening walls."
>   —Longfellow.

TWO figures emerge with a nimbus of glory from the tragedy of the Crimean War. One is that of the great Russian engineer, Todleben, with powerful brow, and face of iron sternness, and eyes that flash as with the keen sparkle of a sword. The other is the slender, modest figure of an English lady, with downcast eyes and pensive brow, and the dress of a nurse. It is Florence Nightingale, whose woman's brain and hand added an element so graci... to the memory of those sad days. And of these two figures, who will

MISS FLORENCE NIGHTINGALE

From a photograph by The London Stereoscopic Company

doubt that "the angel of the hospitals," as she was called, won a finer and more enduring fame than the hero of the trenches?

What a passion of mingled wrath and pity was kindled in Great Britain when the story was known of the brave men dying untended in the hospitals at Scutari or Kululi, or perishing of cold and hunger in the trenches about Sebastopol, can be easily imagined. There were over 13,000 sick in the hospitals. The death-rate at Scutari was forty-two per cent., in the Kululi Hospital it rose to fifty-two per cent. Four patients out of every five who underwent amputation died of hospital gangrene. The doctors showed all the devotion the world has learned to expect from them when face to face with human suffering; but they were few in number, were denied the common appliances of the sick-room, and were bound as with iron fetters by a brainless routine. Pen pictures of scenes in the British hospitals might be selected from Russell's "Letters to the *Times*," which, for their graphic horror, are almost without parallel in literature. They picture scenes which recall the circles of Dante's Inferno. Medicines and medical appliances lay wasted on the beach at Varna, or forgotten in the holds of vessels in Balaclava Harbour, while wounded British soldiers in the great hospital of Scutari were perishing with wounds undressed, and amidst filth which would have disgraced a tribe of savages.

A wave of amazed pity, flavoured with generous wrath, swept over Great Britain when all this was realised. Money was poured into the Patriotic Fund till it rose to more than a million sterling. Medical stores were sent out by the ton. The medical staff was multiplied till there was one doctor for every ninety-five soldiers in the entire British force. The trouble, however, had never arisen from a deficiency of supplies, but only from a bankruptcy of brains and method in their use. The army was being strangled by a system which was omnipotent for mischief, but well-nigh helpless for any useful service. But the sufferings of the British sick, and the insanitary hell into which the British hospitals had sunk, thrilled the hearts of all women in the three kingdoms with a half-fierce pity, and to Mr. Sidney Herbert belongs the distinction of turning the fine element of that pity into a useful force, which wrought in a few brief months one of the most beneficent miracles recorded in the history of army nursing. He saw that what the hospitals needed was woman's quick wit, swift pity, and faculty of patient service. Offers to go out and nurse the dying British soldiers were poured in upon the War Office from tender-hearted women of every rank of life.

Pity, however, had to be organised and wisely led, and Sidney Herbert turned to Florence Nightingale, asking her if she would go to the East, carrying the resources of Great Britain in the palm of her woman's hand, and organise a nursing service in the great hospital at Scutari. A letter from Florence Nightingale offering her services, crossed Mr. Herbert's letter asking if she would give them.

Florence Nightingale was the daughter of a wealthy English household, but born in Florence, and taking her name from that city. In St. Thomas's Hospital, London, stands her statue. She wears the dress of a nurse, and carries in her hand a nurse's night-lamp. The figure is tall and slender, not to say fragile; the face is refined, with a look of reserve upon it—"a veiled and silent woman" she has been called. The living face, however, would kindle with a strange luminousness in conversation, and the dark and steady eyes took what a keen observer has described as a "star-like brightness." That Florence Nightingale was a woman of fine intellect, clear judgment, and heroic quality of will cannot be doubted. Dean Stanley, indeed—not given to cheap praise—has called her "a woman of commanding genius," and her accomplishments tell how swift and penetrating was her intelligence. She spoke French, German, Italian, was a good classic, and had all the social gifts of her order. But all her genius ran in womanly channels. She proved herself, in the Crimea, it is true, to have great powers of administration. Her intelligence had a certain crystalline quality which, within a certain range, made questions that puzzled statesmen easy to her. She hated shallowness and pretence. Although she widened indefinitely the area of woman's work, she did not in the least belong to the order of "new women." To her own sex she wrote, "If you are called to man's work, do not exact a woman's privileges—the privilege of inaccuracy, of weakness. Ye muddle-heads! Submit yourselves to the rules of business as men do, by which alone you can make God's business succeed; for He has never said that He will give His success and His blessing to inefficiency, to sketchy and unfinished work."

But it was into the channel of nursing that Florence Nightingale poured the full strength of her nature. Every woman, she said, has sooner or later some other human life dependent upon her skill as a nurse; and nursing, she insisted, was an art, nay, one of the finest of all arts. Here is her version of the matter:—

"Nursing is an art, and if it is to be made an art, it requires as exclusive a devotion, as hard a preparation, as any painter's or sculptor's work; for what is having to do with dead canvas or cold marble compared with having to do with the living body—the temple of God's Spirit? It is one of the Fine Arts. I had almost said the finest of the fine arts."

Florence Nightingale practised what she preached. Born to the ease and luxury of a rich woman's life, she yet turned aside and spent ten years studying nursing as an art, first at the great Moravian Hospital at Kaiserworth, next with the Sisters of St. Vincent de Paul in Paris. Then she organised a Home for Sick Governesses in London. Then came the opportunity of her life in the call to the East.

On October 21, 1854, she sailed with a band of thirty-eight nurses—of whom ten were Roman Catholic Sisters of Mercy, and fourteen members of an Anglican sisterhood—for Scutari. "I am naturally a very shy person," she says: certainly she had a keen horror of parade, and she started with her gallant band without public notice or farewell. At Boulogne, however, it became known that this company of ladies, with their uniform dark dress, were nurses on their way to the Crimea, and the white-capped fisherwomen of the place thronged round them, and carried their luggage to the railway station, scornfully refusing to let a man so much as touch an article! The band of heroines reached Scutari on November 5, the very day of Inkermann!

The great barrack hospital there was a huge quadrangle, a quarter of a mile on each face; its corridors, rising storey above storey, had a linear extent of four miles. The hospital when the nurses landed held 2300 patients; no less than two miles, that is, of sick-beds—beds foul with every kind of vileness. The mattresses were strewn two deep in the corridors, the wards were rank with fever and cholera, and the odour of undressed wounds. And to this great army of the sick and the dying, the wounded from Inkermann in a few hours were added, bringing the number up to 5000. Into what Russell calls "the hell" of this great temple of pain and foulness moved the slight and delicate form of this English lady, with her band of nurses.

Instantly a new intelligence, instinct with pity, aflame with energy, fertile with womanly invention, swept through the hospital. Clumsy male devices were dismissed, almost with a gesture, into space. Dirt became a crime, fresh air, and clean linen, sweet food, and soft hands a piety. A great kitchen was organised which provided well-cooked food for a thousand men. Washing was a lost art in the hospital; but this band of women created, as with a breath, a great laundry, and a strange cleanliness crept along the walls and beds of the hospital. In their warfare with disease and pain these women showed a resolution as high as the men of their race showed against the grey-coated battalions of Inkermann, or in the frozen trenches before Sebastopol. Muddle-headed male routine was swept ruthlessly aside. If the commissariat failed to supply requisites, Florence Nightingale, who had great funds at her disposal, instantly provided them herself, and the heavy-footed officials found the swift feet of these women outrunning them in every path of help and pity. Only one flash of anger is reported to have broken the serene calm which served as a mask for the steel-like and resolute will of Florence Nightingale. Some stores had arrived from England; sick men were languishing for them. But routine required that they should be "inspected" by a board before being issued, and the board, moving with heavy-footed slowness, had not completed its work when night fell. The stores were, therefore, with official phlegm, locked up, and their use denied to the sick. Between the needs of hundreds of sick men, that is, and the comforts they required was the locked door, the symbol of red tape. Florence Nightingale called a couple of orderlies, walked to the door, and quietly ordered them to burst it open, and the stores to be distributed!

It is not to be wondered at that she swiftly established a sort of quiet and feminine despotism, before which all official heads bowed, and to which all clumsy masculine wills proved pliant. In that sad realm of pain it was fitting that woman—and such a woman!—should be queen. Florence Nightingale, moreover, was strong in official support. She had the whole War Office, with its new head, behind her. She had an even mightier force with her—the sympathy and conscience of the whole nation. In the slender figure and gentle face of this one woman, as she moved with tireless feet through the gloomy wards of that great hospital, the pity of England for her dying sons took, so to speak, concrete shape. Woe to the official who had ventured to thwart her!

It thrills one still to read of the strange passion of half-worshipping loyalty this gentlewoman aroused in every one about her. A little ring of English gentlemen gathered round the hospital to do her behest. One young fellow, not long from Eton, made himself her "fag." Orderlies and attendants ran at her whisper, and were somehow lifted to a mood of chivalry by the process. As for the patients, they almost worshipped her. Macdonald, who administered the fund the *Times* had raised for the service of the sick and wounded, draws a picture of Florence Nightingale in Scutari:—
"As her slender form glides quietly along each corridor, every poor fellow's face softens with gratitude at the sight of her. When all the medical officers have retired for the night, and silence and darkness have settled down upon miles of prostrate sick, she may be observed alone with a little lamp in her hand, making her solitary rounds." It is on this picture—the pitying woman carrying her nurse's lamp through the long corridors where 5000 sick and wounded are lying—that the imagination of Longfellow has fastened:—

"As if a door in heaven should be
Opened, and then closed suddenly,
　　The vision came and went,
　　The light shone and was spent.

On England's annals, through the long
Hereafter of her speech and song,
　　That light its rays shall cast
　　From portals of the past.

A Lady with a Lamp shall stand
In the great history of the land,
　　A noble type of good
　　Heroic womanhood."

It was, perhaps, in the operating-room that Florence Nightingale showed in its highest form the mastery she obtained over the spirits of her soldier patients. This fragile English lady was known, many times, to toil for twenty hours continuously amid her band of nurses and her miles of patients; yet a still sorer tax upon her strength must have been to stand in the dreaded and blood-stained room where the surgeon's knife was busy. But the poor soldier, stretched upon the table, as he looked at the slender figure of the lady nurse—standing with clasped hands but steadfast eyes and pitying smile, enduring the pain of witnessing his pain—drew fortitude from the sight. A soldier told Sidney Herbert that the men watched for her coming into the ward, and though she could not speak to all, "we could kiss her shadow as she passed!"

Nor was the devotion on the part of the men confined to Florence Nightingale. Every member of her band of nurses, and of the band which Miss Stanley afterwards led to the hospital at Therapia, kindled it in a greater or lesser degree. "Oh," said one poor dying soldier to the nurse he saw bending over his pallet, "you are taking me on the way to heaven; don't forsake me now!" The soldiers kept, in a sense, their warlike temper—they were hungry for news from the front. Dying men would ask, "Has Sebastopol fallen? I would like to have been in it at the last." But the presence of the nurses had a strange refining influence over all the inmates of that huge temple of pain and of death. At Scutari men ceased to swear, and forgot to grumble. "Never," said Florence Nightingale, "came from any one of them any word or any look which a gentleman would not have used. The tears come into my eyes," she wrote afterwards, "as I think how, amid scenes of loathsome disease and death, there rose above it all the innate dignity, gentleness, and chivalry of the men."

The miracle wrought by this band of nurses—this entrance of woman into the hell of British hospitals in the East—is capable of being expressed in cold statistics. They found the death-rate in the great hospital at Scutari 52 per cent.; they brought it down to 2 per cent.!

Kinglake says that the part played by male officials and by Florence Nightingale's band of nurses in the hospitals of the Crimea constituted an interesting trial of both brain power and speed between the two sexes; and he is inclined to pronounce, with emphasis, that in this duel of wits the feminine brain comes out best. Women supplied exactly that "agile brain power, that organising or governing faculty" which the state needed, but which its male officials at the moment failed to supply. "The males at that time in England," he says, "suffered from a curious lameness in the use of brain power." They had lost the faculty of initiative, and were slaves to custom.

There is truth in all this, no doubt; but the real secret of the triumph woman won in this contest is found in the fact that the field of battle was a sick chamber, and the foes were pain, fever, and foulness. In that realm woman is queen by right divine. The male officials of the period saw only their "system," and were intent on working it. The nurses at Scutari cared nothing for that abstraction, a "system"; they saw only their patients and were resolute to save them. Kinglake, as an example of the male way of treating the problem, dwells on the medical commission which the Duke of Newcastle sent out to report on the hospitals in the East. Some 10,000 sick and wounded were perishing from mingled neglect and stupidity, and three doctors were sent out to "report" on the situation to the department in London—a process which would occupy three months, during which period half, at least, of this great army of sufferers would perish! Women went out not to explore or to "report," but to scrub floors, cook food, administer medicines, turn chaos into order, and filth into cleanliness. So while the men were "reporting" on the evil, the swift pity and practical genius of woman mended it.

Florence Nightingale remained in the Crimea till the last British soldier had left its shores. She stole back to England as silently as she had left it. But the public gratitude found her out and broke upon her in a generous tempest. A Memorial Fund of £50,000 was raised: she would not take a penny of it, but devoted it to founding schools for the training of nurses in the great London hospitals. To-day as the ships sail past the cliffs of Balaclava, where once three nations met in battle, a gigantic cross shows clear against the sky on the summit of one of the hills. The cross bears the inscription, "Lord, have mercy upon us," and was erected by Florence Nightingale herself as the only memorial she wished of her labours. But Florence Nightingale needs no memorial. She founded, to quote Kinglake, "a gracious dynasty that still reigns supreme in the wards where sufferers lie." The Geneva Convention was held within ten years of Florence Nightingale's labours in the East, and now its red cross, gleaming on every modern battlefield since, is, in a sense, Florence Nightingale's monument. She still lives, a white-haired invalid, well-nigh eighty years old, and when her gentle life ends, one of the noblest careers lived by a woman in modern history will come to a close.

THE END

Printed by BALLANTYNE, HANSON & Co.
Edinburgh & London

BY THE SAME AUTHOR.

Adopted as a Prize-Book by the School Board for London.
CHOSEN FOR HOLIDAY READING AT HARROW AND WINCHESTER.

*SEVENTH EDITION. Crown 8vo, 6s.
With Sixteen Portraits and Eleven Plans.*

DEEDS THAT WON THE EMPIRE.
HISTORIC BATTLE SCENES.

Extract from Author's Preface.

THE tales here told are written, not to glorify war, but to nourish patriotism. They represent an effort to renew in popular memory the great traditions of the Imperial race to which we belong. . . . Each sketch is complete in itself; and though no formal quotation of authorities is given, yet all the available literature on each event described has been laid under contribution. The sketches will be found to be historically accurate.

OPINIONS OF THE PRESS.

The Spectator.—"Not since Macaulay ceased to write has English literature produced a writer capable of infusing such life and vigour into historical scenes. The wholesome and manly tone of Mr. Fitchett's book is specially satisfactory. . . . The book cannot but take the reader by storm wherever it finds him."

The Review of Reviews.—"The book is one which makes the breath come quick, and the throat to bulge, and the eyes to grow moist. It is a splendid book, a book not unworthy of its splendid theme. It is veritable genius that shines in these straightforward stirring stories, genius aflame with inspiration, and aglow with a great enthusiasm."

The Times.—"'Deeds that Won the Empire' is admirably conceived and written. Wolfe's striking feat of arms at Quebec, Hawke's splendid victory in Quiberon Bay, Busaco, Albuera, the Nile, the action of the *Shannon* and *Chesapeake*, with other memorable fights by sea and land, are vividly described. Mr. Fitchett has not sacrificed historical accuracy to dramatic effect, and his words ring true."

The Bookman.—"There is no bluster, no brag, no nauseous cant about a chosen people, but there is a ringing enthusiasm for endurance, for dashing gallantry, for daring and difficult feats, which generous-hearted boys and men will respond to quickly. There is not a flabby paragraph from beginning to end."

The World.—"Quite one of the best books that we have come across this season. . . . The portraits of England's heroes are all taken from authentic sources, and are as admirably produced as are the dozen or so plans of famous battles that add to the usefulness of this capital book."

The School Guardian.—"We can very strongly recommend this book both for boys and girls. It is a well-written narrative of historic battle scenes by sea and land. The accounts of Waterloo and Trafalgar are excellent, and show that the writer has well and carefully studied the material at his disposal."

The Leeds Mercury.—"Quite a wonderful book in its way. It will answer its purpose, that of nourishing true patriotism. Nothing could be written more clearly or carefully."

The Westminster Gazette.—"The account of these famous incidents in British history is written with a knowledge, a verve, and a restraint which are worthy of the highest praise. There is nothing Jingo about the book; its effect can be nothing but good."

The Graphic.—"A stirring chronicle of British valour—a first-rate gift for a patriotically-minded lad."

The Belfast News Letter.—"So fascinatingly rendered as to enlist immediately the sympathies of readers. Boys will find in this publication genuine material to interest them material that will at once educate and benefit them."

The Shipping Gazette.—"A volume that may be placed in the hands of any lad, with a full confidence that, while certain to interest, its influence can scarcely be otherwise than of a distinctly healthy order."

The St. James's Budget.—"A book which deserves to be placed in the hands of every thinking British boy, who in future years will have to puzzle out for himself the methods by which the glory and greatness of our Empire are to be maintained."

LONDON: SMITH, ELDER, & CO., 15 WATERLOO PLACE, S.W.

SMITH, ELDER, & CO.'S PUBLICATIONS.

A SIMPLE GRAMMAR OF ENGLISH NOW IN USE. By JOHN EARLE, M.A., Rector of Swanswick; Rawlinsonian Professor of Anglo-Saxon in the University of Oxford; Author of "English Prose: its Elements, History, and Usage," "The Philology of the English Tongue," &c. Crown 8vo, 6s.

NEW AND CHEAPER EDITION OF GARDNER'S "HOUSEHOLD MEDICINE." Thirteenth Edition. With numerous Illustrations. Demy 8vo, 8s. 6d.

GARDNER'S HOUSEHOLD MEDICINE AND SICK-ROOM GUIDE: A Description of the means of Preserving Health, and the Treatment of Diseases, Injuries, and Emergencies. Revised and expressly Adapted for the Use of Families, Missionaries, and Colonists. By W. H. C. STAVELEY, F.R.C.S., Eng.

MRS. E. B. BROWNING'S LETTERS. Edited, with Biographical Additions, by FREDERIC G. KENYON. Third Edition. 2 vols. with Portraits. Crown 8vo, 15s. net.

"It is not too much to say that these volumes are the first adequate contribution which has been made to a real knowledge of Mrs. Browning. . . . The inestimable value of the collection is that it contains not merely interesting critical writing, but the intimate expression of a personality."—*Athenæum.*

MRS. BROWNING'S COMPLETE WORKS. New and Cheaper Edition. Complete in 1 volume, with Portrait and Facsimile of a "Sonnet from the Portuguese." Large crown 8vo, bound in cloth, with gilt top, 7s. 6d.

*** This Edition is uniform with the 2-Volume Edition of Robert Browning's Complete Works.

"This appears opportunely just now when Mrs. Browning's letters have been attracting attention, and is all the more welcome in that it is the first really complete edition of the poetess's works. . . . In form, as well as in substance, the volume will be a welcome addition to many a library and bookshelf."—*Times.*

THE WAR OF GREEK INDEPENDENCE, 1821-1833. By W. ALISON PHILLIPS, M.A., late Scholar of Merton College, Senior Scholar of St. John's College, Oxford. With Map. Large crown 8vo, 7s. 6d.

"We sincerely commend Mr. Alison Phillips' 'History of the Greek War of Independence' to all readers who have had their attention turned to that country of late. . . . We have met few books better calculated to clear the mind of cant on a subject concerning which much cant has of late been talked."—*St. James's Gazette.*

FRIENDSHIP'S GARLAND. By MATTHEW ARNOLD. Second Edition. Small crown 8vo, bound in white cloth, 4s. 6d.

"All lovers of Matthew Arnold and of genuine humour will hail with delight the republication of 'Friendship's Garland.' . . . The book is written throughout in the highest possible spirits, and there is not a dull page in it."—*Daily News.*

FRANCE UNDER LOUIS XV. By JAMES BRECK PERKINS, Author of "France under the Regency." 2 vols. Crown 8vo, 16s.

"A very good book. . . . Mr. Perkins' tracing out of the foreign policy of France through the wars which did so much to break down her power and the prestige of her crown is very clear and intelligent, and his judgment appears to be generally sound."—*Times.*

A BROWNING COURTSHIP, and other Stories. By ELIZA ORNE WHITE, Author of "The Coming of Theodora," &c. Small post 8vo, 5s.

INDIAN FRONTIER POLICY: An Historical Sketch. By General Sir JOHN ADYE, G.C.B., R.A., Author of "Recollections of a Military Life." With Map. Demy 8vo, 3s. 6d.

ELECTRIC MOVEMENT IN AIR AND WATER. With Theoretical Inferences. By Lord ARMSTRONG, C.B., F.R.S., LL.D., &c. With Autotype Plates. Imperial 4to, £1, 10s. net.

"One of the most remarkable contributions to physical and electrical knowledge that have been made in recent years. . . . The illustrations are produced in a superb manner, entirely worthy of so remarkable a monograph."—*Times.*

GABRIELE VON BULOW, Daughter of Wilhelm von Humboldt. A Memoir compiled from the Family Papers of Wilhelm von Humboldt and his Children, 1791-1887. Translated by CLARA NORDLINGER. With Portraits and a Preface by Sir EDWARD B. MALET, G.C.B., G.C.M.G., &c. Demy 8vo, 16s.

"Miss Nordlinger's excellent translation gives English readers an opportunity of becoming acquainted with a very charming personality, and of following the events of a life which was bound up with many interesting incidents and phases of English history."—*Times.*

LONDON: SMITH, ELDER, & CO., 15 WATERLOO PLACE, S.W.

NEW EDITION OF W. M. THACKERAY'S WORKS.

IN COURSE OF PUBLICATION IN THIRTEEN MONTHLY VOLUMES.

Large Crown 8vo, Cloth, Gilt Top, 6s. each.

THE BIOGRAPHICAL EDITION

OF

W. M. THACKERAY'S COMPLETE WORKS.

THIS NEW AND REVISED EDITION

COMPRISES

ADDITIONAL MATERIAL and HITHERTO UNPUBLISHED LETTERS, SKETCHES, and DRAWINGS

Derived from the Author's Original Manuscripts and Note-Books,

AND EACH VOLUME INCLUDES A MEMOIR, IN THE FORM OF AN INTRODUCTION,

BY MRS. RICHMOND RITCHIE.

The following will be the order of the Volumes:—

1. **VANITY FAIR.** With 20 Full-page Illustrations, 11 Woodcuts, a Facsimile Letter, and a New Portrait. [*Ready.*
2. **PENDENNIS.** With 20 Full-page Illustrations and 10 Woodcuts. [*Ready.*
3. **YELLOWPLUSH PAPERS,** &c. With 24 Full-page Reproductions of Steel Plates by GEORGE CRUIKSHANK, 11 Woodcuts, and a Portrait of the Author by MACLISE. [*Ready.*
4. **THE MEMOIRS OF BARRY LYNDON: The Fitzboodle Papers,** &c. With 16 Full-page Illustrations by J. E. MILLAIS, R.A., LUKE FILDES, A.R.A., and the Author, and 14 Woodcuts. [*Ready.*
5. **SKETCH BOOKS.**—The Paris Sketch Book; The Irish Sketch Book; Notes of a Journey from Cornhill to Grand Cairo, &c. &c. With 16 Full-page Illustrations, 39 Woodcuts, and a Portrait of the Author by MACLISE. [*On August 15.*
6. **CONTRIBUTIONS TO 'PUNCH,'** &c. With 20 Full-page Illustrations, 26 Woodcuts, and an Engraving of the Author from a Portrait by SAMUEL LAURENCE. [*On Sept. 15.*
7. **THE HISTORY OF HENRY ESMOND; and THE LECTURES.** With 20 Full-page Illustrations by GEORGE DU MAURIER, F. BARNARD, and FRANK DICKSEE, R.A., and 11 Woodcuts. [*On Oct. 15.*
8. **THE NEWCOMES.** With 20 Full-page Illustrations by RICHARD DOYLE, and 11 Woodcuts. [*Ready.*

9. **CHRISTMAS BOOKS,** &c.
10. **VIRGINIANS.**
11. **PHILIP,** &c.
12. **DENIS DUVAL,** &c.
13. **MISCELLANIES,** &c.

THE BOOKMAN.—"In her new biographical edition Mrs. Richmond Ritchie gives us precisely what we want. The volumes are a pleasure to hold and to handle. They are just what we like our ordinary every-day Thackeray to be. And prefixed to each of them we have all that we wish to know, or have any right to know, about the author himself; all the circumstances, letters, and drawings which bear upon the work."

From the **ACADEMY.**—"Thackeray wished that no biography of him should appear. It is certain that the world has never ceased to desire one, hence the compromise effected in this edition of his works. Mrs. Ritchie, his daughter, will contribute to each volume in this edition her memories of the circumstances under which her father produced it. Such memoirs, where complete, cannot fall far short of being an actual biography."

From the **DAILY CHRONICLE.**—"We shall have, when the thirteen volumes of this edition are issued, not indeed a biography of Thackeray, but something which will delightfully supply the place of a biography, and fill a regrettable gap in our literary records."

*** *A Prospectus of the Edition, with Specimen pages, will be sent post free on application.*

LONDON: SMITH, ELDER, & CO., 15 WATERLOO PLACE, S.W.

SMITH, ELDER, & CO.'S PUBLICATIONS.

ISABELLA THE CATHOLIC, QUEEN OF SPAIN: her Life, Reign, and Times, 1451-1504. By M. LE BARON DE NERVO. Translated from the Original French by Lieut.-Colonel TEMPLE-WEST (Retired). With Portraits. Demy 8vo, 12s. 6d.

"Neither too long nor too short, not overladen with detail nor impoverished from lack of matter, and is at the same time ample and orderly enough to satisfy the ordinary student."—*Daily Telegraph*.

POT-POURRI FROM A SURREY GARDEN. By Mrs. C. W. EARLE. With an Appendix by Lady CONSTANCE LYTTON. Fifteenth Edition. Crown 8vo, 7s. 6d.

"Intelligent readers of almost any age, especially if they are concerned in the management of a country household, will find these pages throughout both suggestive and amusing."—*Times*.

NEW AND CHEAPER EDITION OF "THE RENAISSANCE IN ITALY."
In 7 volumes, large crown 8vo, with 2 Portraits.

THE RENAISSANCE IN ITALY. By JOHN ADDINGTON SYMONDS.

1. **The Age of the Despots.** With a Portrait. Price 7s. 6d.
2. **The Revival of Learning.** Price 7s. 6d.
3. **The Fine Arts.** Price 7s. 6d.
4 & 5. **Italian Literature.** 2 vols. Price 15s.
6 & 7. **The Catholic Reaction.** With a Portrait and an Index to the 7 vols. Price 15s.

THACKERAY'S HAUNTS AND HOMES. By EYRE CROWE, A.R.A. With Illustrations from Sketches by the Author. Crown 8vo, 6s. net.

☞ NOTE.—The Edition of the Work for sale in this country is limited to 260 copies.

THE ANNALS OF RURAL BENGAL. From Official Records and the Archives of Native Families. By Sir W. W. HUNTER, K.C.S.I., C.I.E., LL.D., &c. New, Revised, and Cheaper Edition (the Seventh). Crown 8vo, 7s. 6d.

"One of the most important as well as most interesting works which the records of Indian literature can show."—*Westminster Review*.

FROM GRAVE TO GAY: being Essays and Studies concerned with Certain Subjects of Serious Interest, with the Puritans, with Literature, and with the Humours of Life, now for the first time Collected and Arranged. By J. ST. LOE STRACHEY. Crown 8vo, 6s.

"Undeniably clever, well-informed, brightly written, and in many ways interesting."—*Times*.

COLLECTED CONTRIBUTIONS ON DIGESTION AND DIET. With an Appendix on the Opium Habit in India. By Sir WILLIAM ROBERTS, M.D., F.R.S. Second Edition. Crown 8vo, 5s.

HISTORY IN FACT AND FICTION. By the Hon. A. S. G. CANNING, Author of "Lord Macaulay: Essayist and Historian," "The Philosophy of Charles Dickens," &c. Crown 8vo, 6s.

"An intensely interesting book. . . . I do not think that I ever saw the difficulties of the Eastern question in so clear a light as I did after reading the short chapter which Mr. Canning devotes to it."—*Pall Mall Gazette*.

THROUGH LONDON SPECTACLES. By CONSTANCE MILMAN. Crown 8vo, 3s. 6d.

"Altogether a very pleasant and companionable little book."—*Spectator*.

SIR CHARLES HALLÉ'S LIFE AND LETTERS. Being an Autobiography (1819-60), with Correspondence and Diaries. Edited by his Son, C. E. HALLÉ, and his Daughter, MARIE HALLÉ. With 2 Portraits. Demy 8vo, 16s.

"The volume is one of the most interesting of recent contributions to the literature of music. . . . A strong sense of humour is manifest in the autobiography as well as in the letters, and there are some capital stories scattered up and down the volume."—*Times*.

THE MEMOIRS OF BARON THIÉBAULT (late Lieutenant-General in the French Army). With Recollections of the Republic, the Consulate, and the Empire. Translated and Condensed by A. J. BUTLER, M.A., Translator of the "Memoirs of Marbot." 2 vols. With 2 Portraits and 2 Maps. Demy 8vo, 28s.

"Mr. Butler's work has been admirably done. . . . These memoirs abound in varied interest, and, moreover, they have no little literary merit. . . . For solid history, bright sketches of rough campaigning, shrewd studies of character, and lively anecdote, these memoirs yield in no degree to others."—*Times*.

PREHISTORIC MAN AND BEAST. By the Rev. H. N. HUTCHINSON, Author of "Extinct Monsters," "Creatures of Other Days," &c. With a Preface by Sir HENRY HOWORTH, M.P., F.R.S., and 10 Full-page Illustrations. Small demy 8vo, 10s. 6d.

"A striking picture of living men and conditions as they once existed. . . . It combines graphic description with scientific accuracy, and is an admirable example of what a judicious use of the imagination can achieve upon a basis of established facts."—*Knowledge*.

LONDON: SMITH, ELDER, & CO., 15 WATERLOO PLACE, S.W.

SMITH, ELDER, & CO.'S PUBLICATIONS.

SONGS OF ACTION. By Conan Doyle. Second Impression. Small crown 8vo, 5s.

"Dr. Doyle's 'Songs' are full of movement. They have fluency, they have vigour, they have force. Everybody should hasten to make acquaintance with them."—*Globe.*

MR. GREGORY'S LETTER-BOX, 1813-1830. Edited by Lady Gregory. With a Portrait. Demy 8vo, 12s. 6d.

EGYPT IN THE NINETEENTH CENTURY; or, Mehemet Ali and his Successors until the British Occupation in 1882. By Donald A. Cameron, H.B.M.'s Consul at Port Said. With a Map. Post 8vo, 6s.

THE LIFE OF SIR JOHN HAWLEY GLOVER, R.N., G.C.M.G. By Lady Glover. Edited by the Right Hon. Sir Richard Temple, Bart., G.C.S.I., D.C.L., LL.D., F.R.S. With Portrait and Maps. Demy 8vo, 14s.

COLLECTIONS AND RECOLLECTIONS. By "One who has kept a Diary." Sixth Impression. Demy 8vo, 16s.

"The most interesting diary that has been published for years."—*Truth.*

THE LIFE OF LORD LAWRENCE. By R. Bosworth Smith, M.A., late Fellow of Trinity College, Oxford; Assistant Master at Harrow School, Author of "Mohammed and Mohammedanism," "Carthage and the Carthaginians," &c. Revised and Cheaper Edition, being the Sixth Edition. 2 vols., large crown 8vo, with 2 Portraits and 2 Maps, 21s.

LIFE OF SIR HENRY LAWRENCE. By Major-General Sir Herbert Benjamin Edwardes, K.C.B., K.C.S.I., and Herman Merivale, C.B. With 2 Portraits. 8vo, 12s.

LIFE OF LIEUT.-GENERAL SIR JAMES OUTRAM. By Major-General Sir Frederic J. Goldsmid, C.B., K.C.S.I. Second Edition. 2 vols. demy 8vo, 32s.

THE LIFE OF MAHOMET. From Original Sources. By Sir Wm. Muir, K.C.S.I. Third Edition, with a New Map and several Illustrations. 8vo, 16s.

By the same Author.

THE MAMELUKE OR SLAVE DYNASTY OF EGYPT, 1260-1517 A.D. With 12 full-page Illustrations and a Map. 8vo, 10s. 6d.

THE MERV OASIS. Travels and Adventures East of the Caspian during the Years 1879-80-81, including Five Months' Residence among the Tekkes of Merv. By Edmond O'Donovan, Special Correspondent of the *Daily News*. In 2 vols. demy 8vo, with Portrait, Maps, and Facsimiles of State Documents, 36s.

MERV. A Story of Adventures and Captivity. Epitomised from "The Merv Oasis." By Edmond O'Donovan, Special Correspondent of the *Daily News*. With a Portrait. Crown 8vo, 6s.

ESSAYS ON THE EXTERNAL POLICY OF INDIA. By the late J. W. S. Wyllie, C.S.I., India Civil Service, sometime Acting Foreign Secretary to the Government of India. Edited, with a brief Life, by Sir W. W. Hunter, B.A., LL.D. With a Portrait of the Author. 8vo, 14s.

THE ANNALS OF RURAL BENGAL. From Official Records and the Archives of Ancient Families. By Sir W. W. Hunter, LL.D. Vol. I. The Ethnical Frontier. Fifth Edition. Demy 8vo, 18s. Also the new, revised, and cheaper edition (the seventh). Crown 8vo, 7s. 6d.

By the same Author.

ORISSA; or, The Vicissitudes of an Indian Province under Native and British Rule. Being the Second and Third Volumes of "Annals of Rural Bengal." With Illustrations. 2 vols. demy 8vo, 32s.

A LIFE OF THE EARL OF MAYO, Fourth Viceroy of India. 2 vols. Second Edition. Demy 8vo, 24s.

THE INDIAN EMPIRE: its Peoples, History, and Products. Third and Standard Edition. With Map. Demy 8vo, 25s.

London: SMITH, ELDER, & CO., 15 Waterloo Place, S.W.

SMITH, ELDER, & CO.'S PUBLICATIONS.

A YEAR IN THE FIELDS. Selections from the Writings of JOHN BURROUGHS. With Illustrations from Photographs by CLIFTON JOHNSON. Crown 8vo, 6s.
"The book is an excellent example of its kind, pleasant, chatty, and readable. . . . Fresh and graphic, instinct with country sights, scents, and sounds."—*Land and Water.*
"The book is pleasant reading, and Mr. Burroughs is a true lover of Nature."—*Athenæum.*

THE MONEY-SPINNER, and other Character Notes. By H. SETON MERRIMAN, Author of "The Sowers," "With Edged Tools," &c.; and S. G. TALLENTYRE. With 12 Full-page Illustrations by ARTHUR RACKHAM. Second Edition. Crown 8vo, 6s.
"We have many bad books, and many goody-goody books, but few good books; this is one of them."—Mr. JAMES PAYN in the *Illustrated London News.*

SELECTED POEMS OF WALTER VON DER VOGELWEIDE, THE MINNESINGER. Done into English Verse by W. ALISON PHILLIPS, M.A., late Scholar of Merton College, and Senior Scholar of St. John's College, Oxford. With 6 Full-page Illustrations. Small 4to, 10s. 6d. net.
"There is in the outpourings of the famous Minnesinger a freshness and a spontaneity that exercise an irresistible charm. . . . Mr. Phillips deserves thanks from all lovers of poetry for bringing him before the world again in so acceptable a form."—*Times.*

A HISTORY OF THE HEBREW PEOPLE FROM THE DIVISION OF THE KINGDOM TO THE FALL OF JERUSALEM IN 566 B.C. By CHARLES FOSTER KENT, Ph.D., Associate-Professor of Biblical Literature and History, Brown University. With Maps and Chart. Crown 8vo, 6s.
*** This Second Volume completes the Work.

ENGLISH PROSE: its Elements, History, and Usage. By JOHN EARLE, M.A., Rector of Swanswick, formerly Fellow and Tutor of Oriel College, Professor of Anglo-Saxon in the University of Oxford. 8vo, 16s.

THE HISTORIC NOTE-BOOK; with an Appendix of Battles. By the Rev. E. COBHAM BREWER, LL.D., Author of "The Dictionary of Phrase and Fable," "The Reader's Handbook," &c. Crown 8vo, over 1000 pp., 7s. 6d.

GEOLOGICAL OBSERVATIONS ON THE VOLCANIC ISLANDS AND PARTS OF SOUTH AMERICA, visited during the Voyage of H.M.S. *Beagle.* By CHARLES DARWIN, M.A., F.R.S. Third Edition. With Maps and Illustrations. Crown 8vo, 12s. 6d.

THE STRUCTURE AND DISTRIBUTION OF CORAL REEFS. By CHARLES DARWIN, M.A., F.R.S., F.G.S. With an Introduction by Professor T. G. BONNEY, D.Sc., F.R.S., F.G.S. Third Edition. Crown 8vo, 8s. 6d.

HAYTI; or, The Black Republic. By Sir SPENSER ST. JOHN, G.C.M.G., formerly Her Majesty's Minister Resident and Consul-General in Hayti, now Her Majesty's Special Envoy to Mexico. Second Edition, revised. With a Map. Large crown 8vo, 8s. 6d.

THE REIGN OF QUEEN VICTORIA: a Survey of Fifty Years of Progress. Edited by T. HUMPHRY WARD. 2 vols. 8vo, 32s.

A COLLECTION OF LETTERS OF W. M. THACKERAY, 1847-1855. With Portraits and Reproductions of Letters and Drawings. Second Edition. Imperial 8vo, 12s. 6d.

A JOURNAL KEPT BY DICK DOYLE IN THE YEAR 1840. Illustrated by several hundred Sketches by the Author. With an Introduction by J. HUNGERFORD POLLEN, and a Portrait. Second Edition. Demy 4to, 21s.

THE INGENIOUS GENTLEMAN, DON QUIXOTE OF LA MANCHA. By MIGUEL DE CERVANTES SAAVEDRA. A Translation, with Introduction and Notes, by JOHN ORMSBY, Translator of "The Poem of the Cid." Complete in 4 vols. 8vo, £2, 10s.

SHAKESPEARE. Certain Selected Plays Abridged for the Use of the Young. By SAMUEL BRANDRAM, M.A. Oxon. Fourth and Cheaper Edition. Large crown 8vo, 5s.
*** Also the 9 Plays separately, crown 8vo, neatly bound in cloth limp, price 6d. each.

SHAKSPEARE COMMENTARIES. By Dr. G. G. GERVINUS, Professor at Heidelberg. Translated, under the Author's superintendence, by F. E. BUNNETT. With a Preface by F. J. FURNIVALL. Fifth Edition. 8vo, 14s.

THE STORY OF GOETHE'S LIFE. By GEORGE HENRY LEWES. Second Edition. Crown 8vo, 7s. 6d.

LONDON: SMITH, ELDER, & CO., 15 WATERLOO PLACE, S.W.

"A work absolutely indispensable to every well-furnished library."
— The Times.

Royal 8vo. Price 15s. each net, in cloth; or in half-morocco, marbled edges, 20s. net.

VOLUMES 1-56 (ABBADIE-TOLLET) OF THE

DICTIONARY OF NATIONAL BIOGRAPHY

Edited by LESLIE STEPHEN and SIDNEY LEE

Volume I. was published on January 1st, 1885, and a further Volume will be issued quarterly until the completion of the work.

NOTE.—A Full Prospectus of "The Dictionary of National Biography," with Specimen Pages, may be had upon application.

FROM A RECENT NOTICE OF THE WORK IN "THE WORLD."

"The present instalment of this really great work is fully equal in every respect to its predecessors. Mr. Sidney Lee and his staff of contributors, indeed, have left nothing undone which the reader could wish or expect them to do, and the publishers may be congratulated on the approaching conclusion of an enterprise of which the success is as conspicuous as its merits, and in the department of literature to which it belongs unparalleled and unprecedented."

TRUTH.—"I am glad you share my admiration for Mr. Stephen's *magnum opus*—THE MAGNUM OPUS OF OUR GENERATION—'The Dictionary of National Biography.' A dictionary of the kind had been attempted so often before by the strongest men—publishers and editors—of the day, that I hardly expected it to succeed. No one expected such a success as it has so far achieved."

THE ATHENÆUM.—"The latest volumes of Mr. Stephen's Dictionary are FULL OF IMPORTANT AND INTERESTING ARTICLES. . . . Altogether the volumes are good reading. What is more important, the articles, whether they are on small or great personages, are nearly all up to the high standard which has been set in the earlier portions of the work, and occasionally above it."

SATURDAY REVIEW.—"From the names we have cited it will be seen that great pains have been taken with that portion of the Dictionary which relates to modern times, and this has been rightly done; for often nothing is more difficult than to find a concise record of the life of a man who belonged to our own times or to those just preceding them. Consistently enough, the Editor has been careful to keep the work reasonably up to date."

THE SPECTATOR.—"As each volume of the Dictionary appears, its merits become more conspicuous. . . . The book ought to commend itself to as wide a circle of buyers as the 'Encyclopædia Britannica.'"

THE MANCHESTER EXAMINER AND TIMES.—"We extend a hearty welcome to the latest instalment of a most magnificent work, in which both the editing and the writing appear still to improve."

THE QUARTERLY REVIEW.—"A 'DICTIONARY OF NATIONAL BIOGRAPHY' OF WHICH THE COUNTRY MAY BE JUSTLY PROUD, which, though it may need correcting and supplementing, will probably never be superseded, and which, in unity of conception and aim, in the number of the names inserted, in fulness and accuracy of details, in the care and precision with which the authorities are cited, and in the bibliographical information given, will not only be immeasurably superior to any work of the kind which has been produced in Great Britain, but will as far surpass the German and Belgian biographical dictionaries now in progress as the two important undertakings are in advance of the two great French collections, which until lately reigned supreme in the department of Biography."

The Rev. Dr. Jessop in the *Nineteenth Century*.—"The greatest literary undertaking that has ever been carried out in England. . . . We shall have a Dictionary of National Biography such as no other nation in Europe can boast of, and such as can never be wholly superseded, though it will need to be supplemented for the requirements of our posterity."

THE LANCET.—"The usefulness, fulness, and general accuracy of this work become more and more apparent as its progress continues. It is a classic work of reference as such, WITHOUT ANY COMPEER IN ENGLISH OR PERHAPS ANY OTHER LANGUAGE."

THE PALL MALL GAZETTE.—"As to the general execution, we can only repeat the high praise which it has been our pleasing duty to bestow on former volumes. To find a name omitted that should have been inserted is well-nigh impossible."

LONDON: SMITH, ELDER, & CO., 15 WATERLOO PLACE, S.W.

ROBERT BROWNING'S WORKS
AND "LIFE AND LETTERS"

THE COMPLETE WORKS OF ROBERT BROWNING. Edited and Annotated by AUGUSTINE BIRRELL, Q.C., M.P., and FREDERIC G. KENYON. In 2 vols. large crown 8vo, bound in cloth, gilt top, with a Portrait-Frontispiece to each volume, 7s. 6d. per volume.

*** An Edition has also been printed on Oxford India Paper. This can be obtained only through booksellers, who will furnish particulars as to price, &c.

UNIFORM EDITION OF THE WORKS OF ROBERT BROWNING. Seventeen Volumes, small crown 8vo, lettered separately, or in set binding, price 5s. each.

This edition contains Three Portraits of Mr. Browning, at different periods of life, and a few illustrations.

CONTENTS OF THE VOLUMES

1. PAULINE: and SORDELLO.
2. PARACELSUS: and STRAFFORD.
3. PIPPA PASSES: KING VICTOR AND KING CHARLES: THE RETURN OF THE DRUSES: and A SOUL'S TRAGEDY. With a Portrait of Mr. Browning.
4. A BLOT IN THE 'SCUTCHEON: COLOMBE'S BIRTHDAY: and MEN AND WOMEN.
5. DRAMATIC ROMANCES: and CHRISTMAS-EVE AND EASTER-DAY.
6. DRAMATIC LYRICS: and LURIA.
7. IN A BALCONY: and DRAMATIS PERSONÆ. With a Portrait of Mr. Browning.
8. THE RING AND THE BOOK. Books 1 to 4. With Two Illustrations.
9. THE RING AND THE BOOK. Books 5 to 8.
10. THE RING AND THE BOOK. Books 9 to 12. With a Portrait of Guido Franceschini.
11. BALAUSTION'S ADVENTURE: PRINCE HOHENSTIEL-SCHWANGAU, Saviour of Society: and FIFINE AT THE FAIR.
12. RED COTTON NIGHT-CAP COUNTRY: and THE INN ALBUM.
13. ARISTOPHANES' APOLOGY, including a Transcript from Euripides, being the Last Adventure of Balaustion: and THE AGAMEMNON OF ÆSCHYLUS.
14. PACCHIAROTTO, and How he Worked in Distemper: with other Poems: LA SAISIAZ: and THE TWO POETS OF CROISIC.
15. DRAMATIC IDYLS, First Series: DRAMATIC IDYLS, Second Series: and JOCOSERIA.
16. FERISHTAH'S FANCIES: and PARLEYINGS WITH CERTAIN PEOPLE OF IMPORTANCE IN THEIR DAY. With a Portrait of Mr. Browning.
17. ASOLANDO: Fancies and Facts: and BIOGRAPHICAL AND HISTORICAL NOTES TO THE POEMS.

A SELECTION FROM THE POETICAL WORKS OF ROBERT BROWNING. FIRST SERIES, crown 8vo, 3s. 6d. SECOND SERIES, crown 8vo, 3s. 6d.

POCKET VOLUME OF SELECTIONS FROM THE POETICAL WORKS OF ROBERT BROWNING. Small fcap. 8vo, bound in half-cloth, with cut or uncut edges, price 1s.

THE LIFE AND LETTERS OF ROBERT BROWNING. By Mrs. SUTHERLAND ORR. With Portrait, and Steel Engraving of Mr. Browning's Study in De Vere Gardens. SECOND EDITION, crown 8vo, 12s. 6d.

LONDON: SMITH, ELDER, & CO., 15 WATERLOO PLACE, S.W.

POPULAR NOVELS.

Each Work complete in One Volume, Crown 8vo, price Six Shillings.

By HENRY SETON MERRIMAN.
RODEN'S CORNER. 3rd Edition.
IN KEDAR'S TENTS. 8th Edition.
THE GREY LADY. With 12 Full-page Illustrations.
THE SOWERS. 19th Edition.

By A. CONAN DOYLE.
THE TRAGEDY OF THE KOROSKO. With 40 Full-page Illustrations.
UNCLE BERNAC. 2nd Edition. With 12 Full-page Illustrations.
RODNEY STONE. With 8 Full-page Illustrations.
THE WHITE COMPANY. 19th Edition.

By S. R. CROCKETT.
THE RED AXE. With 8 Full-page Illustrations. 2nd Edition.
CLEG KELLY, ARAB OF THE CITY. 33rd Thousand.

By Mrs. HUMPHRY WARD.
HELBECK OF BANNISDALE. 3rd Edition.
SIR GEORGE TRESSADY. 3rd Edition.
MARCELLA. 16th Edition.
ROBERT ELSMERE. 27th Edition.
THE HISTORY OF DAVID GRIEVE. 9th Edition.

By STANLEY J. WEYMAN.
THE CASTLE INN. With a Frontispiece. 2nd Edition.

By Mrs. E. RENTOUL ESLER.
THE WARDLAWS.

By Miss THACKERAY.
OLD KENSINGTON.
THE VILLAGE ON THE CLIFF.
FIVE OLD FRIENDS AND A YOUNG PRINCE.
TO ESTHER, and other Sketches.
BLUEBEARD'S KEYS, and other Stories.
THE STORY OF ELIZABETH; TWO HOURS; FROM AN ISLAND.
TOILERS AND SPINSTERS, and other Essays.
MISS ANGEL; Fulham Lawn.
MISS WILLIAMSON'S DIVAGATIONS.
MRS. DYMOND.

By CLIVE PHILLIPPS-WOLLEY.
ONE OF THE BROKEN BRIGADE.

By ALEXANDER INNES SHAND.
THE LADY GRANGE.

By the Rev. J. E. C. WELLDON.
GERALD EVERSLEY'S FRIENDSHIP. A Study in Real Life. 4th Edition.

By ARCHIE ARMSTRONG.
UNDER THE CIRCUMSTANCES.

By the Rev. COSMO GORDON LANG.
THE YOUNG CLANROY: A Romance of the '45.

By W. CARLTON DAWE.
CAPTAIN CASTLE: A Story of the South Sea. With a Frontispiece.

By Mrs. DE LA PASTURE.
DEBORAH OF TOD'S. 3rd Edition.

By ANNA HOWARTH.
JAN: An Afrikander. 2nd Edition.

By FRANCIS H. HARDY.
THE MILLS OF GOD.

By HAMILTON DRUMMOND.
FOR THE RELIGION.

By ARCHER P. CROUCH.
SEÑORITA MONTENAR.

By J. A. ALTSHELER.
A SOLDIER OF MANHATTAN.

By OLIVE BIRRELL.
THE AMBITION OF JUDITH.

By PERCY FENDALL and FOX RUSSELL.
OUT OF THE DARKNESS.

By A. E. HOUGHTON.
GILBERT MURRAY.

By ADAM LILBURN.
THE BORDERER.

By Mrs. BIRCHENOUGH.
DISTURBING ELEMENTS.

By PERCY ANDREAE.
THE SIGNORA: A Tale.
THE MASK AND THE MAN.

By R. O. PROWSE.
A FATAL RESERVATION.

By LORD MONKSWELL.
KATE GRENVILLE.

By SARAH TYTLER.
KINCAID'S WIDOW.

By LADY VERNEY.
LLANALY REEFS.
LETTICE LISLE. With 3 Illustrations.

LONDON: SMITH, ELDER, & CO., 15 WATERLOO PLACE, S.W.

SMITH, ELDER, & CO.'S NEW BOOKS.

THE LETTERS OF ROBERT BROWNING AND ELIZABETH BARRETT BARRETT. 1845-1846. With 2 Portraits and 2 Facsimile Letters. 2 vols., crown 8vo, 21s.
⁎ *These Volumes are uniform with "The Letters of Elizabeth Barrett Browning."*

THE LIFE OF CHARLES STEWART PARNELL, 1846-1891. By R. BARRY O'BRIEN, Author of "Fifty Years of Concessions to Ireland." With a Portrait, a View of Avondale, and a Facsimile Letter. 2 vols., large post 8vo, 21s.

A LIFE OF WILLIAM SHAKESPEARE. By SIDNEY LEE, Editor of "The Dictionary of National Biography." With 2 Portraits of Shakespeare, a Portrait of the Earl of Southampton, and Facsimiles of Shakespeare's known Signatures. Crown 8vo, 7s. 6d.

SIR FRANK LOCKWOOD: a Biographical Sketch. By AUGUSTINE BIRRELL, Q.C., M.P. With 2 Portraits, 10 Full-page Illustrations, and 2 Facsimile Letters. THIRD EDITION. Large crown 8vo, 10s. 6d.

RHODESIA AND ITS GOVERNMENT. By H. C. THOMSON, Author of "The Chitral Campaign," and of "The Outgoing Turk." With 8 Illustrations and a Map. Large crown 8vo, 10s. 6d.

THE POETICAL WORKS OF ROBERT BRIDGES. Volume I. Small crown 8vo, 6s. CONTENTS—Prometheus the Firegiver; Eros and Psyche; and The Growth of Love.

CHARLES LAMB AND THE LLOYDS. Edited by E. V. LUCAS. With Portraits and a Facsimile Letter. Small Post 8vo, 6s.

PAGES FROM A PRIVATE DIARY. Reprinted from the *Cornhill Magazine*. Crown 8vo, 6s.

INTRODUCTION TO THE STUDY OF THE RENAISSANCE. By Mrs. LILIAN F. FIELD. Crown 8vo, 6s.

THE SEPOY MUTINY AS SEEN BY A SUBALTERN FROM DELHI TO LUCKNOW. By Colonel EDWARD VIBART. With 2 Portraits, a Plan, and 10 Illustrations. Large crown 8vo, 7s. 6d.

BRITISH RULE AND MODERN POLITICS. An Historical Study. By the Hon. A. S. G. CANNING, Author of "The Divided Irish," "History in Fact and Fiction," &c. Large crown 8vo, 7s. 6d.

IDLEHURST. A Journal kept in the Country. By JOHN HALSHAM. Crown 8vo, 6s.

THE CRUISE OF THE "CACHALOT": Round the World after Sperm Whales. By FRANK T. BULLEN, First Mate. With 8 Illustrations and a Chart. Large post 8vo, 8s. 6d.

SKETCHES AND STUDIES IN ITALY AND GREECE. By the late JOHN ADDINGTON SYMONDS. NEW EDITION, in Three Series. Large crown 8vo, 7s. 6d. each.

NEW AND CHEAPER EDITION OF "AURORA LEIGH."

AURORA LEIGH. By ELIZABETH BARRETT BROWNING. With an Introduction by ALGERNON CHARLES SWINBURNE, and a Frontispiece. Crown 8vo, cloth, gilt top, 3s. 6d.

THE ROSE AND THE RING. By W. M. THACKERAY. NEW AND CHEAPER EDITION. Square 16mo, 2s. 6d.

NEW EDITION OF "THE RING AND THE BOOK."

THE RING AND THE BOOK. By ROBERT BROWNING. With 2 Portraits and 12 Full-page Illustrations. Large crown 8vo, 8s. 6d.

MRS. PERKINS'S BALL. By M. A. TITMARSH. With 22 Coloured Illustrations. Fcp. 4to, 7s. 6d.
⁎ *A Reprint in the Original Form of Thackeray's Popular Christmas Story.*

LONDON: SMITH, ELDER, & CO., 15 WATERLOO PLACE, S.W.

www.ingramcontent.com/pod-product-compliance
Lightning Source LLC
Chambersburg PA
CBHW032031220426
43664CB00006B/439